Music and society

Music and society

*the politics of
composition, performance and reception*

edited by
RICHARD LEPPERT and SUSAN McCLARY

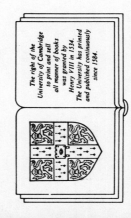

The right of the
University of Cambridge
to print and sell
all manner of books
was granted by
Henry VIII in 1534.
The University has printed
and published continuously
since 1584.

CAMBRIDGE UNIVERSITY PRESS

Cambridge
New York   Port Chester
Melbourne   Sydney

Published by the Press Syndicate of the University of Cambridge
The Pitt Building, Trumpington Street, Cambridge CB2 1RP
32 East 57th Street, New York, NY 10022, USA
10 Stamford Road, Oakleigh, Melbourne 3166, Australia

© Cambridge University Press 1987

First published 1987
First paperback edition 1989

Printed in Great Britain at
the University Press, Cambridge

British Library cataloguing in publication data
Music and society: the politics of composition,
performance and reception.
1. Music society
I. Leppert, Richard II. McClary, Susan
780'.07   ML3795

Library of Congress cataloguing in publication data
Music and society.
Index.
1. Music and society. I. Leppert, Richard
II. McClary, Susan.
ML3795.M78   1987   780'.07   86-31672

ISBN 0 521 32780 6 hard covers
ISBN 0 521 37977 6 paperback

ME

Contents

Illustrations

Contributors

SIMON FRITH is a senior lecturer in Sociology at the University of Warwick and the author of *Sound effects: youth, leisure and the politics of rock 'n' roll*. As a freelance rock critic he has written for numerous newspapers and magazines on both sides of the Atlantic. From 1982–6 he was rock critic of the London *Sunday Times*, and he currently writes a monthly music column in *The Village Voice*. His most recent research has been on the influence of art schools and art education on British pop music.

RICHARD LEPPERT, co-editor, is Professor of Humanities at the University of Minnesota. His training is in musicology and art history; his scholarship is focused on the iconography of music. His publications include *The theme of music in Flemish paintings of the seventeenth century* and *Arcadia at Versailles: noble amateur musicians and their musettes and hurdy-gurdies at the French court (c. 1660–1789)*. He is currently completing a monograph socio-cultural history of upper-class amateur musicians in eighteenth-century England.

SUSAN McCLARY, co-editor, is Associate Professor of Musicology and a member of two research centers (Center for Advanced Feminist Studies and Center for Humanistic Studies, for which she was Acting Director, 1985–6) at the University of Minnesota. Her research focuses on the ways in which music both articulates and shapes social values, and her publications include essays on seventeenth-century music, Mozart, and new music. She serves as a frequent consultant to arts organizations on matters related to new forms of music, dance, and theater, and she has recently composed a music-theater piece, *Susanna does the elders*.

JOHN MOWITT is Assistant Professor of Humanities and English at the University of Minnesota. His work primarily reflects interests in the history and theory of critical method as well as the problematic of the cultural constitution of subjectivity. He has published recently on rhetoric, the cinematic apparatus, and the discipline of the humanities. His current research centers on an effort to clarify the relation between writing and subjectivity embodied in the 'text' as a literary object.

JOHN SHEPHERD is Associate Professor of Music and a Member of the Centre for Communication Culture and Society at Carleton University, Ottawa. He is the author of *Tin Pan Alley* and a co-author of *Whose music? A sociology of musical languages*, and he has published extensively in the areas of the sociology and aesthetics of music, popular music and the sociology of music education. He served as Executive Secretary of the International Association for the Study of Popular Music, 1983–7.

ROSE ROSENGARD SUBOTNIK is currently Visiting Associate Professor of Music at the Graduate Center of The City University of New York. She will join the faculty of the School of Music at the University of Minnesota in the fall of 1987. She formerly taught at the University of Chicago, where she was a Guggenheim Fellow. She has published numerous articles on interdisciplinary aspects of music, including essays on Kant, Adorno, musical semiotics, and the problem of musical criticism.

JANET WOLFF is Reader in Sociology of Culture at the University of Leeds, where she was also co-founder, and first Director, of the Centre for Cultural Studies in 1985. Her work is in the sociology of art, cultural studies, and women and the arts, and her publications include: *Hermeneutic philosophy and the sociology of art*, *The social production of art*, *Aesthetics and the sociology of art*, and *The art of women* (forthcoming). She has also co-edited a number of volumes, the most recent of which (co-edited with John Seed) is a collection of essays on class, culture and the visual arts in the North of England in the nineteenth century.

Introduction

The past fifteen years have witnessed a major transformation in the ways in which the arts and humanities are studied. Influenced by such socially and politically grounded enterprises as feminism, semiotics and deconstruction, both the artifacts considered worthy of analysis and the questions asked of canonized works of art have changed radically. These changes, especially evident in studies of literature, film, and visual art, in turn have led to a systematic investigation of the implicit assumptions underlying critical methods of the last two-hundred years, including prominently the assumption that art constitutes an autonomous sphere, separate and insulated from the outside social world.

While the lasting effects of this transformation are impossible to predict and its value and significance is hotly debated and negotiated at the moment,[1] it seems safe to propose that humanistic scholarship will not soon return to the models of self-contained aesthetic enhancement that had characterized it at earlier stages – or at least, if it does, such a return will be marked indelibly as a politically informed choice. Moreover, to the extent that the arts produced during this same time period have been

---

[1] For recent statements attempting to dismiss or undermine the critical methods of this re-evaluation, see Norman Cantor, 'The real crisis in the humanities today', *The New Criterion*, 3/10 (June, 1985), pp. 28–38, and William J. Bennett, *Reclaiming a legacy* (National Endowment for the Humanities, November, 1984). For a more direct critique of the positions presented in this volume, see Edward Cowan's letter to *Opus* (April, 1986), pp. 3–4, responding to Joseph Horowitz's article on the Music and Society Conference, 'Musical mavericks fume and blaspheme in Minnesota' (October, 1985), pp. 15–17.

shaped by similar questions and influences, making sense of today's art world demands a full range of the new critical methods.

The only one of the arts that has remained largely untouched by such redefinitions of method and subject matter in its academic discipline is music. For the most part, the discourse of musical scholarship clings stubbornly to a reliance on positivism in historical research and formalism in theory and criticism, with primary attention still focused almost exclusively on the canon. Nevertheless, a few signs that musicology (if not music theory) might be changing along lines pioneered in literary studies have recently appeared. Joseph Kerman's Contemplating music, for instance, exposes with admirable clarity both the historical and ideological factors that contributed to the entrenchment of positivism and formalism in American universities.[2] Richard Norton's Tonality in Western culture seeks to redefine the central musical language of the 'Great Composers' such that it can be understood as a social construct, rather than as the universal it is frequently asserted to be.[3] In Great Britain, where sociology of the arts has found greater acceptance in the academy, studies by Christopher Ballantine, Christopher Small, and Alan Durant each problematize the inherited boundaries of music scholarship and propose other, more fruitful models to replace them.[4]

The essays in Music and society raise a series of complementary questions, foremost among which is that of autonomy itself: the notion that music shapes itself in accordance with self-contained, abstract principles that are unrelated to the outside social world. Not surprisingly, the classic formulations of this issue by Theodor Adorno[5] and Walter Benjamin[6] are repeatedly engaged as well – as points of departure, as support, as models, or as paradigms that themselves are in need of critical examination.

2 Joseph Kerman, Contemplating music: challenges to musicology (Cambridge, Mass., 1985), English edition as Musicology (London, 1985). Kerman deals extensively in this study with the ideological implications of the canon, and even considers briefly the absence of feminist and deconstructive criticism in musicology (p. 17).

3 Richard Norton, Tonality in Western culture (University Park, Penn., 1984).

4 Christopher Ballantine, Music and its social meanings (New York, 1984); Christopher Small, Music – society – education (London, 1980); Alan Durant, Conditions of music (Albany, 1984).

5 See especially Theodor Adorno, Introduction to the sociology of music, trans. E.B. Ashton (New York, 1976); Philosophy of modern music, trans. Anne G. Mitchell and Wesley V. Blomster (New York, 1973); Prisms, trans. Samuel Weber and Shierry Weber (1967; reprint ed. Cambridge, Mass., 1981); and 'On the fetish character in music and the regression of listening', The essential Frankfurt School reader, eds. Andrew Arato and Eike Gebhardt (New York, 1978), pp. 270–99. The essays by Susan McClary and John Mowitt deal most directly with Adorno.

6 The work of Benjamin most frequently invoked is 'The work of art in the age of mechanical reproduction', Illuminations, trans. Harry Zohn, ed. Hannah Arendt (New York, 1969), pp. 217–52. The Adorno–Benjamin controversy is re-examined in considerable detail in Mowitt's piece.

Briefly stated, the disciplines of music theory and musicology are grounded on the assumption of musical autonomy. They cautiously keep separate considerations of biography, patronage, place and dates from those of musical syntax and structure. Both disciplines likewise claim objectivity, the illusion of which is possible only when the questions considered valid are limited to those that can, in fact, be answered without qualification. The ideology of autonomy also informs the conventional musical reception of the 'music lover' who listens to music precisely in order to withdraw from the real world and to experience what is taken to be authentic subjectivity.

In order to begin making connections between the substance of music and social values, it is necessary first to try to discover the reasons (historical, social, psychological) that its consumers and practitioners cling so tenaciously to the principle of artistic autonomy and to analyze how belief in musical autonomy has shaped the methods, questions, and answers in the reigning histories and theories of music. For alternative models can be proposed and elaborated only after such deconstruction of established paradigms has occurred.

Janet Wolff's Foreword addresses most directly the concept of autonomy in several of the arts through the nineteenth and twentieth centuries, and she discusses many of the reasons why critics of the other arts have called it into question. In the course of her exposition, she also remarks that music does not present any special problems vis-à-vis its non-representational character and socio-cultural analysis. That remark introduces one of the more interesting tensions of the volume, for most of the essays argue at least implicitly in opposition to this position. Insofar as other art forms are in one way or another abstract or non-representational, Wolff is, of course, correct. But historically, music has been viewed by Western culture by means of an unproblematized paradigm which assumes music's non-representational character as the *sine qua non* from which all further study proceeds. That is a very different position from which to begin analysis than for most other art forms. To what extent does music parallel the other arts in its relationship to society, and to what extent might it indeed constitute a special case? These questions appear throughout the volume, along with the variety of answers that befit the first stages of a new area of inquiry.

A second issue addressed in this collection involves the reinterpretation of Western music along lines suggested by the elimination of the precept of musical autonomy. For it is one thing to decide that music and society are integrally connected and another to demonstrate in concrete detail how that connection is manifested. The essays by McClary, Leppert, Subotnik and Shepherd all are concerned with presenting alternative models to the reading of music history and music criticism – models that strive to permit social context and musical discourse to inform one another. This series of particular case studies addresses such matters as the articulation of social values in specific musical repertoires and the function of music in social contexts as a means of transmitting dominant ideology. Because such artic-ulations and functions differ widely from time to time and from place to place, each case study requires a different set of observations, relevant source materials, and techniques. In all instances, these essays contribute historical insights as well as self-conscious reflections on method.

Susan McClary uses the celebrations of the 1985 Bach tercentenary as her point of departure. In the course of accounting for Bach's prestigious posi-tion in contemporary musical reception, she explores the ways in which music functions differently from literature or the visual arts in Western consciousness (in particular tracing its claim to autonomy back to the Greeks), the peculiar privileging of eighteenth-century cultural products in the current crisis of humanism, the political battles in music theory over definitions of order versus noise, the strategies of silencing alternative voices (of women, of ethnic minorities, of popular culture, of the avant-garde) by means of the classical tradition, and the reification of meaning that necessarily attends the canonization of the Bach repertory. Her thesis is grounded in a historically self-reflexive analysis of two very different examples of Bach's composition (one instrumental, one vocal), treated not simply as organized sounds but rather as instances of socially circumscribed discourses. Her analysis provides a foundation for reinterpretations of Bach's music in performance, and it clarifies the social and musical implica-tions for our own time inherent in the deification of Bach and the uncriti-cal acceptance of his works.

Richard Leppert concentrates on visual representations (especially por-traits in oil) of British residents in India in the eighteenth and nineteenth centuries which include notable reference to music. By this means, and also by a discussion of the ideological functions of musical instruments in domestic gender relations, he suggests the uses of music in the economic and social colonization program carried out by the English in India. He reads the 'texts' and 'subtexts' of these images in conjunction with arche-typal examples of European Enlightenment music-theory treatises which, in their dual appeal to nature and reason, make tonality appear both universal and objectively superior to any other kind of musical system. Leppert thus demonstrates inherent political and ideological agendas motivating the claim to autonomy in music and disguised in the gentility of portraits and in the apparent theoretical abstraction of the treatises.

Rose Rosengard Subotnik addresses the piano music of Chopin, a repertory essential to those who would claim music to be devoid of ideological content. She begins with a detailed consideration of autonomy versus contingency in music; she places this issue within the context of debates in academic musicology surrounding methodological positivism and historical contextualism and the implications of both for musical–historical studies. She follows with an examination of contingency in the music of Chopin (thereby challenging its claim to autonomy) by analyzing Chopin's compositional strategies. She proposes that Chopin's music articulates an alternative sense of reality (especially as regards time structuring and social order) than that expressed by other contemporaneous classical music and explores the ways in which the composer is able to manipulate his inherited musical language in order to make this intelligible.

John Shepherd's concern is to understand how the politically personal is articulated from within the internal processes of music and to elaborate a theoretical model whereby 'the parameters of timbre, pitch and rhythm, in both "classical" and "popular" musics, can be linked to male hegemonic processes of gender typing and of cultural reproduction and resistance.' In a discussion of male–female gender relations and cultural reproduction, he stresses that male hegemony is essentially visually constituted. As such, male hegemony has a problematic relationship to sound and especially to music: whereas vision implies separation and distancing, music implies precisely the opposite, namely, the integrative and relational. He argues that timbre 'appears to constitute the nature of sound itself' and that 'the texture, the grain, the tactile quality of sound brings the world into us and reminds us of the social relatedness of humanity . . . Symbolically, it *is* our existence.' He further argues that the issue of timbre tends to be marginalized by formal music theory, which concentrates almost exclusively on pitch in its obsession with objective, rational, visual (masculine) control. Having established timbre as a crucial semiotic dimension in music, Shepherd goes on to compare timbre in 'classical' and 'popular' (especially 'heavy-metal' and 'soft-core' rock) musics and the ways in which these and other repertories manipulate sonorities – the sound itself – to articulate (gender-related) meaning.

John Shepherd's article heralds the third issue explored in the volume: the categories of 'serious' and 'popular' music. These categories are called into question and even collapsed, not only in Shepherd's essay, but also in the chapter by Simon Frith. Traditionally, popular music has been regarded as utilitarian, devoid of aesthetic value, while 'serious' music has been viewed as wholly aesthetic, free of the taint of utility, purpose, or interestedness. The collapse of these conventional categories has several methodological implications. Their demise calls for a historical account of the ideological function of such categories, and it also suggests – or even demands – a crossover of methods: that is, the aesthetic dimension of popular music becomes visible at the same time that the social and political functions of 'serious' music become unavoidable.

In other words, these two repertories, which were previously held as polar opposites, are put on the same methodological footing and are subjected to the same kinds of questions. It is not coincidental, in fact, that such a collapse in academic categories should happen at a time when musical production itself no longer observes such segregation. To the contemporaries of Philip Glass, Laurie Anderson, Steve Reich, Brian Eno, Glenn Branca, and David Byrne, such distinctions seem arbitrary at best, elitist and exclusionary at worst.[7]

Frith's essay reconstructs a set of criteria that underlie the popular evaluation of rock music and suggests an agenda by means of which we can begin to discern how rock articulates meaning, how it organizes our collective sense of time and memory, how it contributes to the social construction of individual identities, and how it is able to be at once socially grounded and resistant to mainstream social norms. He establishes the locus for aesthetic judgment and value in rock music by addressing not only the problematics of its relationship to the demands of the marketplace (the record companies) but also to rock's relationship with its audience of listeners and how that audience is formed. Frith's aesthetic, then, is grounded in society and history and is thus always contingent and problematized by its function as a mass market commodity. At the same time he emphasizes that the 'good' rock song transcends the apparent limitations of its commercial pedigree and posits the means by which this occurs.

The fourth issue examined focuses on the influence of technology and music-distribution patterns on current perceptions and receptions of music. So long as music is understood essentially as autonomous, abstract pitch relationships, then the technologies that produce and reproduce the sounds and the institutions that decide what to perform, publish, broadcast, and so forth remain invisible – or inaudible. They are regarded simply as the means by which the composer's subjectivity comes into contact with

7 For studies that attempt to deal with both 'serious' and 'popular' repertories together on the same footing, see Durant, *Conditions*; Billy Bergman and Richard Horn, *Recombinant do-re-mi: frontiers of the rock era* (New York, 1985); and John Rockwell, *All American music: composition in the late twentieth century* (New York, 1983).

that of the listener and that mystical union of composer and listener seemingly will admit of no actual mediation.

Once the processes of mediation become matters for discussion, however, the components of that mystical union fall apart. And perhaps the most disturbing loss in the fragmentation of the traditional model is that of subjectivity itself. The prized illusion that one owns at least one's perceptions, feelings, and individuality gives way to the realization that one is fundamentally shaped by socially produced, reproduced, and transmitted images.

These problems are repeatedly engaged in the volume, but most especially by John Mowitt. Mowitt's essay, whose title bears homage to Walter Benjamin's classic study, investigates various ramifications of electronic technology in sound production, recording, reproduction, and consumption. Introducing the category of 'a structure of listening', he argues for 'the priority of reception within the social determination of musical experience'. He places musical experience within the context of memory and develops a thesis which recognizes not only the social character of subjectivity, but also the fact that experience itself takes place within a cultural context organized by institutions and practices. His ultimate purpose is to raise political issues, in particular to 'sketch out the emancipatory dialectic of contemporary musical reception' relative to electronic technological processes that dominate one or more stages of music's production and reception in the 'developed' world.

Mowitt formulates his argument around a well-known television advertisement, the phenomenon of the recording studio, and the relation of both to cultural formation and consumption. He delineates the ways in which recording organizes the experience of reception, and he posits that the very conditions of reception actually *precede* the moment of production. He draws attention to the importance of seeing as a supplement to hearing, thus complementing a position held by John Shepherd – but also problematizing it, in that Mowitt holds that this primacy is actually in decline. In examining the cultural experience of reception he engages the famous Adorno–Benjamin debate that centered on the cultural experience of mechanically reproduced art and the political implications of the difference between art to be received in a state of contemplation (traditional art forms – 'masterpieces') and that ideally received in a state of 'distraction' (mechanically reproduced art – the photograph, the film – or, for Adorno, mass-marketed popular music, which for him led to 'regressive listening'). Mowitt ends his essay by formulating the ways in which a bit-centered electronic technology, in spite of its 'corporate imprint', permits a reorganization for the ways in which we both receive and produce music, precisely because this technology renders meaningless the previous auratic differentiation between the original and the copy.

Many other issues, equally significant and equally urgent, are not examined extensively in this volume. For instance, it does not deal with the relationships between music and society in non-Western cultures. This omission should not be taken as evidence of ethnocentrism, however. To the contrary, the questions and methods that recur throughout the volume are especially indebted to models developed by ethnomusicologists. For the most part, unfortunately, the findings of ethnomusicology have been acceptable to historical musicology only insofar as they concern *other* cultures. In other words, recognizing that other musics are bound up with social values does not necessarily lead to the conclusion that *our* music likewise might be: more often it simply results in the chauvinistic, ideological reaffirmation of the superiority of Western art, which is still widely held to be autonomous. This volume intends in part to break down the methodological gap between Western musicology and ethnomusicology by demonstrating how Western music, classical and popular alike, is as dependent on social structures and practices as is any other music.

The volume touches only lightly on questions about the music of women, and ethnic and racial minorities. (Feminist issues are treated most directly by Shepherd; McClary includes a section of feminist criticism; Leppert briefly addresses the relationship of domestic gender relations to music. The music of Black musicians is touched upon by both Shepherd and Mowitt, and Leppert's essay deals at length with the imperialist and racist dimensions of Western art and aesthetics.)

It is our hope that the theoretical models presented here have the effect of opening criticism and scholarship to topics that have been blindspots of traditional musicology, many of which were not expressly considered in this volume. As was suggested above, the old historical and theoretical paradigms have to be re-evaluated, modified, or even discarded if the musics of marginalized peoples are to be received on the same methodological footing as the music of the European canon. And that, finally, is our aim.

To begin to acknowledge the ideologies behind the claim to autonomy, the positivism and formalism of the academic disciplines of music, the conventional categories of serious and popular culture, and the impact of technological mediation on present-day perception and reception is to be forced to abandon the traditional uses of Western classical music. But, at the same time, it is to grasp how very central music is to our understanding of ourselves. Music passes from the separate sphere of the marginal-if-beautiful into the realities of the social world. If music thereby loses its aura, it is granted both the powers and responsibilities of a genuinely politi-cal medium.

RICHARD LEPPERT
SUSAN McCLARY

University of Minnesota

Acknowledgments

We wish to express our thanks to our contributing authors, who also participated in the international conference at the University of Minnesota in April 1985 for which initial versions of the essays in this volume were produced. We are grateful to the Graduate School, University of Minnesota, for its generous financial support of this project. Particular thanks is due Mrs Marlos Rudie and Ms Monika Stumpf for their help in manuscript preparation and the myriad other labors associated with seeing the book through to the end. Finally, we express our gratitude to our editor at Cambridge, Ms Penny Souster, for her support and professionalism every step of the way, and to our text editor at Cambridge, Ms Victoria Cooper.

University of Minnesota

RICHARD LEPPERT
SUSAN McCLARY

Foreword
The ideology of autonomous art

JANET WOLFF

The notion that Art – at least Great Art – transcends the social, the political and the everyday has been under attack for fifteen years or so, in a concerted development of work across a number of disciplines. These disciplines include the relatively new areas of cultural studies, film studies and feminist analysis, as well as the sociology of the arts, the social history of art, and minority voices within departments of English and other literatures. In all the interdisciplinary activity around these developments (new journals, conferences, courses and degrees), music is strangely absent. It is as though music claims a particular exemption from the sociological critique of culture, retaining its special quality as transcendent and autonomous.

The papers in this volume represent an important breakthrough in the study of music by challenging the notion of music as autonomous. But it is crucial to understand where this ideology of autonomous art originated, both in general and with regard to music. In this Foreword, I shall review some of the recent work which has been done on the historical construction of 'aesthetic autonomy', contrasting this with the actual social and ideological nature of all cultural products. I will then go on to consider the relative absence of music from this critical work, and look at some of the possible reasons for its apparent exemption. In particular, I want to examine the argument that music is less amenable to sociological or social-historical analysis because of its abstract or non-representational nature, and to suggest that music is not, in fact, unique in these characteristics: certain other art forms are equally abstract and non-representational.

1

Moreover, even with regard to literature and representational painting, I would argue that an analysis which is restricted to the interpretation of what is represented at the level of content, character and narrative is inadequate. To that extent, music does not present any additional problems which would render sociological analysis impossible.

In England during the past few years there have been heated debates about the nature, and the future, of art education. A major focus of argument, for example at the Royal College of Art in London, has been the relationship between art and design, and between art and industry. Any suggestions that art education should be relevant to the needs of industry and business have been met with that outraged reaction which invariably occurs when the sanctity and purity of Art seem to be challenged. A practical art education is incompatible with the still dominant notion that Art is an individual creation, the result of creative talent and particular inspiration, which could only be contaminated and impeded by any extra-aesthetic concerns.

Without wanting in any way to appear to be defending the specifically Thatcherite inflection of the current argument in favor of the relevance of the arts (as opposed, for example, to the very different intentions behind the nineteenth-century version of William Morris and of the Arts and Crafts Movement), I do think it is worth pointing to the totally unexamined premises on which the would-be saviors of Creativity base their defense. One relevant piece of historical information, which has been lost in the general commitment to a timeless conception of Art, is the fact that contemporary art education originated in a close relationship with industry. The schools of art and design in Britain were set up as the product of a Government Select Commission in 1835, whose concern was with design in manufacture.[1] The ideological premise that the arts ideally work outside the constraints of specific commission and of political or economic imperatives thus postdates even that relatively recent moment in the cultural formation of the industrial bourgeoisie.

The Romantic notion of the autonomy of art, which is still dominant in the late twentieth century, is essentially a product of nineteenth-century ideology and social structure. However, as Arnold Hauser and others have clearly shown, it was preceded, and enabled, by developments much earlier, and in particular by the rise, in the late Renaissance and since, of the notion of the 'artist', as distinct from the craftsperson. Hauser suggests that Michelangelo was the first 'modern artist', not in the sense that there was

[1] See, for example, Nicholas Pearson, *The state and the visual arts: a discussion of state intervention in the visual arts in Britain, 1760–1981* (Milton Keynes, 1982).

something particular about his work which was unprecedented, but because he was associated with important changes in status and conditions of production which promoted the individual artist as creator of his work. These included: the end of dependence on the guilds; improved economic situation; abandonment of the requirement that the artist provide a guarantor for a contract; and emancipation from direct commission. Central to the new conception of art and of the artist, and closely tied to the parallel development of humanist thought, is 'the discovery of the concept of genius, and the idea that the work of art is the creation of an autocratic personality, that this personality transcends tradition, theory and rules, even the work itself'.[2] Over the following centuries, the individualism of the liberal-humanist thought associated with mercantile capitalism and with the bourgeoisie confirmed and reinforced the aesthetic ideology of the artist as sole and privileged originator of the cultural work.

The contemporary version of this conception, however, would not have been possible without the specific developments in the social relations of cultural production in the nineteenth century. The dissolution of the bond between artist/author and patron was more or less completed under industrial capitalism, and the artist, like other kinds of producers, was compelled to operate through the market – producing works and looking for buyers. This literal freedom from constraint (which was, of course, also the cause for many other kinds of unfreedom and new constraints) completed the image of the artist as detached from society, as working in total independence from external pressures, and as expressing his or her own personality in the work of art. Essential to this development was the growth of numerous cultural institutions which effectively mediated between the free-floating artist and potential patrons: dealers, critics, publishing houses, journals and so on. (The transformation of production of fine arts was paralleled by changes in literature, for it was also the case that much writing before the eighteenth century was produced under some form of direct patronage.)[3] Thus the actual situation of the artist/author from the mid-nineteenth century helped to produce the myth that art is an activity which transcends the social. In the twentieth century, this myth has been sustained by the continued marginal existence of cultural producers, and by the persistence and proliferation of specialized arts institutions and personnel – publishers, agents, museum curators, arts editors, and even arts-funding bodies.

[2] Arnold Hauser, *The social history of art*, trans. in collaboration with the author by Stanley Godman (1951; reprint ed. London, 1962), II, p. 61.

[3] See Diana Laurenson, 'The writer and society', *The sociology of literature*, Diana Laurenson and Alan Swingewood (London, 1972), in particular pp. 91–116.

Finally, the idea of aesthetic autonomy has been multiply compounded by the authority of academic disciplines, notably art history, literary criticism, and aesthetics itself. The development of the notion of the artist as creative personality and free intellectual worker was endorsed by the birth of an art history which focused on artists and their work. Vasari's *Lives of the painters* (1550) is the most important early example of this tradition. The discipline of art history, to this day, has been largely a history of great artists and of great works or movements. Apart from certain relatively marginal writers, the mainstream of art history, at least in the English-speaking world, has retained and reinforced a conception of fine art as transcending the social and the historical by virtue of its status *as* art. Until the recent development of a more critical art history (informed by Marxism and feminism), there was little attempt to comprehend artistic production in its political and social context or to examine the very notion of aesthetic autonomy.

Literary criticism, too, has developed, in its rather shorter history, as an approach which sanctifies a particular literary canon in isolation from its material and social conditions of production and reception. Tony Davies has suggested that 'literature, literary ideology and literary history "came into being" at the same moment', namely the 1860s,[4] that they legitimate one another, and that they were central, through the system of education, to the ideological formation of the unity of the English bourgeoisie. The work of Marxist critics like Terry Eagleton and Francis Mulhern has shown how the academic study of literature continues to operate as ideology, despite, or rather because of, its passionate insistence on its detachment from ideology and on the non-ideological nature of the texts it studies.[5] Here, too, the myth of aesthetic autonomy, itself the product of specific historical developments, is guaranteed by the academic discipline which takes 'literature' as its legitimate object. And aesthetics – the philosophy of art – colludes in this exercise, since this discipline also exists in a symbiotic relationship with the idea of 'Art' as comprehensible in terms which are purely intrinsic.[6]

[4] Tony Davies, 'Education, ideology and literature', *Red Letters*, 7 (1978), p. 7. Reprinted in Tony Bennett *et al.*, eds., *Culture, ideology and social process* (London, 1981), pp. 251–60.

[5] Terry Eagleton, *The function of criticism: from The Spectator to post-structuralism* (London, 1984); Francis Mulhern, *The moment of Scrutiny* (London, 1979).

[6] The contradictory features of the concept of 'autonomy' have been discussed recently by Peter Bürger, *The theory of the avant-garde*, trans. Michael Shaw (Minneapolis, 1984). Bürger (p. 35) explores the paradox that, in contemporary bourgeois society, art is *in fact* autonomous (i.e., art has become separated from other aspects of social life), while at the same time the ideology of autonomy has to be attacked in order to expose the very production *of* this autonomy. In this he follows Theodor Adorno, *Aesthetic theory*, trans. G. Lenhardt

Culture, however, is a social product, and the study of culture and the arts must accordingly be sociologically informed. Here it is only possible to indicate some of the social processes which have been involved in the production of art. The social and economic factors relevant to the understanding of art include: contemporary forms of patronage; dominant institutions of cultural production and distribution (workshops, academies, art schools, publishers, galleries, concerts, music publishers, broadcasting companies, and so on – each of which has its own social history and specific social relations); the relationship of the State to cultural production (censorship, control of certain institutions, funding); the sociology of cultural producers (background, class, gender); and the nature and constitution of consumers (literacy rates, availability of cheap materials as a result of improvements in printing, reproduction and other technological developments, social divisions among audiences/viewers/readers).[7] The history of any art is a history of the interplay of these many factors.

I have already indicated the way in which 'Art' itself is a historically specific fact, produced in particular and contingent social circumstances. It can also be shown that the division between 'high art' and both 'popular art' and the so-called 'lesser arts' (decorative arts and crafts) is based on social, rather than aesthetic, distinctions. Paul DiMaggio has demonstrated, for example, how the arts in early nineteenth-century Boston were a promiscuous mix of levels, genres and styles, which played to and were enjoyed by audiences from a wide range of social backgrounds. 'Museums were modelled on Barnum's . . .: fine art was interspersed among such curiosities as bearded women and mutant animals, and popular entertainments were offered for the price of admission to a clientèle that included working people as well as the upper middle class . . . Moses Kemball's Boston Museum exhibited works by such painters as Sully and Peale alongside Chinese curiosities, stuffed animals, mermaids and dwarves.'[8] By the last quarter of the nineteenth century, the divisions between high and popular culture with which we are familiar had been clearly made, and these divisions were firmly grounded in class divisions.

A parallel process of differentiation had also been occurring in England,

(London, 1984), p. 320. Habermas has recently made a similar point concerning art's actual autonomy from society, and the dilemmas this produces. See Jürgen Habermas, 'Modernity versus postmodernity', *New German Critique*, 22 (Winter, 1981), pp. 3–14.

[7] For examples of this type of work, see Milton C. Albrecht *et al*., eds., *The sociology of art and literature: a reader* (London, 1970); and Howard Becker, *Art worlds* (Berkeley and Los Angeles, 1982).

[8] Paul DiMaggio, 'Cultural entrepreneurship in nineteenth-century Boston: the creation of an organizational base for high culture in America', *Media, Culture and Society*, 4/1 (1982), p. 34.

where the pre-industrial cultural pursuits, enjoyed on a cross-class basis, were gradually replaced by a class-specific culture, the high arts of music, theater and literature being the province of the upper-middle and middle classes, and the popular cultural forms of music hall, organized sport and popular literature providing the entertainment of the lower classes. In this process, too, the elimination of traditional cultural activities, and the introduction of new, urban-based entertainments, has to be seen in relation to the developing and problematic relationship between the bourgeoisie and the working class: the increase in what have been called 'rational recreations' was part of the effort made by the new ruling class to control the working class and to legitimate its own rule.[9]

The distinction between high art and the lesser arts has, historically, been closely tied to gender difference in the production of culture. Just over ten years ago, an American feminist art historian asked the question, 'Why have there been no great women artists?'[10] and it has been a large part of the project of the feminist social history of art to try to find an answer. It is evident that the relative invisibility of women in the history of the arts is the result of a variety of exclusionary practices, changing from one period to another, but always discriminating against women. In the history of painting, for example, women artists have had difficulty in gaining admission to guilds and workshops, been excluded from membership of the academies, and been barred from the life class. Even in the history of literature, where, of course, there have been rather more female practitioners, there is plenty of evidence of institutional and ideological constraints on women. With the growing prestige of the novel in the nineteenth century, publishers increasingly favored male novelists over female novelists.[11] And critical practice, in literature and indeed in all the arts, has consistently undermined, neutralized and dismissed work by women.[12] In the fine arts, those areas in which women did come to outnumber men – flower painting, embroidery, and so on – were consequently downgraded in status (in a process with which we are very familiar). A recent book on the history of

[9] For example, see Robert W. Malcolmson, *Popular recreations in English society 1700–1850* (Cambridge, 1973).

[10] Linda Nochlin, 'Why have there been no great women artists?', *Art and sexual politics: women's liberation, women artists, and art history*, eds. Thomas B. Hess and Elizabeth C. Baker (New York, 1973), pp. 1–43.

[11] Gaye Tuchman and Nina Fortin, 'Edging women out: some suggestions about the structure of opportunities and the Victorian novel', *Signs: Journal of Women in Culture and Society*, 6/2 (1980), pp. 308–25.

[12] See Elaine Showalter, 'Women writers and the double standard', *Woman in sexist society: studies in power and powerlessness*, eds. Vivian Gornick and Barbara K. Moran (New York, 1971), pp. 452–79.

embroidery documents the involvement of men in this practice in earlier centuries, and the evolving association of the craft with domesticity and femininity, as well as the concomitant decline in prestige of this work, from the seventeenth century, and particularly during the nineteenth century.[13]

The social basis of cultural practices and institutions is still central to the analysis of the arts in the twentieth century. Several writers have found useful the term 'cultural capital', taken from the work of the French sociologist, Pierre Bourdieu, to describe the way in which different social groups use culture as a kind of capital, confirming their social position, excluding other social groups, and guaranteeing the reproduction of these social divisions from one generation to another.[14] The contemporary sociology of art, like the social history of art, can explore and expose the social bases of those divisions between art forms which are generally presented as purely aesthetic. Rock music is not (at least so far) cultural capital; neither is pottery-making. Soap opera on television does not rank with mainstream theater in the hierarchy of the arts. Science fiction, detective novels and romances have not yet appeared on the syllabuses of many university English degrees (except perhaps in one or two more progressive establishments, and then as optional courses, marginal to the traditional canon). In all this, the maintenance of an elite culture and of the traditional preserve of 'high art' operates at the symbolic level to reinforce the social power of a particular minority. But the challenge of the social-historical analysis of culture throws into disarray the dominant discourse, raising apparently insoluble problems of aesthetic judgment, cultural policy, and, on the practical level, arts funding. When the contingent nature of the ranking of the arts becomes clear, it is a little more problematic to continue to insist that the work of the Royal Shakespeare Company just *is* better than that of a local political theater group ('better' too being a socially-located judgment produced by those accredited with the power to make universal aesthetic pronouncements).

So far, I have talked about the institutions and social relations in which culture is produced and consumed. I have not considered the text itself – the painting, the novel, the film. It will not be surprising, however, to find that the text bears the traces of those historical processes in which it originates. A good deal of the recent work in the sociology of the arts has been the critical analysis of texts, which, moving away from art historical

[13] Rozsika Parker, *The subversive stitch: embroidery and the making of the feminine* (London, 1984).
[14] Pierre Bourdieu, *Distinction: a social critique of the judgement of taste* (London, 1984); see also Paul DiMaggio and Michael Useem, 'The arts in class reproduction', *Cultural and economic reproduction in education: essays on class, ideology and the state*, ed. Michael W. Apple (London, 1982), pp. 181–201.

and literary critical discussions of style and of internal characteristics of works of art, attempts to interpret the meaning of these works in terms of the social and ideological categories represented in them. Art is always ideological, not in the sense that it contains a political message, but in that its meanings are the literary/visual/filmic representation of the extra-aesthetic. The way in which women are depicted in the fine arts is integrally bound up with the way in which they are perceived in a patriarchal culture. (It is important to add that this is a two-way relationship; painting does not just 'reflect' social reality, but is also involved in its production.) The concerns of the nineteenth-century novel, as well as its formulation of issues and its silences, are the concerns of the wider society in which it was produced. The corollary of this, more recently emphasized by work on 'reception aesthetics', is that the meaning read *from* texts will be to some extent that produced by their readers/audiences. Insofar as texts are complex, offering the possibility of a variety of interpretations, then new readers will interpret through the perspective of their own experience and world-view. Meaning is never fixed, and reading is always re-reading.[15]

The idea of aesthetic autonomy, constructed in specific historical and social circumstances, and reinforced by the critical and ideological practices of certain academic disciplines, is beginning to disintegrate. We should not exaggerate the extent to which this socio-critical work has gained acceptance and incorporation within the mainstream of the disciplines of art history and literary criticism. Nevertheless, the sociological approach is now reflected in a large, and growing, amount of important analytical and historical work. Its use by increasing numbers of writers and teachers, and its representation in courses, texts and conferences, constitutes a major challenge to the traditional modes of thought.

The striking exception to all this, until recently, has been music. It is rare to find courses on music in interdisciplinary degrees of cultural studies. Cross-disciplinary journals which publish essays on the sociology of the arts do not often include pieces on music. And most work which has been done on what might be called a 'sociology of music' remains at the level of institutional analysis, audience research or social history. The sociology of music in the United States includes studies of the internal relations of an opera company, and of a symphony orchestra; of the nature of conducting as a profession; and of types of patronage of music.[16] An interesting histor-

[15] See Robert C. Holub, *Reception theory: a critical introduction* (New York, 1984); Terry Eagleton, *Literary theory: an introduction* (Minneapolis, 1983), chapter 2: 'Phenomenology, hermeneutics, reception theory'; and Hans Robert Jauss, *Toward an aesthetic of reception*, trans. Timothy Bahti (Minneapolis, 1982).

[16] Rosanne Martorella, 'The relationship between box office and repertoire: a case study of

ical study has explored the development of concert life in European capital cities in relation to the rise of the middle class, with its particular social calendar and social life, and its 'invention' of domesticity.[17] Scholars of popular music have usually looked at the music industry and at those who use music (sociology of youth culture), or they have analyzed music through its lyrics.[18]

For both popular and classical music, there is hardly any work so far on the ideological nature of musical 'texts', that is, of the music itself, although, interestingly, one of the founding fathers of sociology, Max Weber, did attempt to analyze music (harmony, the dominant seventh, scale systems, and so on) in terms of the progressive rationalization of society.[19] There have been some exceptions to this, particularly in very recent years,[20] but on the whole the ideology of autonomy still rules in the study of music. This may be partly explained by the more specialized and technical knowledge which sociologists and social historians untrained in musi-

[17] opera', *Sociological Quarterly*, 18/3 (1977), pp. 354–66; and also Robert Faulkner, 'Orchestra interaction: communication and authority in an artistic organization'; Jack B. Kamerman, 'The rationalization of symphony orchestra conductors' interpretive styles'; and Stephen R. Couch, 'Patronage and organizational structure in symphony orchestras in London and New York'; all in *Performers and performances: the social organization of artistic work*, eds. Jack B. Kamerman and Rosanne Martorella (New York, 1983).

[18] William Weber, *Music and the middle class: the social structure of concert life in London, Paris and Vienna* (London, 1975). See also Alice M. Hanson, *Musical life in Biedermeier Vienna* (Cambridge, 1985).

[19] For example, Richard A. Peterson and David G. Berger, 'Cycles in symbol production: the case of popular music', *American Sociological Review*, 40/2 (1975), pp. 158–73; also Simon Frith, *Sound effects: youth, leisure and the politics of rock 'n' roll* (London, 1981); Dick Hebdige, *Subculture: the meaning of style* (London, 1979), and Alan Durant, *Conditions of music* (Albany, 1984), chapter 6: 'Rock today: facing the music'.

[19] Max Weber, *The rational and social foundations of music*, trans. and ed. Don Martindale, Johannes Riedel, and Gertrude Neuwirth (Carbondale and London, 1958). The work of Theodor Adorno on the sociology of music also stands out as a major exception to this generalization. See, for instance, his *Introduction to the sociology of music*, trans. E. B. Ashton (New York, 1976), and *Prisms*, trans. Samuel Weber and Shierry Weber (1967; reprint ed. Cambridge, Mass., 1981).

[20] See, for instance, Jacques Attali, *Noise: the political economy of music*, trans. Brian Massumi (Minneapolis, 1985); John Blacking, *How musical is man?* (Seattle, 1973); Dave Laing, *One chord wonders: power and meaning in punk rock* (Milton Keynes, 1985); Susan McClary, 'Pitches, expression, ideology: an exercise in mediation', *Enclitic*, 7 (1983), pp. 76–87; Richard Norton, *Tonality in Western culture* (University Park, Penn., 1984); John Shepherd et al., *Whose music? A sociology of musical languages* (London, 1977); Christopher Small, *Music – society – education* (London, 1977); Rose Rosengard Subotnik, 'Adorno's diagnosis of Beethoven's late style: early symptom of a fatal condition', *Journal of the American Musicological Society*, 29 (1976), pp. 242–75, and 'The historical structure: Adorno's "French" model for the criticism of nineteenth-century music', *19th Century Music*, 2 (1978), pp. 36–60; Leo Treitler, 'History, criticism, and Beethoven's Ninth Symphony', *19th Century Music*, 3 (1980), pp. 193–210, and '"To worship that celestial sound": motives for analysis', *Journal of Musicology*, 1 (1982), pp. 153–70.

cology feel unable to engage in and thus inhibited from approaching.[21] Yet, apart from the mystique surrounding music, there is nothing to prevent anyone from learning about harmony and composition, and since there are plenty of people who have this expertise – musicians, music critics, and music historians – there must be other reasons why the idea of autonomy continues to attach to music so much more tenaciously than to the other arts.

In the sociological study of the arts, it is literature which has proved the most amenable to analysis in terms of ideology-critique and textual semiotics. It appears that the literary text, with its range of characters, narrative line, and linguistic codes, provides a subject-matter which can easily be discussed in terms of social-historical 'types' (Engels, Lukács), class worldviews (Lucien Goldmann),[22] or bourgeois forms of theater (Raymond Williams).[23] That is, the content of the literary text is very often the basis of a socio-critical study. Similarly, in the case of representational painting, the sociological de-coding is likely to depend on character/person depicted or narrative/event portrayed: the nude as part of patriarchal culture,[24] the growing problems of class relations as manifested in changing portrayals of rural workers,[25] or Goya's paintings and engravings as expressing the social and political contradictions of Bourbon Spain.[26] Representational and figurative arts do present one obvious level of interpretation by which we can connect the social and ideological to what is represented in the text.

Music, on the other hand, is abstract and non-representational. (I am, of course, ignoring music with words or lyrics – songs, opera, popular music – on the assumption that what is problematic is not the analysis of the linguistic, but the de-coding of the music itself.) Music does not represent bourgeois characters, gender relations, or political conflicts, at least in any literal or visible manner. For this reason, it is often argued that music somehow does transcend the social and the contingent in ways which literature, film and representational painting do not. I want to conclude by contesting this claim, in order to suggest that the non-representational character of music is no explanation for its exemption from sociological analysis.

21 See Frith, *Sound effects*, p. 13, on his own lack of 'the vocabulary and techniques of musical analysis'.
22 Lucien Goldmann, *The hidden god: a study of tragic vision in the Pensées of Pascal and the tragedies of Racine*, trans. Philip Thody (London, 1964).
23 Raymond Williams, 'Social environment and theatrical environment: the case of English naturalism', *Problems in materialism and culture* (London, 1980), pp. 125–47.
24 John Berger, *Ways of seeing* (Harmondsworth, 1972).
25 John Barrell, *The dark side of the landscape: the rural poor in English painting 1730–1840* (Cambridge, 1980).
26 Gwyn A. Williams, *Goya and the impossible revolution* (London, 1976).

In the first place, music is not the only apparently non-representational art. Abstract painting is similarly resistant to socio-critical analysis. How can we talk about the ideology of a painting by Rothko? What we *can* do, of course, is locate the development of abstract art in the particular social-political-historical moment of its development, and investigate the institutional and other social factors which promoted its success.[27] (An analogous sociology of music is similarly unproblematic.) The real issue is whether the paintings themselves are available for a critical reading. And this has been attempted by certain analysts, who have discussed the formal characteristics of works which themselves produce meaning.[28] Certain types of modern and 'post-modern' dance, which have consciously abandoned character and story-line, must also be interpreted by means of other categories. So music is not unique in presenting a challenge to sociological method, insofar as it is what is generally called 'abstract.'

Secondly, it is becoming increasingly clear that representational art as much as non-representational art is inadequately comprehended in an analysis which deals only with content, character and narrative. The development of structuralist and semiotic modes of analysis has demonstrated that meaning is constructed at a variety of levels. The ideology of the novel is contained in the literary devices and stylistic aspects of the text as well as in the story. Feminist critics have shown, for instance, how the patriarchal nature of writing is constituted both in dominant narrative structure and literary conventions (types of heroine, for example), and in structural features of the available genres and literary and linguistic limitations.[29] Raymond Williams has described the class nature of mid-nineteenth-century writing in terms both of content and of literary style.[30] Nicos Hadjinicolaou has argued that we must locate 'visual ideology' at the level of style and pictorial conventions as much as at the level of narrative.[31] And the semiotics of theater explores the way in which aesthetic and extra-

[27] See, for example, Peter Fuller, 'The fine arts after modernism', *New Left Review*, 119 (1980), pp. 42–59; reprinted in Peter Fuller, *Beyond the crisis in art* (London, 1980), pp. 44–67. See also Fred Orton and Griselda Pollock, 'Avant-gardes and partisans reviewed', *Art History*, 4/3 (1981), pp. 305–27; and Serge Guilbaut, *How New York stole the idea of modern art: abstract expressionism, freedom, and the Cold War* (Chicago, 1983).

[28] Peter Fuller, 'American painting since the last war', and 'John Hoyland', *Beyond the crisis in art*, pp. 70–97, and 56–67, respectively.

[29] Judith Fetterley, *The resisting reader: a feminist approach to American fiction* (Bloomington and London, 1978); Jean E. Kennard, *Victims of convention* (Hamden, Conn., 1978); and Catherine Belsey, *The subject of tragedy: identity and difference in Renaissance drama* (London, 1985).

[30] Raymond Williams, 'Notes on English prose: 1780–1950', *Writing in society* (London, 1983), pp. 67–118.

[31] Nicos Hadjinicolaou, *Art history and class struggle* (London, 1978), especially chapters 7 and 8.

aesthetic meaning is produced not only in text and performance, but also through proxemics, kinesics, dress, gesture, language and numerous other codes.[32] Similarly, the semiotics of television alerts us to the visual, aural and sound (music) codes, rather than operating solely with character and dialogue.[33]

My argument is that all of these considerations bridge the gap between music and the other arts. For, as we now know, the sociological critique of culture involves a complex de-coding of the representational and the non-representational, the linguistic and the non-linguistic, the narrative and the formal. Music does not present any special problems in this respect. My optimistic conclusion, then, is that the sociology of music may benefit from what we have learned from developments in other areas of cultural studies, and that our inhibitions about dismantling the 'autonomy' of music may begin to disappear. The papers which follow in this volume constitute a valuable contribution to this task.

32 Keir Elam, *The semiotics of theatre and drama* (London, 1980).
33 John Fiske and John Hartley, *Reading television* (London, 1978); Umberto Eco, 'Towards a semiotic inquiry into the television message', *Communication studies: an introductory reader*, eds. John Corner and Jeremy Hawthorn (London, 1980), pp. 131–49.

The blasphemy of talking politics during Bach Year

SUSAN McCLARY

Introduction

The last great Bach Year, 1950 (the bicentennial of Bach's death), inspired the undertaking of many monuments of Bach scholarship we now find indispensible. The *Neue Bach Ausgabe* was initiated,[1] and it was during the course of preparing that new edition that the profound revision of Bach's compositional chronology began to emerge.[2] We now know, for instance, that his cantata composition was concentrated in a very few years, that his production of instrumental music occurred throughout his career, that he was far more ambivalent about his position as a church musician than had previously been recognized.[3] Moreover, our interest in the performance practices of early music intensified at that time, resulting in the proliferation of first-rate performers devoted to carefully reconstructed renderings of Bach's music.

But of all these extraordinary contributions to our understanding of Bach, my favorite souvenir of that last Bach Year remains Adorno's 'Bach defended against his devotees'.[4] In this classic essay, Adorno set forth a

[1] *Neue Bach Ausgabe*, ed. Johann-Sebastian-Bach-Institut, Göttingen, and Bach-Archiv, Leipzig (Kassel and Basel, 1954–).

[2] See Georg von Dadelsen, *Beiträge zur Chronologie der Werke Johann Sebastian Bachs* (Trossingen, 1958), and Alfred Dürr, 'Zur Chronologie der Leipziger Vokalmusik J.S. Bach', *Bach Jahrbuch*, 44 (1957), pp. 5–162.

[3] See, for instance, Robert Marshall, 'Bach the progressive: observations on his later works', *The Musical Quarterly*, 62 (1976), pp. 313–57, and Friedrich Blume, 'Outlines for a new picture of Bach', *Music and Letters*, 44 (1963), pp. 214–27.

[4] Theodor Adorno, *Prisms*, trans. Samuel Weber and Shierry Weber (1967; reprint ed. Cambridge, Mass., 1981), pp. 133–46.

model of how Bach's music might be understood in social contexts: both Bach's own and those of subsequent (especially post-war) generations. Unlike the other new directions for Bach scholarship suggested in the 1950s, however, Adorno's insights have had negligible impact on musicology or on the common reception of Bach.[5] Indeed, as 1985 (the tercentenary of Bach's birth) arrived, it became clear that the matters that concerned Adorno had changed very little in the intervening thirty-five years – except, perhaps, to move even farther in directions Adorno would recognize with the ironic satisfaction a paranoid derives from seeing worst-possible scenarios fully realized.

As a scholar classified as a Baroque music specialist, I participated during 1985 in several Bach Year celebrations: panel discussions in which my contributions were modest attempts at resituating Bach in his social, political, ideological context. To my overwhelming joy (again as paranoid confronted with worst-possible scenario), I was told outright by prominent scholars that Bach (unlike 'second-rate' composers such as Telemann) had *nothing* to do with his time or place, that he was 'divinely inspired'; that his music works in accordance with perfect, universal order and truth. One is permitted, in other words, to deal with music in its social context, but only if one agrees to leave figures such as Bach alone. Thus the time seems ripe to take up Adorno's enterprise, to re-examine the ways in which Bach's music can be said to bear the imprint of its social origins, to reconsider the place of Bach's music in present-day culture.

I shall begin by inquiring how and why music is treated differently than the other arts in our culture and also by examining our preconceptions and ideological uses of eighteenth-century music, Bach's in particular. By way of contrast, the second section will present a sketch of Bach's social context and discuss two of his compositions in order to demonstrate the kinds of insights that can be gleaned from socially grounded interpretation. In the final section, I shall consider what is to be gained by dealing with Bach in political terms.

The Pythagorean dilemma

Why should the act of talking about music – especially Bach's – in a political context be regarded as blasphemous? To some extent, music's history of

5 See, however, Laurence Dreyfus, 'Early music defended against its devotees: a theory of historical performance in the twentieth century', *The Musical Quarterly*, 69 (1983), pp. 297–322.

reception parallels that of literature and the visual arts in that it was displaced during the course of the nineteenth century to a 'separate sphere', replete with pseudo-religious rituals and attitudes.[6] At the very moment that music was beginning to be produced for a mass bourgeois audience, that audience sought to legitimize its artifacts by grounding them in the 'certainty' of another, presumably more absolute, realm – rather than in terms of its own social tastes and values.

I wish to argue, however, that music has a much longer history of claiming autonomy from social practice – indeed a history that can be traced at least as far back as Pythagoras and the discovery of a correspondence between harmonious tones and numerical proportions.[7] (Later theorists found similar correspondences between triads – the building blocks of the tonality of the bourgeois era – and properties of physical acoustics[8] or attempted to validate compositions on the basis of their apparently mechanical generation from pitch class sets.)[9] In other words, from very early times up to and including the present, there has been a strain of Western culture that accounts for music in non-social, implicitly metaphysical terms. But parallel with that strain (and also from earliest times) is another which regards music as essentially a human, socially grounded, socially alterable construct.[10] Most polemical battles in the history of music theory and criticism involve the irreconcilable confrontation of these two positions.

[6] See, for instance, Jacques Barzun, *The use and abuse of art* (Princeton, 1974); Janet Wolff, *Aesthetics and the sociology of art* (London, 1983); Terry Eagleton, *Literary theory* (Minneapolis, 1983), and *The function of criticism* (London, 1984); and Susan McClary's series, 'Historical deconstructions and reconstructions' in the *Minnesota Composers Forum Newsletter*, especially 'The roots of alienation' (June, 1982), 'Autonomy and selling out' (June, 1983), and 'The living composition in social context' (February and March, 1984).

[7] What we know of Pythagoras' philosophy was transmitted principally through Philolaus, Plato, and Aristotle. See the discussion in Richard Norton, *Tonality in Western culture* (University Park, Penn. and London, 1984), pp. 80–104.

[8] As much as they may differ in specific argument, the two most influential theories of tonality, those by Rameau and Schenker, agree at least in their desire to account for tonality on a non-social basis. See Jean-Philippe Rameau, *Traité de l'harmonie* (Paris, 1722), trans. Philip Gossett (New York, 1971), and Heinrich Schenker, *Der freie Satz* (Vienna, 1935), trans. Ernst Oster (New York and London, 1979). For discussions linking these to the Pythagorean position see Norton, *Tonality*, pp. 22–55, and Susan McClary, 'The politics of silence and sound', the afterword to Jacques Attali, *Noise: the political economy of music*, trans. Brian Massumi (Minneapolis, 1985), pp. 150–2.

[9] See Allen Forte, *The structure of atonal music* (New Haven, 1973), and David Epstein, *Beyond Orpheus* (Cambridge, Mass., 1979).

[10] Plato deals seriously in the *Republic* with the ethical dimensions of various kinds of musical practice and considers some to be socially beneficial, others to be pernicious. Major stylistic changes in the history of Western music have frequently been accompanied by justifications indicating that new styles are products of changes in social values. For instance, the polemics of the early seventeenth-century 'seconda pratica' assert that abstract rules of

Clearly, my sympathies are with the latter position. But since I consider the problem to lie in that fundamental difference, I would like to explore briefly why the Pythagorean model, with all its subsequent manifestations, is so seductive.

Music enters through the ear – the most vulnerable sense organ. It cannot be closed or used selectively: one can avert one's eyes from the decor of an elevator but not one's ears from its Muzak. And especially in Western culture, in which the visual and the verbal are privileged as sources of knowledge, sound and music tend to slip around and surprise us.[11] The impact of the phenomenon seems immediate: one appears to experience concretely and intimately whatever the music dictates.

Moreover, music appears to be non-representational, at least as representation is usually construed. Unlike literature or the visual arts (which at least make use of characters, plots, color, and shapes that resemble phenomena in the everyday world and that can be referred to by means of ordinary language), music seems to be generated from its own self-contained, abstract principles. It is obviously much easier to demonstrate the content (both literal and ideological) of stories and pictures than of patterns of tones, for which most people have no verbal vocabulary and therefore no conscious cognition.

In music one enters a strange rarified world in which, for instance, the phenomenon of a db can move one to tears, can appear either to affirm (as though inevitably, absolutely) one's expectations or to shatter one's most fundamental beliefs.[12] Now a db all by itself in the real, extra-musical world signifies nothing. It can only do so by appearing in a highly structured, ordered context – a context dependent on norms, rules, and those apparently self-contained, abstract principles known explicitly only by initiated practitioners.

Thus, on the one hand, we have a priesthood of professionals who learn principles of musical order, who come to be able to call musical events by name and even to manipulate them; and, on the other hand, we have a

harmony no longer govern the new music, but rather considerations of text and passionate expression influence its composition. See Monteverdi's foreword to his *Fifth book of madrigals* (1605) as it was glossed by his brother, Giulio Cesare, in *Scherzi musicali* (1607) in *Source readings in music history*, ed. Oliver Strunk (New York, 1950), pp. 405–12. Schoenberg's move into 'atonality' was understood by him at times as a new abstract order, but at other times as a self-conscious rejection of bourgeois values. See Carl Schorske's account in *Fin-de-siècle Vienna* (New York, 1981), pp. 344–64.

11 See, for instance, Don Ihde, *Listening and voice: a phenomenology of sound* (Athens, Ohio, 1976).

12 See, for instance, the discussion of the function of the db in Schubert's Impromptu, Op. 90, No. 1 in Susan McClary, 'Pitches, expression, ideology: an exercise in mediation', *Enclitic*, 7 (1983), pp. 76–86.

laity of listeners who respond strongly to music but have little conscious critical control over it. Because non-professional listeners usually do not know how to account intellectually for how music does what it does, they respond either by mystifying it (ascribing its power to extra-human sources – natural or implicitly supernatural) or by domesticating it (trivializing or marginalizing it, asserting that it does not really bear meaning).

Neither priest nor consumer truly wants to break the spell: to reveal the social grounding of that magic. Thus the priesthood prattles in its jargon that adds a metaphysical component to the essence of music and abdicates responsibility for its power; and listeners react as though mystically – not wanting to attribute to mere mortals the power to move them so. For if one recognizes the power of music to manipulate through unknown means, one at least wants to believe that human hands are not working the controls. Or, conversely, if one is working the controls, one most understandably wants to deny responsibility, to displace it elsewhere. Both musician and layperson collude in this mystification, both resist establishing connections between the outside, social world and the mysterious inner world of music.

If one feels comfortable and identifies with what is being articulated in a particular kind of music, one is likely to be happy ascribing to it universality and extra-human truth. It is only when one is dissatisfied with that music and its implicit social agenda – when, for instance, one's own voice is being silenced by its prestige and its claim to universal autonomy – that the music's ideological constructedness will become an issue: a *political* issue. In other words, advocates of dominant culture tend to take refuge in a neo-Pythagorean position (that is, 'we didn't make this up: this is simply the order of things'). Opponents to reigning order, however, rightly seek to deconstruct its social ideology.

Jacques Attali, in his book *Noise*,[13] develops a means of deciphering socio-political agendas in apparently self-contained music by focusing on the dialectic between order on the one hand and violence on the other. Music must have some degree of order: otherwise it reduces to undifferentiated noise. But it must also have some elements that deviate at least occasionally from that order, or else there is no semblance of motion, no interest, no art. Different repertories arrange themselves variously on a continuum between pure order and pure noise, depending both on the values of the society within which they are produced and also on those of the musicians who compose or even perform the music. By understanding as ideological constructs both the norms of a repertory and also the devia-

[13] Originally published as *Bruits: essai sur l'économie politique de la musique* (Paris, 1977).

tions against those norms in particular compositions, one can begin to discern the most fundamental principles of social order of a period as well as individual strategies of affirmation and opposition.

One can also begin to distinguish between two very different groups of people who participate in music: (1) those who seek to immerse themselves in what they wish to regard as the pure order of music in order to escape what they perceive as the chaos of real life and (2) those who turn to music in order to enact or experience vicariously the simulacrum of opposition to the restrictiveness of real life (with 'real life' represented by those abstract though socially grounded norms). The ways in which one composes, performs, listens, or interprets are heavily influenced by the need either to establish order or to resist it.

We find ourselves today embedded in a society that is very anxious to secure for itself order in the face of potential or actual violence, in the face of pluralistic claims of the right to cultural production. Our theories of music (the means by which institutions train musicians) try to account for all events in a piece of music as manifestations of self-contained order, rather than as a more complex dialectical relationship between conventional norms and codes on the one hand and significant particularities and strategies on the other. And, consciously or not, our performance practices for the most part are designed to produce literal, note-perfect, reassuring but inert renditions of virtually all musics, whether originally affirmative or oppositional.

The music that dominates the concert repertory today is that of the eighteenth-century Enlightenment: the music that was first shaped in accordance with the social values of the stabilizing middle class.[14] This music appears (at least on some levels) to present itself as harmonious, perfect, organic, unified, formally balanced, capable of absorbing and resolving all tensions.[15] In this way, it is very much unlike either the music produced in the seventeenth century (which celebrates in its fragmented structures, its illegitimate dissonances, and in its ornate, defiant arabesques the disruptive, violent struggles of the emerging bourgeoisie against the norms of the church and the aristocracy)[16] or in the nineteenth century (which dramatizes the conflicts between the subjective self and the con-

14 See Susan McClary, 'The rise and fall of the teleological model in Western music', to be published in *The paradigm exchange* (Minneapolis, 1987), and Norton, *Tonality*, pp. 169–230. Compare Terry Eagleton's account of the rise of the novel as a similar means of securing cultural hegemony for the English middle class in *The rape of Clarissa* (Minneapolis, 1982).

15 See Susan McClary, 'A musical dialectic from the Enlightenment: Mozart's Piano Concerto in G Major, K. 453, movement II', *Cultural critique* 4 (Fall, 1986), pp. 129–69.

16 See McClary, 'Politics', pp. 154–6.

straints of bourgeois society).[17] In the music of both the seventeenth and nineteenth centuries the ideological dimensions are far more evident, because their symbolic enactments of social antagonisms are to a large extent the message.

But, in fact, no less ideological are the 'classics', which pretend (at least on some levels) to be manifestations of perfect, absolute, universal form and truth. Surely the overt defiance of eighteenth-century convention that begins in Beethoven means to be unmasking precisely this claim. And even within what we frequently like to perceive as the pure order of eighteenth-century music itself, the tension between order (indeed, competing claims to legitimate order) and deviation – if not outright violence – is readily apparent if we permit ourselves to hear it.[18]

Bach's music as social discourse

This is the case even with the great, universal Bach, whose music is so widely thought to transcend the conditions of his time, place, career, and personality. However, once we understand each of the styles Bach appropriated as an articulation of a set of social values, then we can begin to detect details in his celebrated stylistic synthesis that connect his particular eclectic mode of composition with his thorny social and professional relationships and even with his situation with respect to the broader political context.

To begin with the larger picture, Bach's collected works could only have been produced by someone occupying a de-centered position with respect to acknowledged, mainstream musical cultures. As a German, he belonged to a society that had long been culturally colonized – by the music of the church and later, in the secular realm, by Italian opera and the musical manifestations of French Absolutism.[19] Others of his contemporaries

[17] See Theodor Adorno, 'Spätstil Beethovens', and 'Schubert' in *Moments musicaux* (Frankfurt, 1964), pp. 13–36; Morse Peckham, *Beyond the tragic vision: the quest for identity in the nineteenth century* (New York, 1962); Rose Rosengard Subotnik, 'Adorno's diagnosis of Beethoven's late style: early symptom of a fatal condition', *Journal of the American Musicological Society*, 29 (1976), pp. 242–75, and 'The historical structure: Adorno's "French" model for the criticism of nineteenth-century music', *19th Century Music*, 2 (1978), pp. 36–60; and McClary, 'Pitches'.

[18] See McClary, 'Musical dialectic' and also the discussion of Bach's Brandenburg Concerto No. 5, below.

[19] See Christoph Wolff's article on Bach, *The new Grove dictionary of music and musicians*, ed. Stanley Sadie, 20 vols. (London, 1980), I, pp. 785–840, for a presentation of Bach's career that is sensitive to social contexts. See also Barbara Schwendowius and Wolfgang Dömling, eds., *Johann Sebastian Bach: life – times – influence* (Kassel, 1976), trans. John Coombs, Lionel Salter and Gaynor Nitz (Hamburg, 1977).

aligned themselves with one or another of the dominant options and wrote more or less systematically within its genres and for its market.[20] But Bach chose to retain his marginalized position, to appropriate all available musical discourses while clinging fiercely to his own German heritage, and to forge perhaps not so much a unified totality as a set of eclectic hybrids.

To have thus flown in the face of each of his spheres of influence required a certain kind of personality. Bach's career was mapped on the same forcefield of attractions and ambivalences as his style collection: never willing to commit himself entirely to any single context and its attendant ideology, he continued to shuttle among them, creating antagonisms with superiors while acting out possible means of reconciliation among these various contradictions only within his music.[21]

Seen against this social backdrop, the music itself ceases to appear as the pure mathematical order often suggested by theorists. For the styles Bach assembles are not simply different with respect to surface mannerisms: each has its own peculiar quality of moving through time. To combine in a single composition the on-rushing goal orientation of the Italian opera or concerto with the more sober, static, contrapuntal ideal of the German Lutheran repertory and the motion-arresting graces of French dance is to produce at times a highly conflicted procedure.[22] Yet Bach's genius lies in his ability to take these components that are highly charged – both ideologically and with respect to dynamic musical impulse – and to give the impression of having reconciled them.

Examples

I would like now to demonstrate how this synthetic procedure is manifested in two of Bach's compositions: the first movement of the Brandenburg Concerto No. 5 and Cantata 140, *Wachet auf*. My approach differs fundamentally from those of mainstream music theory which, because it is in search of deep-structural universals, disregards the idiosyncrasies of pieces – or regards them as surface difficulties to be explained away, to be reduced back to the norm.

This is not to say that I am uninterested in norms. Since signification in

[20] Handel, for instance, adopted far more fully the genre of Italian opera and later altered his style to fit the changing tastes of English audiences.

[21] A very high proportion (indeed most) of the surviving documents written by Bach are connected with disputes with authorities. These are collected in *The Bach reader*, ed. and trans. Hans T. David and Arthur Mendel (New York, 1945).

[22] See the discussion below of Bach's cantata *Wachet auf*.

music is in part a product of the socially invested meanings of the individual elements themselves, both of these presentations will require that their components be discussed to some extent in the abstract: it is only up against the norms and semiotic conventions of a style that the strategies of an individual piece can be perceived as significant. Thus the reconstruction of both the norms and the semiotic codes upon which a piece relies is essential.[23] But inasmuch as every piece of music assembles and problematizes very different elements of the shared semiotic code, the interpretive process is by definition both ad hoc (it derives its strategies from the specific demands and features of the individual composition) and dialectical (it strives to account for particularities in terms of the norms they affirm or oppose).

1. *Brandenburg Concerto No. 5, first movement*[24]

a. *Tonality*

On the most basic level, this concerto is a tonal composition (as are most of Bach's pieces). Tonality is, in short, a set of structural and syntactical procedures that emerged in Western music during the course of the seventeenth century and that underlies the concert music of the eighteenth and nineteenth centuries.[25] It is so familiar to us that we often accept it as 'the way music is supposed to go', though its career of rise and decline happens to articulate through musical terms the course of the European bourgeoisie.[26]

Tonality as a procedure relies on the interaction between at least two mutually dependent levels: a background progression and surface strategies. Each informs the other and makes the other meaningful. The background progression is responsible for giving the impression of long-term

[23] We are fortunate in that there existed in the eighteenth century an area of inquiry that strongly resembles semiotics, known today as the *Affektenlehre* or doctrine of the affections. Theorists such as Bach's contemporary, Johann Mattheson, in *Der vollkommene Capellmeister* (Hamburg, 1739), trans. Ernest Harriss (Ann Arbor, 1981), systematically codified both the various signs available for constructing representations of the affections and also the ways in which they could be combined in composition.

[24] The *Concerts avec plusieurs instruments* (French name, Italian forms, German dedication) were presented in autograph to the Margrave of Brandenburg in 1721. Bach had written them, however, between 1718 and 1721 for performance by his own ensemble at Cöthen, where he was employed. The fifth of them is thought to have been the last of the set to be composed.

[25] See Christopher Small, *Music – society – education* (2nd ed. rev., London, 1980), especially chapters 1, 3 and 4.

[26] See Norton, *Tonality*, and McClary, 'Rise and fall'.

coherence. Normally it begins in a home-key called the tonic, proceeds through a series of other keys (each of which is articulated heavily by a cadence), and returns at the end to re-affirm the tonic. The surface activities in a piece of tonal music are concerned with sustaining dynamic tension between the points of arrival that punctuate the background progression. This is largely accomplished by means of a complex harmonic syntax that continually implies what the next cadence in the background ought to be – while deferring the actual arrival until the composer sees fit to produce it.

This process is intensively <u>teleological</u> in that it draws its power from its ability to make the listener desire and finally experience the achievement – usually after much postponed gratification – of predetermined goals. It also seems rational, in that the harmonic procedures are always regulated and controlled by the constraints of tonal harmonic convention. The social values it articulates are those held most dear by the middle class: beliefs in progress, in expansion, in the ability to attain ultimate goals through rational striving, in the ingenuity of the individual strategist operating both within and in defiance of the norm.

In Bach's early eighteenth century, there were several different dialects of tonal procedure. The music of the German Lutheran sphere made use of tonal procedures in some respects (especially the harmonic strategies of implying and postponing goals),[27] but this repertory had other priorities (for instance, long-term structures based on traditional chorale melodies rather than on strictly 'logical', abstract background progressions) that resisted total conversion to tonal procedures. The French musical establishment under Louis XIV recognized all too well the destabilizing, exuberant, subversive character of tonality and tried to prevent its infiltration; the braking quality of French Baroque music (so peculiar to our tonally-trained ears) is the result of its attempt to appropriate the rational power of tonality while constantly draining off its energy.[28]

<hr>

[27] There had been several moments of Italian influence in Germany before this time. In the early seventeenth century, Praetorius employed the polychoral Venetian style, Schein adapted the affective extremes of the madrigal to the sacred motet, and Schütz experimented with these as well as with monody and *stile recitativo* in the context of Lutheran church music. Influence of the later seventeenth-century Italian *bel canto* style is evident in the music of Buxtehude and others.

[28] While French musical style was not of particular concern in Italy, the flamboyant, noisy Italian style was a prominent political issue in France, where it was heatedly discussed and often even banned. See Robert Isherwood, *Music in the service of the king* (Rochester, 1973), for a discussion of the connections between musical institutions and politics in the French court. For contemporary French polemics comparing Italian and French musical styles in terms of a noise/order dichotomy, see François Raguenet, *Parallèle des Italiens et des Français* (Paris, 1702), and *Le Cerf de la Viéville, Seigneur de Freneuse, Comparaison de la musique*

The dynamic procedures just described are most characteristic of Italian music. Bach came into contact with the Italian musical language in the 1710s by way of the fashionable Vivaldi concertos being circulated throughout Europe,[29] and, to a great extent, he adopted it as his principal tongue. Yet (like many who write or speak primarily in a second language) his strategies continually treat tonal procedures as a construct, always under scrutiny, always being informed by the properties of the native tongue.

The opening movement of the Brandenburg Concerto No. 5 qualifies as a tonal composition. Its background progression opens in a key it unambiguously defines as its tonic (D Major), proceeds through a number of other keys (in order: A Major, B Minor, and F♯ Minor), then returns to re-establish the tonic key, thus achieving tonal closure. And throughout, its surface harmonic syntax is unrelentingly devoted to directing the ear to the next goal, instilling desire in the listener for attainment of that goal, and playing with (teasing and postponing, gratifying) the expectation of imminent closure. I will deal with Bach's more unusual strategies in fuller detail below.

b. *Concerto grosso procedure*

The movement's formal structure likewise is indebted heavily to the model Vivaldi developed and made popular. The concerto grosso involves two principal performing media: a large, collective force (the concerto grosso – literally, the 'big ensemble') and one or more soloists. These two forces enact metaphorically – and as a spectacle – the interactions between individual and society.

The fact that this genre developed in the early eighteenth century is not surprising, given that it so systematically addresses the tensions between the dynamic individual and stable society – surely one of the most important issues of the increasingly prominent middle class. By contrast, the medium favored by the sixteenth century was equal-voiced polyphony in which the harmony of the whole was very carefully regulated. The seventeenth century saw the emergence of solo genres (sonata, cantata, opera) that celebrate individuality, virtuosity, dissonance, and extravagant dynamic motion. In the eighteenth century, most musical genres testify to a widespread interest in integrating the best of both those worlds into one in

italienne et de la musique française (Paris, 1705), selections of both translated in *Source readings*, ed. Strunk, pp. 473–507.

[29] Bach studied Vivaldi's collection of concertos, *L'Estro armonico* (Amsterdam, 1712), shortly after they were published. He not only made arrangements of several of these pieces for organ and wrote many Vivaldi-style concertos himself, but he applied its formal principles to almost every other genre with which he was concerned.

which social harmony and individual expression are mutually compatible. The concerto, the new formalized opera aria, and the later sonata procedure all are motivated by this interest.

The standard Vivaldi-style concerto grosso movement begins with the presentation by the large group of a stable block of material, the ritornello. A ritornello represents a microcosm of the entire movement: it defines the tonic and principal thematic material, introduces at least a moment of instability in its middle, and then returns to the stable tonic and closing material to conclude. True to its name ('the little thing that returns'), it reappears throughout the piece to punctuate points of arrival in the background progression, thus throwing the unfolding structure into high relief. Such movements also end with a restatement of the ritornello, which articulates broadly the re-establishment of tonal and thematic order.

In a concerto grosso, the soloist enters between statements of the ritornello. This soloist is almost invariably a virtuosic exhibitionist, the individualism of which flaunts the collectivity of the larger ensemble. It is the active agent in the piece — it is primarily responsible for dynamic motion, for destabilization, the striving toward and achievement of each successive goal (which the large group greets and punctuates with a ritornello).

The convention itself, then, comes with an agenda attached. Given the high value placed on closure in eighteenth-century style, we already know prior to any particular piece (1) that the group will represent stability and the soloist, individual mobility; (2) that the two forces will operate dialectically — with the soloist providing movement, desire, and noise, the group acknowledging and appropriating the soloist's achievements; (3) that regardless of the oppositional tensions between the two in the course of the piece, the tonic key area and the group ritornello will have the last word — thus containing or absorbing the excesses of the soloist; and (4) that individual expression and social harmony will finally be demonstrated to be compatible.

The first movement of Brandenburg Concerto No. 5 shapes itself in accordance with these principles: it begins with a full-ensemble ritornello, alternates ritornello fragments with materials from the soloists in the body of the movement, and concludes with a complete statement of the opening ritornello (Ex. 1).

But the movement starts to present its own problems when the soloists enter. It begins as though it is going to be a concerto for solo flute and violin, but it soon becomes clear that there is a darkhorse competitor for the position of soloist: the harpsichord. Because today we are so accustomed to keyboard concertos, our senses are perhaps dulled to what

Ex. 1: Schematic overview of movement [* = missed cadence or failed closure]

mm. 1–9	mm. 9–19	mm. 19–20	mm. 20–9	mm. 29–31	mm. 31–9	mm. 39–42
Ritornello I	Soloists	*Rit. IIa*	Soloists	*Rit. IIb*	Soloists	*Rit. III*
D Major	DM to AM	AM	AM	AM	AM to Bm	Bm

mm. 42–58	mm. 58–61	mm. 61–101	mm. 101–2	mm. 102–21	mm. 121–5	mm. 125–36
Soloists	*Rit. IV*	Soloists	*Rit. V*	Soloists	*Rit. VIa*	Soloists
Bm to DM	DM*	DM, F#m, AM	AM	AM to DM	DM*	DM

mm. 136–9	mm. 139–54	mm. 154–219	mm. 219–27
Rit. VIb	Soloists	*Harpsichord cadenza*	*Rit. VII*
DM*	DM	[DM]	DM

this emergence of the harpsichord as a soloist signified in terms of the norms in Bach's day. And since this use of the harpsichord turns out to be one of the most unusual and most critical elements in the movement, a word on the conventional early eighteenth-century functions of the harpsichord is in order.

c. Harpsichord

Harpsichords are almost invariably present in Baroque ensembles, but they normally play a service role. They are part of the continuo section, along with a melodic bass instrument, that provides the normative harmonic and rhythmic foundation for the group. Baroque ensembles cannot do without the continuo, but it usually blends in with the background like a custodian that, in insuring continuity, permits the expressive liberties of the soloists. Yet it is frequently the composer or group leader – the brains of the operation – who occupies the position of harpsichordist. Thus as self-effacing as the role may seem, the harpsichordist is often a Svengali or puppet master who quietly works the strings from behind the keyboard.

Anyone who has served as an accompanist knows the almost complete lack of recognition that comes with that position. As an active keyboardist, Bach was very familiar with this role and – if the narrative of this piece can serve as an indication – with its attendant rewards and frustrations. For in this concerto (in which he would have played the harpsichord part himself),[30] he creates a 'Revenge of the continuo player': the harpsichord begins in its rightful, traditional, supporting, norm-articulating role but then gradually emerges to shove everyone else, large ensemble and conventional soloists alike, out of the way for one of the most outlandish displays in music history. The harpsichord is the wild card in this deck that calls all the other parameters of the piece – and their attendant ideologies – into question.

d. Discussion

The premises of the styles within which Bach has chosen to operate (tonality and concerto grosso procedure) presuppose both the simulacrum of dynamic motion and ultimate reconciliation, closure, collective order. The specific characters in Bach's narrative are:

(1) the large ensemble and its ritornello, which is confident (note the self-assured arpeggiation of the opening), unified, slightly smug (the repetition of each note of the unison arpeggio yields a quality of complacency or self-satisfaction), and self-contained (Ex. 2);

Ex. 2: Brandenburg Concerto No. 5, mm. 1–9

Allegro

Flute

Solo violin

Violin

Viola

Violoncello

Violone

Cembalo concertato

accompagnamento

[30] The scoring for the concerto is unusual in that it requires only one violin part instead of the normal two. Bach ordinarily played viola with his group, but if he were occupied with the virtuosic harpsichord part, there would be one string player missing from his standard ensemble. See Friedrich Smend, *Bach in Köthen* (Berlin, 1951), p. 24.

Talking politics during Bach Year

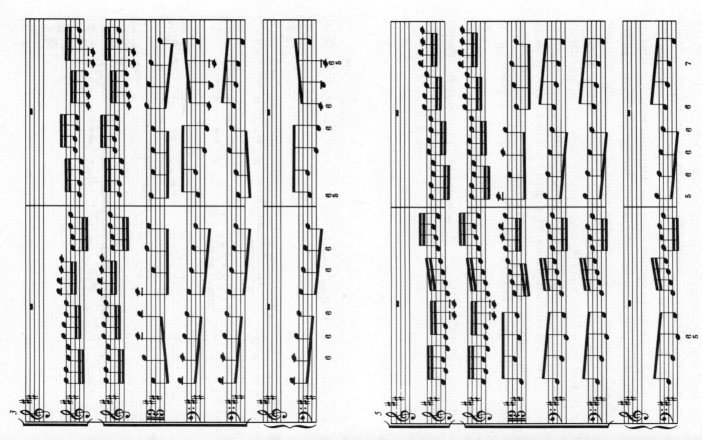

Ex. 2: (cont.)

(2) the conventional soloists – the flute and violin, which are marked by eighteenth-century semiotics as somewhat sentimental (Ex. 3: note the elaborate ornamental filagree of mm. 13–16, the conventional sighs of mm. 20–1) and yet dynamic enough to accomplish modulations to other keys;

(3) the harpsichord, which first serves as continuo support (see Ex. 2) then begins to compete with the soloists for attention (Ex. 4a), and finally overthrows the other forces in a kind of hijacking of the piece (Ex. 4b).

I use the word 'overthrow' because the harpsichord's solo emergence is written so as *not* to appear as an orderly event in the planned narrative. The ritornello seems to know how to deal with the more well-behaved soloists, how to appropriate, absorb, and contain their energy. But in the passage just prior to the cadenza (the extensive harpsichord solo), Bach composes the parts of the ensemble, flute, and violin to make it appear that *their* piece has been violently derailed. They drop out inconclusively, one after another, exactly in the way an orchestra would if one of its members started making up a new piece in the middle of a performance. Their parts no

Talking politics during Bach Year

Ex. 3: mm. 9–22

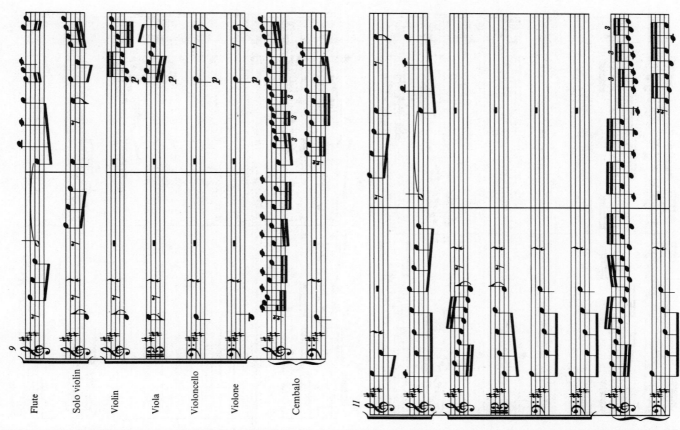

Flute

Solo violin

Violin

Viola

Violoncello

Violone

Cembalo

Ex. 3: (cont.)

Talking politics during Bach Year

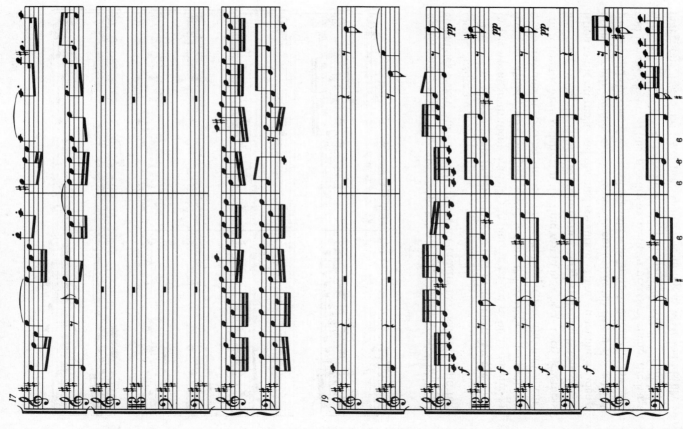

Ex. 3: (*cont.*)

longer make sense. They fall silent in the face of this affront from the ensemble's lackey, and all expectations for orderly reconciliation and harmonic closure are suspended.

The cadenza is extremely unusual in several respects. First, it is presented by the wrong instrument: initially the piece appeared to be a concerto for sentimental flute and violin, yet the cadenza is delivered by a frenzied continuo instrument. Second, it occupies a full quarter of the movement's entire length. Most cadenzas at the time would have been a very few measures long – a slightly elaborate prolongation and preparation before capitulation to the ritornello and the final resolution. Third, sustaining a cadenza of this length requires extraordinary ingenuity. Recall that if the soloist's pace should slacken, the ensemble could leap in (theoretically in any case) and impose closure. Thus in order to maintain necessary energy the harpsichord part must resort to increasingly deviant strategies – chromatic inflections, faster and faster note values – resulting in what sounds like a willful, flamboyant seventeenth-century toccata: in its opposition to the

Talking politics during Bach Year

Ex. 4a: mm. 47–8

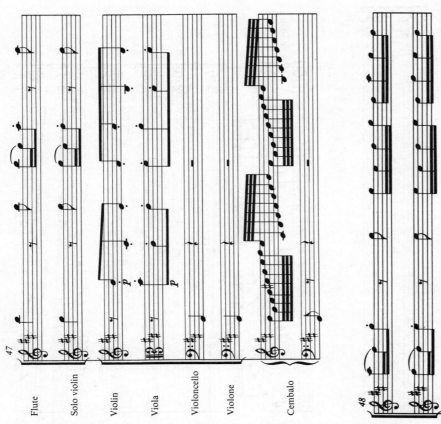
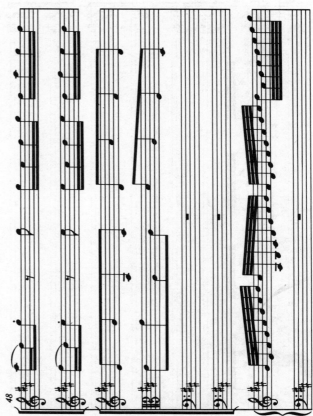

Flute

Solo violin

Violin

Viola

Violoncello

Violone

Cembalo

Ex. 4b: mm. 151-5

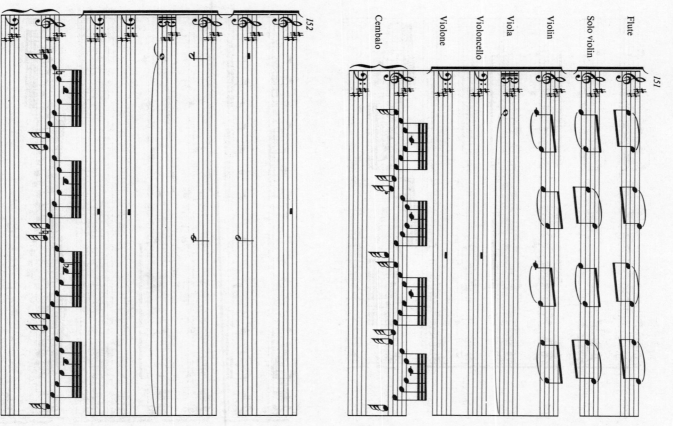

Talking politics during Bach Year

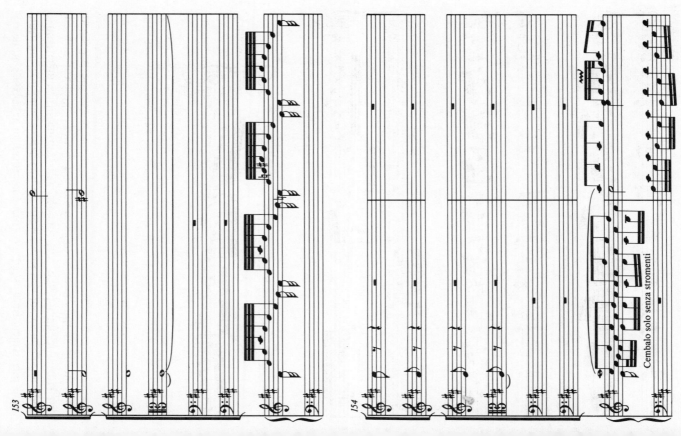

Cembalo solo senza stromenti

ensemble's order, it unleashes elements of chaos, irrationality, and noise until finally it blurs almost entirely the sense of key, meter, and form upon which eighteenth-century style depends (Ex. 5a). Finally, it relents and politely (ironically?) *permits* the ensemble to re-enter with its closing ritornello (Ex. 5b).

Ex. 5a: mm. 196–214

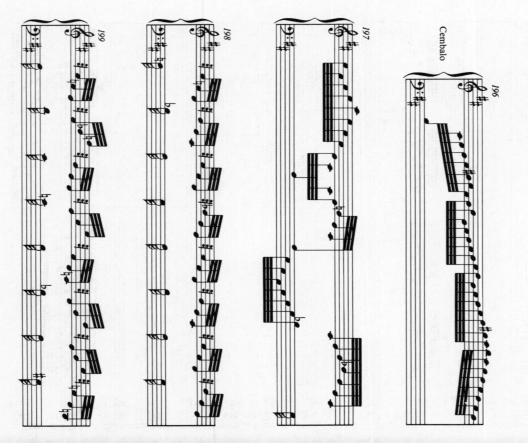

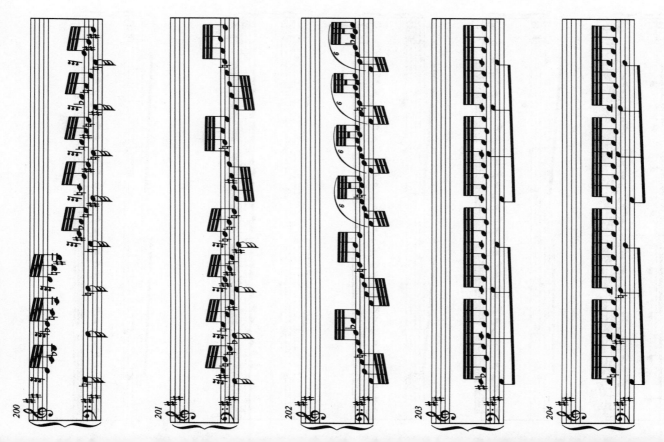

Talking politics during Bach Year

Ex. 5a: (cont.)

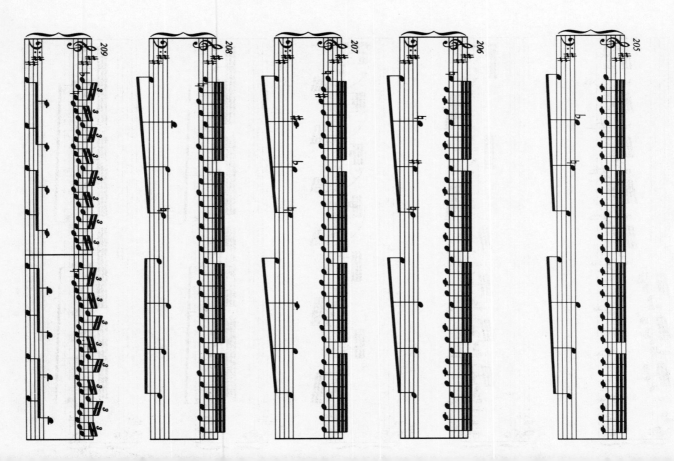

Talking politics during Bach Year

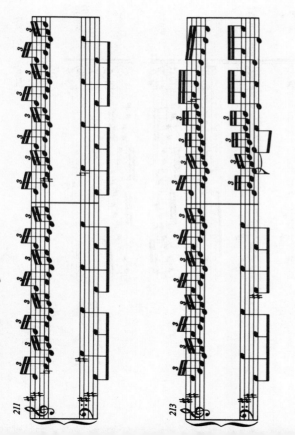

Ex. 5b: mm. 215–19

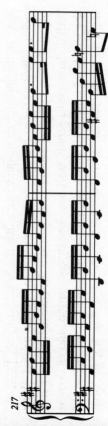

Ex. 5b: (*cont.*)

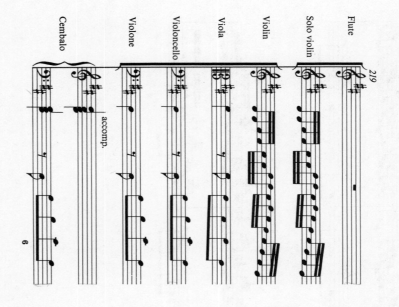

On the surface, closure is attained; but the subversive elements of the piece seem far too powerful to be contained in so conventional a manner. We are relieved at this closure (the alternative seems to be madness) but surely also somewhat troubled by its implications. The usual nice, tight fit between the social norm, as represented by the convention of concerto procedure, and specific content is here highly problematized. Certainly social order and individual freedom are possible, but apparently only so long as the individuals in question – like the sweet-tempered flute and violin – abide by the rules and permit themselves to be appropriated. What happens when a genuine deviant (and one from the ensemble's service staff yet!) declares itself a genius, unconstrained by convention, and takes over? We readily identify with this self-appointed protagonist's adventure (its storming of the Bastille, if you will) and at the same time fear for what might happen as a result of the suspension of traditional authority.

Bach thus articulates very powerfully precisely the dilemma of an ideology that wants to encourage freedom of expression while preserving social harmony. The possibility of virtual social overthrow, and the violence implied by such overthrow, is suggested in the movement, and the reconciliation of individual and social hierarchy at the end – while welcome – may seem largely motivated by convention. To pull this dramatization back within the limits of self-contained structure and order may seem to avoid the dilemma, but it does so at the expense of silencing the piece. For Bach is here enacting the exhilaration as well as the risks of upward mobility, the simultaneous desire for and resistance of concession to social harmony.

2. *Wachet auf*[31]

The shaping principles of both tonality and concerto (and their attendant ideologies) are operative in Cantata 140 as well. But because the cantata is tied to a clear extra-musical, liturgical tradition, Bach also has available to him in the writing of the cantata an explicit semiotic code of conventional signs and associations. It is thus possible to become far more specific with regard to signification in the cantata than in the strictly instrumental concerto. Yet Bach's compositional process never is reducible to the assembling of ready-made meanings. As is the case with all of his pieces, meaning is produced by virtue of particular choices and contextual juxtapositions. I would like here to address a cluster of issues that are engaged by Bach in the cantata: national identity, orthodoxy/Pietism, and gender construction.

a. *National identity*

Bach had access to three distinguishable national styles, each with its own social priorities, codes, ways of understanding and organizing the world. The Italian style had been associated with virtuosity and theatricality since the early seventeenth century. Its practitioners had developed carefully during that period (1) a code by which various flamboyant emotion-types could be constructed and (2) the goal-oriented motion described above in the section on tonality. The French, by contrast, had produced most of

[31] The cantata is designated for the twenty-seventh Sunday after Trinity – an occasion that occurred but twice (1731 and 1742) during Bach's mature career. It is thus thought to have been written in 1731 and probably repeated in 1742. The chorale on which the cantata is based, 'Wachet auf', was written by Philipp Nicolai in the late sixteenth century. The librettist is unknown. See Alfred Dürr, *Die Kantaten von Johann Sebastian Bach* (Kassel, 1971), pp. 531–5, and also the *Norton critical scores* edition of the cantata, with commentary by Gerhard Herz (New York, 1972).

their officially recognized music in the context of Louis XIV's absolutist court. Much of it was self-consciously anti-Italian: in particular the emotional dimension of Italian music was regarded as excessive and the onrushing quality of motion as dangerously close to chaos.[32] In this rarified world in which Platonic order and regimented dance ruled, music was restrained both in its expressivity (for the sake of *bon goût*) and in its characteristic quality of motion. Whereas the aim of Italian music was to sustain tension as long as possible, continually deferring relaxation to moments of orgasmic release, the French constantly drained off excess tension, often once or twice per measure, leaving only enough energy to provide a modicum of movement.

German music in the eighteenth century was heavily influenced by both Italian and French modes of composition. Several waves of Italian style had washed over Germany since the early seventeenth century, and each left a kind of hybrid behind in its wake.[33] French music had likewise been imported, especially by the nobility who aspired to emulate the example of Versailles.[34] What remained constant and recognizable in German music was the traditional tie to the Lutheran liturgy. Regardless of the stylistic surface of this music, to the extent that it incorporated chorale melodies it was still identifiably German.

Moreover, the dedication to chorale-based composition resulted in other, more specifically musical characteristics. For instance, if one was committed to utilizing a sixteenth-century, pre-tonal chorale as the structural underpinning for a movement, the formal demands of the chorale's cadential patterns had to be adjusted to the demands of conventional tonal background progressions – or vice versa. One had to decide whether to abide by the ways of God (as represented by the chorale's archaic – or 'irrational' – characteristics),[35] to follow the ways of Man (as represented by Italianate

32 See n. 28.
33 See n. 27.
34 According to his son, C.P.E., while Bach was a student in Lüneburg he had some access to the Francophile ducal court in Celle and became familiar with the French style there.
35 See, for instance, Bach's Cantata No. 77, *Du sollt Gott, deinen Herren, lieben* (Leipzig, 1723). The underlying pre-existent material in the opening movement is the traditional chorale, 'Dies sind die heil'gen zehn Gebot'' ('These are the Holy Ten Commandments'), a modal chorale that is organized irrationally with respect to tonal norms. To compound the difficulty, Bach sets the chorale as a complex canon (a pun on law). The law of God – the old, pre-Enlightenment law – thus circumscribes many times over the movement's procedure. And while it abides by this law, in musical terms it sounds almost arbitrary in its unfolding. For the old law, it seems, is not compatible with the new eighteenth-century bourgeois tonal procedures that we tend to hear as absolute, timeless, and universal. If the movement makes us uneasy, this is no accident. It is meant to demonstrate how far removed our sense of propriety is from God's and to call the believer back from the false security of secular reason to the unfathomable truth of God. The arias that follow in the

tonal convention), or to try to bring about a reconciliation. And the composers of the German church had retained their taste for complex polyphonic counterpoint, in part because the sixteenth-century motet repertory continued to be used in Lutheran services well into the eighteenth century, in part because of a greater commitment to community (as opposed to Italian unimpeded individual – soloistic – progress), and in part because of an implicit, multileveled metaphysics still fashionable among certain of the German intelligentsia.[36] This penchant for imitative layering gave German music a riche, more ponderous quality of motion that becomes obvious when one compares, say, a concerto of Vivaldi with a concerto by Bach written in the 'Italian style'.[37]

A German composer had the option of pursuing these various styles side by side or meshing them in relatively unproblematic ways.[38] Bach often calls attention to the separate implications of the various components of which he makes use and then seems to overcome the dichotomies in order to fashion a world (always centrally German) in which aspects of each style can co-exist. The first movement of *Wachet auf* is a case in point.

The movement is framed as an Italian concerto, with a self-contained orchestral ritornello that opens, punctuates, and concludes the structure (Ex. 6). Yet the tonal motion within the movement (between statements of the ritornello) is determined by the cadential demands of the pre-existent German chorale melody, 'Wachet auf'.[39] This means that the on-going progressive characteristics of the concerto must be made compatible with the repetitive, relatively static AABA structure of the tune. Bach's solution

cantata are humble pleas for God to teach us His ways. This cantata presents an unusual strategy for Bach in that he stresses incompatibility of his sources rather than enacting his more typical synthesis.

36 The collection of sixteenth-century motets *Florilegium portense* (compiled 1603) remained in use in Leipzig, for instance, during Bach's tenure, and Bach became especially drawn to this archaic style in his last years. See Christoph Wolff, *Der stile antico in der Musik Johann Sebastian Bachs* (Wiesbaden, 1968) for a detailed study of Bach's complex relationship with archaic styles.

37 The first movement of Brandenburg Concerto No. 2 is an excellent example of a composition that utilizes Vivaldi's formal model but that renders it far more complex by means of permutations and imitative overlapping among the four soloists. The concerto-like first movement of the Sonata in B Minor for flute and harpsichord, BWV 1030 becomes so convoluted in its contrapuntal overlap that the linear narrative of the Vivaldi model threatens to break down altogether.

38 Handel, for instance, made use of all the national styles with which he had had contact, but he rarely proceeded by juxtaposing self-consciously his various semiotic systems for the sake of forging new meanings – with socio-political implications – from that juxtaposition.

39 The chorale was first published in 1598 and was incorporated (unlike many hymns composed after the canon was established) into official hymnals. It is extremely regular with regard to melodic contour, formal patterning, and cadential articulation – thus there is no musical dilemma inherent in fusing it with eighteenth-century tonal procedures.

satisfies both dimensions while managing to comment on each and even to make the apparent non-fit thematically meaningful.

Ex. 6: Schematic outline of *Wachet auf*, movement 1

mm. 1-17	17-53	53-69	69-105	105-17	117-24	124-7
Rit. I	Chorale, lines 1-3	Rit. II	Chorale, 4-6	Rit. III	Chorale, 7	Rit. IV
EbM	EbM	EbM	EbM	EbM to BbM	EbM	EbM

mm. 127-34	135-56	156-60	161-89	189-205
Chorale, 8	Extended alleluia	Rit. V	Chorale, 9-11	Rit. VI
EbM	Gm to Cm	CM	AbM, Cm, EbM	EbM

The movement also bears, especially at the beginning, essential references to French music – indeed to the original contextual functions of the stylistic borrowings. For the piece sounds initially as though it is going to be a French overture, a genre developed for the ceremonial entrances of the Sun King to his entertainments[40] (Ex. 7). Two details mark the beginning in ways that illustrate Bach's intentions: (1) while French overtures, like most processional genres, are normally in duple meters, this one is in a *triple* meter and (2) the piece is in Eb, the key of *three* flats. This, then, is music for the entrance of a King – but of the Trinitarian King, which is, in fact, the subject of the chorale and cantata text.

As befits French style, the opening four measures are grand but also rather deliberate and static. They move, in other words, like a French piece. Now Bach seems willing on occasion to simulate briefly the quality of motion characteristic of French music. But even in his French-style dance suites, he quickly becomes impatient: once the French reference has been made, he modulates rapidly into the more congenial Italian on-rushing quality of motion.[41] This affective modulation has extremely interesting

40 For further reading on the impact of Louis' personal imagery on the politics of representation and the absolutist state, see Louis Marin, *Le portrait du roi* (Paris, 1981), to be published in translation by University of Minnesota Press. Louis XIV appropriated many of the signs formerly associated with theological authority and suited them to his own use. Here Bach reverses the process and appropriates Louis' images back to theology; but this reversal underscores how close the two semiotic systems were at the time.

41 This modulation from French rigidity to Italianate exuberance occurs repeatedly in Bach's most French genre, the dance suite. For instance, in the Partita in D major for harpsichord (the most self-consciously French of the entire set) virtually every movement operates according to this principle. The opening 'Ouverture' couples a French overture beginning and an Italian concerto continuation; the 'Courante' commences with the regular braking action of Louis' favorite court dance but soon converts to impetuous Italian motion; and the 'Sarabande' takes an extravagant courtly gesture and teaches it to flow. I know of very few movements by Bach in which he maintains a French quality of motion after he has referred to it.

Ex. 7: mm. 1–4

1. Chorale

ideological implications, for Bach is, in effect, continually setting up a rigid aristocratic structure in order to transform it into the dynamic mobility with which he seems to identify.

The Italian ritornello of this German-chorale movement, then, begins as though it will be a French overture; but another motive enters in the fifth measure – syncopated, scattered, and halting at first (Ex. 8a), then increasingly capable of continuous motion until it leads to a quintessentially Italian spill-over (Ex. 8b), contained only at the very end by the return of the dotted French rhythms which brake the energy and conclude (Ex. 8c). And, of course, the French/Italian ritornello as a whole serves as the

Ex. 8a: mm. 5–6

Ex. 8b: mm. 9–10

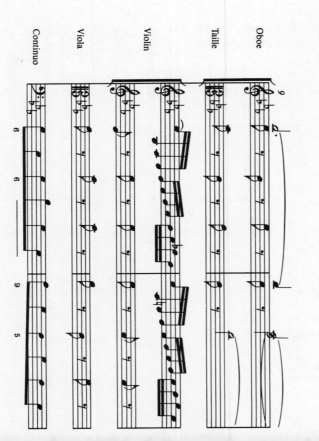

In the terms of the text, the advent of the Trinitarian King is announced, and the sleepers awake and rush excitedly to join the procession. And Bach makes use of all these various elements from his various codes in order to produce a particular quality – that of moving repeatedly from the stasis of the regal or the timeless to the excited goal-oriented expectation of the human congregation and on to a tantalizing foretaste of synthesis or reconciliation.

On one level, the movement is a set of relatively autonomous microcosmic distillations, one nested inside the next, of the cantata's overall plot:

Ex. 9: mm. 17–25

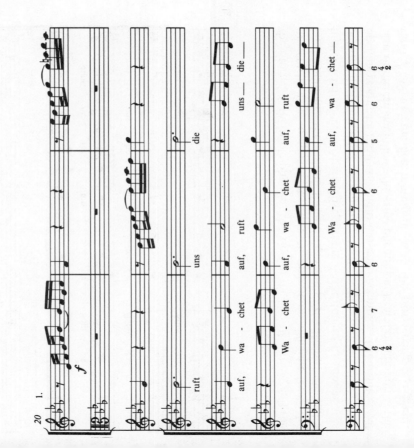

Ex. 9: (cont.)

the ritornello, the triple-phrased A-section of the chorale setting, and the movement as a completed structure all present on different levels the regal beginning, the rushing forward, and the reconciliation. On still a higher level (since final narrative closure — the longed-for union — is deferred until the end of the cantata), this movement converts into a huge opening gesture for the whole multi-movement complex. The architectural plan of the cantata follows the same phenomenological progression as the various layers of the first movement, with this part serving as a grand, French overture, the middle chorale-based movement concerned almost exclusively with the exploration of on-rushingness, and the closing chorale presenting final arrival, absorption into a timeless Lutheran orthodoxy that transcends and contains all the properties (French, Italian, German) that went into its accomplishment (Ex. 10). After hearing such a piece in which so many interlocking levels all finally achieve closure, who could fail to believe in the overdetermination of salvation? In the specifically German plan of salvation?

Ex. 10: Overview of cantata
1. Chorale Fantasia ———— 4. Chorale-based movement
⎣2. Recit.⎦ 3. Duet I ————⎣5. Recit.⎦ 6. Duet II   7. Chorale

The cantata enacts a synthesis of all available national styles in such a way as to appropriate them all and put them in the service of an expressly Lutheran agenda. The monad that contains the whole world is located, significantly, on German soil.

b. Orthodoxy/Pietism

One of the principal ideological disputes with which Bach was continually entangled was that between the more orthodox strains of Lutheranism versus the pietistic.[42] While this split is no longer of pressing interest to us, it did affect Bach's career directly (and, quite frequently, uncomfortably), and it informed his compositional choices.

Very briefly, orthodox congregations were more concerned with collective worship, with doctrine, with the traditional liturgy and hymnody. Elaborate 'art music' (performed by special choirs and instrumentalists and incorporating complex, often secular, styles) was included in services for the 'greater glory'. By contrast, Pietism focused on the personalized relationship between the individual and God. The intervention of elaborate, professionally performed music in that relationship was considered distasteful. Instead, Pietists preferred either straight congregational singing or else, in the context of devotionals, songs in which the lyrics dealt in sentimental – sometimes even erotic – terms with the one-to-one empathy between the Soul and Jesus.[43]

Much of Bach's church music attempts a reconciliation between these two

[42] For more on orthodoxy and Pietism, see Friedrich Blume, *Protestant church music*, trans. in collaboration with Ludwig Finscher *et al.* (London, 1975), Section II, pp. 125–316. For a detailed study of Bach's particular theological situation, see Günther Stiller, *Johann Sebastian Bach and liturgical life in Leipzig* (Berlin, 1970), trans. Herbert Bouman, Daniel Poellot, and Hilton Oswald (St. Louis, 1984).

[43] The chorale 'Wachet auf' is one of the most famous of the personalized Jesus hymns. It is one of the few hymns of Pietist leanings to be canonized in the mainstream chorale tradition, and thus it already suggests the possibility of reconciliation between the orthodox and mystical within itself. See Blume, *Protestant*, p. 140.

positions. On the one hand, most of it clearly falls in the orthodox camp by virtue of its complexity and theatricality, a fact brought to his attention repeatedly by displeased employers of Pietist leanings. But, on the other, he had an insatiable taste, as did many of the writers of cantata libretti, for the vivid, personalized imagery of Pietism. Indeed, the cantata *as a genre* represents a strange fusion between the opera-inspired techniques welcome only in orthodox contexts and the obsessions with Mystical Union, pain, and sentiment that might have seemed repugnant to many of the orthodox. To a Baroque poet or composer, however, this fusion offered an irresistible combination: virtuosity *and* extravagant emotional expression.

The libretto for *Wachet auf* is concerned with integrating both orthodox and pietistic approaches to faith. The structure of the text pursues two parallel strands: the opening, central and concluding movements (which all utilize the traditional chorale melody) address the collective response to the announced advent, while the two Soul/Jesus duets that separate these chorale-based movements involve the individual Christian's response. As we have seen, the collective strand first contains the heralding of the Bridegroom's coming, then the rushing forth of the guests to meet Him, and finally a stable, collective chorale celebrating the arrival. The duets first articulate the Soul's passionate longing for that advent (in explicit bride/groom imagery) and then the mutual bliss of the Union, followed by the concluding chorale in which the congregation, the individual Soul, and Christ are all unified. Both orthodox and Pietist visions of salvation are satisfied. The two camps are thus demonstrated to be mutually compatible. If Bach could not effect such a solution in real life, he could at least enact it through his creative imagination.

c. Gender

Questions concerning the construction of gender rarely enter into discussions of music.[44] The absence of a feminist critique in music is not *necessarily* owing, however, to an anti-woman bias.[45] Until there exists some way

[44] By 'construction' I mean the modes developed in our musical traditions for representing men and women. I am thus assuming that while the sex of an individual is a biological given, the ways in which we understand gender are socially defined and transmitted by – among many other means – music. One of the profound musical achievements of the seventeenth century was the invention of a vocabulary by means of which women characters in operas could be portrayed. That vocabulary is an ideological construct, and it is informed by (male) attitudes of what women are, how they behave and feel, and so forth. Both the code itself and its uses in particular compositions can tell us a great deal about how gender was (and is) socially shaped.

[45] For accounts of how and why American musicology has resisted criticism see Joseph Kerman, *Contemplating music* (Cambridge, Mass., 1985), and Rose Rosengard Subotnik, 'The role of ideology in the study of Western music', *Journal of Musicology*, 2 (1983), pp. 1–12.

of dealing with music in general as a social discourse, gender will remain a non-issue. In this, it is treated no differently than any other matter one might wish to examine critically or ideologically.

The Soul/Jesus duets, however, raise some interesting questions in connection with gender that I would like to discuss. The convention of casting the individual believer as female, incomplete and longing for satisfaction and fulfillment from the divine male, is ancient and Bible-sanctioned. As was mentioned above, it was resurrected and exploited extensively in Pietist poetry concerned with the Mystical Union between the Soul as Bride and Christ as Bridegroom, and it provides one of the two narrative strands of *Wachet auf*.

I am not interested here in bringing charges of 'sexism' against Bach as an individual. He clearly was a product of his time, shaped by attitudes toward religion, politics, and gender then prevalent. It is, however, interesting to note the ways in which Bach brings the musical apparatus of his day to bear on the construction of gender, especially in the first duet.

The duet operates on the conceit that the Soul, unable to perceive Christ's presence or his responses, longs impatiently for him, continually asking when he will arrive. The Soul is presumably gender-free (male souls are also supposed to long in this manner for Christ's coming, after all), yet the musical images Bach uses mark it as specifically female, or as femininity is frequently construed in his – and our – culture, in any case. Put quite simply, the Soul here is a nagging, passive–aggressive wife, insecurely whining for repeated assurances of love and not hearing them when they are proffered (Ex. 11).

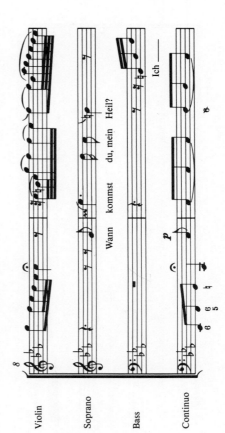

Ex. 11: Movement 2, mm. 8–18

Ex. 11: (cont.)

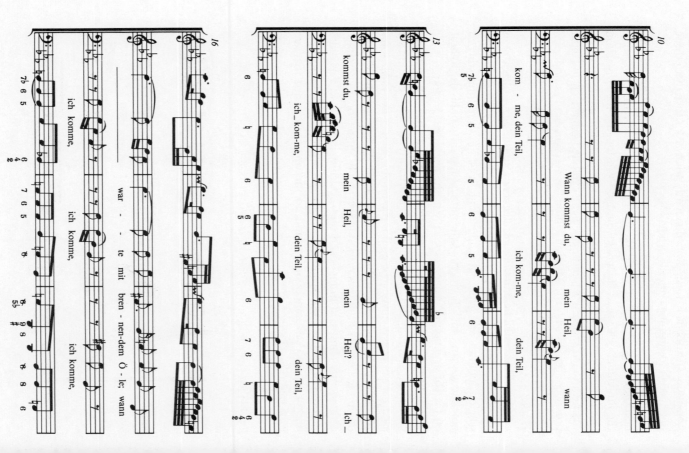

One might counter that this is, in fact, the way we *all* are with respect to the Patriarch, that this is a universal condition. Yet underlying Bach's musical metaphors is an analogy: just as a husband patronizingly puts up with a complaining mate because he knows that her insecurity stems from her emotional dependence, so God tolerates (uni-sex) us and our frailties.

Interestingly, though not really surprisingly, men listening to this duet tend to situate themselves differently with respect to its dialectic than do women. In class discussions I have discovered that the men unself-consciously identify with the male character (with Christ!) and sneer at the Bride's tiresomeness. And the women realize that they are supposed to identify with the Bride but resent the pleading insecurity with which she is portrayed.

That Bach was simply drawing on the stereotypes of female behavior familiar to him and deriving a kind of down-to-earth, homey realism from what was taken to be 'shared truth' – at least among the men in his day – is not in question. Indeed, that is precisely the point. Bach's music is indelibly marked with the concerns and conventional social constructs of his time and place. It is not universal, nor does it represent pure order. Like any product of human social discourse, it is subject to critique – even feminist critique.

Bach reception

Far from appearing universal, Bach's audacious synthesis of all available cultures – with Germany at its center – was not likely to have pleased many of his contemporaries, not even most Germans. Perhaps not surprisingly, he was canonized as representing pure order only after the codes on which his semiotic strategies had relied and their accompanying social contexts had become inactive.[46] Universality was achieved only at the expense of specific, concretely articulated meaning.

The strategy of defining one's own ideology as pure, non-social order clearly is empowering; but it is not entirely advantageous, not even to the artists who most obviously benefit from it. For, as we have seen, such absolutist redefinitions remove whatever was being articulated within the

[46] Bach's music was known to a few connoisseurs in subsequent generations. Van Swieten, for instance, introduced his music (primarily the fugues) to both Mozart and Beethoven, but it was the skilled craftsman and pedagogue in Bach that they admired. By the time Mendelssohn resurrected the *St Matthew Passion* in 1829, the contexts within which Bach had composed it had long vanished. For more on the reception of Bach's music before the Mendelssohn revival, see Gerhard Herz, *Essays on J.S. Bach* (Ann Arbor, 1985), pp. 1–124.

music in terms of signification and convert the composition – or even the repertory as a whole – to the status of icon. If all is perfect order, pure and simple, then no compositional choice can *mean* anything, except by virtue of a kind of closet metaphysics: as evidence of something beyond, which is the source of all perfection.

As is the case with most composers, Bach both revealed his project – throughout his career juxtaposing these widely divergent, ideologically antagonistic styles – and concealed his political agenda in seeming just to be writing notes. His 'devotees,' however, by taking very seriously the claim to autonomy and by having lost access to the codes through which Bach revealed his meanings, have flattened him out into pure order.

Many factors have had a hand in this recasting of Bach as icon: the German nationalists of the early nineteenth century who wanted covertly to colonize the world culturally by means of 'absolute music' (that is, German music with the ideology camouflaged),[47] those nostalgic for periods of strong religious authority;[48] music theorists who derive their rules and norms from the study of his music;[49] the objectivists and combinatorialists of abstract expressionism who claim Bach as their forerun-

[47] The first biographer and advocate of Bach, J.N. Forkel (1802), makes no secret of his nationalistic agenda: 'This undertaking [Bach's biography] is not only of the highest advantage, in every respect, to the art itself, but must contribute more than any other of the kind to the honor of the German name. The works which John [*sic*] Sebastian Bach has left us are an invaluable national patrimony, with which no other nation has anything to be compared.' Forkel continues at some length in this vein. See the translation by 'Mr. Stephenson' (1808) in David and Mendel, eds., *The Bach reader*, p. 296. There is, of course, nothing inappropriate in the promotion of one's national cultural treasures – it is frequently on that basis that canons are constructed. The problem enters only when this interest becomes suppressed.

[48] See Adorno, 'Devotees,' especially pp. 135–6, for a treatment of this mode of reception.

[49] Much of Bach's music was originally designed at least in part for pedagogy: the *Orgel-Büchlein*, the *Well-tempered Clavier*, the *Clavier-Übung*, and the *Art of Fugue* all have obvious educational dimensions. And it was as a teacher, a lone transmitter of the old style of rigorous compositional technique, that Bach was noted in his day and in the generations that followed. (See n. 46.)

But gradually, as familiarity with the codes within which Bach's music operates has eroded, his compositions have been seen not as instances of reconciled tensions but as order, pure and simple. Thus the chorale settings, which to Bach presented the challenge of taking traditional modal melodies and 'rationalizing' them through tonal harmonic syntax, are taken as paradigms of tonal propriety. We take these pieces, in which modal patterns frequently force Bach to resort to outlandish strategies in order to make us believe in their tonal logic, and we teach students that this is how tonality works – without any recognition of the dialectical strain inherent in the genre. Similarly Bach's fugues have been reduced to formula, to structural analysis, and to chord labeling, thus obscuring once again that extraordinary tension between his determination to integrate the old-fashioned multi-leveled polyphonic style with the new on-rushing Italian procedures.

ner;[50] the recording industry that peddles 'authenticity' while sacrificing interpretation to the demands of efficient sound engineering;[51] and performers whose sensibilities have been formed by vastly different cultures and who have no familiarity with – and, indeed, no interest in – Bach's socio-historical context.[52] The result is a politically neutralized cultural figure whose whole opus signifies greatness while none of the events in particular pieces can be said to mean anything at all.

Why do we still need to locate perfection, universality, extra-human truth in this music at the expense of stifling it? What is our sense of the history of the bourgeoisie that we want to cling to its early documents as 'divinely inspired' (a bizarre aspiration, to be sure, for secular humanism), that we do not want them to have been constructed by *us*, that we want our regulations to have extra-human authority – yet to have no god per se onto whom to place the responsibility? In today's crisis of liberal humanism, we appear especially to be trying to hold onto the shreds of evidence for the universal truth-content of bourgeois ideology. And eighteenth-century music seems to offer the best source because it hides its social agenda inside what appear to be pure, self-contained patterns of tones.

Bach's music is especially marked in our culture as a repository of *truth*. Its particular authority is, to be sure, partly owing to its expressly religious

[50] See, for instance, Schoenberg's essay from 1950 on Bach, in *Style and idea*, ed. and trans. Leo Black (Berkeley and Los Angeles, 1975), pp. 393–7. The essay opens as follows: 'I used to say, "Bach is the first composer with twelve tones."' In the same collection, see also 'New music, outmoded music, style and idea', pp. 116–18 and 'National music (2)', p. 173. I by no means intend to criticize Schoenberg for this self-interested appropriation. Indeed, like Adorno (*Devotees*, p. 146), I see this self-empowering reinterpretation as the path away from cultural stagnation. But a new 'misreading' is past due.

[51] The proponents of 'authentic' performance practice in Adorno's day were frequently inept performers located in university musicology programs – thus his sarcastic comments in 'Devotees', pp. 142–6. In the last fifteen years, however, technically proficient performers have begun to participate in early music, and a wide range of highly polished, elaborately produced recordings are now available. In certain respects, new versions of old music have become the current vanguard, satisfying the demand for novelty and thus replacing the need for new music. Many talented young musicians, who in another time would have been composers, devote their efforts to reconstructing this year's definitive, new and improved *Messiah*. 'Authenticity' has become a marketing catchword in this new mass culture industry, with virtually every recording of Baroque music announcing in big letters its particular claim: authentic instruments, authentic score, authentic acoustical setting, or whatever. What often (though not always – see below, n. 60) gets obscured by the obsession for technical and technological perfection is careful interpretation of the music itself. Adorno's statement, p. 144, concerning adequate interpretation remains a powerful guideline.

[52] Some of the leading proponents of 'authentic' early music performance are keenly aware of the necessity of understanding the music within its original social context. See especially Nicolas Harnoncourt's *Musik als Klangrede* (Salzburg and Vienna, 1982). See also Richard Taruskin, Daniel Leech-Wilkinson, Nicholas Temperley, and Robert Winter, 'The limits of authenticity: a discussion', *Early Music*, 12 (1984), pp. 3–25.

subject matter. Much, for instance, is made of Bach's habit of dedicating his music to the Glory of God (though the same people who find great significance in Bach's dedications respond quite differently to the same gesture when delivered by the rock star, Prince).[53] But there is plenty of sacred music available that is not regarded with the same reverence. Why Bach?

As Adorno pointed out in his essay, Bach's music participates fully in musical procedures that are primarily products *not* of a medieval, ritualistic society but of the eighteenth-century Enlightenment bourgeoisie.[54] To be sure, this music abounds with self-conscious archaisms and references to earlier traditions; but the parts that we treasure most – the ones that appear to grant us tastes of what we like to consider universal transcendent truth – are those constructed by means of virtuoso, individualistic defiant techniques of the Italian Baroque: the techniques Bach learned from Vivaldi concertos.

Yet at the same time that this music shapes itself in terms of bourgeois ideology (its goal orientation, obsessive control of greater and greater spans of time, its willful striving, delayed gratification and defiance of norms), it often cloaks that ideology by putting it at the service of an explicit theology. The tonal procedures developed by the emerging bourgeoisie to articulate their sense of the world here become presented as what we, in fact, want to believe they are: eternal, universal truths. It is no accident that the dynasty of Great (bourgeois) Composers begins with Bach, for he gives the impression that *our* way of representing the world musically is God-given. Thereafter, tonality can retain its aura of absolute perfection ('the way music goes') in its native secular habitat. This sleight of hand earned Bach the name 'the fifth evangelist',[55] and his gospel informs and legitimizes the

53 Prince always includes a statement such as 'All thanks 2 God' on his record jackets along with the other acknowledgments. He seems to mean it, even though those unfamiliar with the fusion of physical and divine forms of ecstasy characteristic of Gospel traditions (and, one might add, of Lutheran Pietism) tend to regard these as blasphemous.

54 'Devotees', pp. 135–9.

55 Blume includes this term among others in his attack on theologized notions of Bach in 'Outlines', p. 217. Blume's secularizing of Bach perhaps went a bit too far in denying Bach's commitment to the church, but it succeeded admirably in stimulating a new wave of scholarship that attempts to relocate Bach in his Lutheran setting without undue mystification. Herz 'Toward a new image of Bach', (originally from the 1970 issue of *Bach*, reprinted in his *Essays on Bach*, pp. 149–84) is a direct attempt at refuting Blume's 'Marxism', and Stiller's *Bach and liturgical life in Leipzig* likewise readdresses these issues in great detail. The old mystified Bach lives on, however, in Wilfrid Mellers, *Bach and the dance of God* (New York and Oxford, 1981).

The question is not whether Bach was a believer, but whether his faith caused his music to possess some extrahuman aura. It seems to me quite inescapable that Bach was (among many other things) a Christian; but regardless of how strong his belief, his music remains a human social construct.

remainder of the German canonic tradition, especially the music of the pre-lapsarian Enlightenment (that is, the time when we had it all together rationally, before we began to destroy it with self-indulgent romanticism).

Bach in today's cultural politics

I would now like to invert my title: to address the blasphemy of talking about Bach in a context concentrating primarily on political issues in the current musical scene. Why bother with Bach if one is aware of issues concerning ideological reproduction, if one recognizes the suffocating effect the canon has on those whom it marginalizes? Is it not hypocritical or cowardly to pretend, on the one hand, that one's allegiances are to various forms of post-modern performance and to continue, on the other, to lavish time and energy on the canon?

The fact is that Bach does not go away simply because one refuses to talk about him. Culture is not produced in a vacuum but in a social context with a tradition that, for us, very prominently contains Bach. By turning away to alternative, contemporary forms and leaving him exclusively to his devotees, one may inadvertently contribute to the canon's stranglehold – to the implicit claim by the mainstream that '*we* have truth and universals while *you* only have noise and fads'. Only if those claims, those dominant modes of composition and of reception are scrutinized critically can Bach be perceived in a perspective that permits the music of today to exist on an equal methodological footing.[56]

Let me return for a moment to Adorno and his attack on Bach's devotees. While much of his analysis of ideological tensions in Bach's music and in the reception of that music is extremely insightful and useful, it is difficult fully to endorse his position on how we ought to regard Bach and how we ought, in light of Bach, to proceed. For Adorno is still operating within and on behalf of the autonomous German canon, which he continued to regard as a repository of truth.[57] Adorno's autopsy of Western

[56] By this I do not mean necessarily that Bach and (say) Prince are of equal value, but simply that both need to be critically evaluated in terms of their social contexts, functions, and agendas, that neither is exempt from scrutiny.

[57] Virtually all of Adorno's program is concerned either with discerning the truth articulated in German music from Bach (the fountainhead, as we have seen, of German national music) through Schoenberg or attacking other musics, whether jazz (see 'Perennial fashion – jazz', *Prisms*, pp. 121–32) or Stravinsky (see *Philosophy of modern music*, trans. Anne Mitchell and Wesley Blomster (New York, 1973)).

This concentrated obsession with German culture is understandable, given his own social context, but it presents obstacles to the generalization of his insights. In working with Adorno, one must attempt both to reconstruct the intellectual/political environment

culture and his strategic stance of resignation offer few options and little room to maneuver for the post-World War II artist, especially those (such as blacks and women – indeed, non-Germans) whom he consistently excluded from cultural production. His discussion of Bach seeks on the one hand to relocate Bach's compositional enterprise in a social context but, on the other, to wrest him from the degradation of social reception for the sake of his music's autonomous truth-content.

My problem with current Bach reception is not simply that the devotees have got it all wrong or even that we are spending too much of our finite energies on a repertory 275 years old (though both of those considerations do, in fact, motivate me to some extent), but that the way in which our society regards Bach serves as an obstacle and blinder to new contributions to culture. Thus we must *confront* Bach and the canon and resituate him in such a way as to acknowledge his prominence in musical and non-musical culture while not falling victim to it.

What I am suggesting here is deconstruction as a political act. It is not coincidental that most deconstructive enterprises have centered on classic texts of the eighteenth-century Enlightenment, for, as we have seen, these are the texts (and the musical repertories) that most powerfully articulated the social values of the emergent bourgeoisie under the guise of universal rationality, objectivity, truth.[58] Indeed, so powerful and successful were these articulations – with their hidden ideological underpinnings – that they still shape the ways in which we understand the world and our place as individuals within it.

My proposed project would involve at least three levels. The first is the deconstruction of the canon. For until we can perceive the artifacts of the eighteenth century as human constructs, created in particular social contexts and for particular ideological interests, we cannot, in a sense, be free to produce our own articulations of our own times and interests. The claim to transcendental truth that attaches to Bach and Mozart especially will continue to undercut our efforts until we can begin to define all these various kinds of artistic production as social practice. This program is not intended to reduce Bach's achievement. Indeed, the more one knows about his social and working conditions and the musical codes within which and against which he produced meaning, the more one ought to

within which he formulated his statements and to distill a general methodology that can be applied to repertories excluded by Adorno.

58 See, for instance, Eagleton, *The function of criticism* and *The rape of Clarissa*, deconstructing respectively the institutions of criticism and the novel in eighteenth-century England, and also Jacques Derrida, *Of grammatology*, trans. Gayatri Spivak (Baltimore and London, 1976), pp. 95–316, deconstructing notions of writing in Rousseau.

Ex. 8c: mm. 16–17

introduction that ushers in the true musical king of this cantata: the traditional German chorale melody.

The alternation of static, regal processional music with exuberant, onrushing mobility remains characteristic of the entire movement. A similar effect is drawn from the superimposition of the monolithic, <u>cantus-firmus</u> presentation of the chorale melody and the imitative commentary of the remainder of the choir, though the semiotic associations are different: the chorale stands for the timeless voice of orthodox tradition, while the chattering counterpoint represents human response (Ex. 9).

admire his endeavor, for the compositional choices and inflections in his music will become significant in the sense of *producing socially grounded meaning*, rather than significant as antiquarian relics that have value simply by virtue of possessing 'aura'.

Second, these reinterpretations need to be put into practice. So long as the performances of Bach to which we are subjected are of the pure-order, brain-dead variety, what I have been talking about cannot, in fact, be perceived.[59] In order to make audible the daring syntheses of opposing ideological forces in his compositions, the performer has to be aware of the faultlines in the pieces (that is, how to identify the various components, to be able to render them so as to make their individual qualities of motion heard), and then to *appear* to transcend them by sheer force of will and ingenuity. To play pieces in manners that make accessible the kinds of interpretations suggested above is to contribute insight both into Bach as a human being with desires and frustrations and into the social tensions of his day; to be more responsive to the notation as indicative of highly inflected, significant choices; and to produce a more dramatic, musically compelling reading than is usual.[60] To be sure, those who seek in Bach's music their principal refuge of order become highly indignant with such readings which reintroduce the violent element into his compositions. The greatest blasphemy of all is to perform Bach's music such that it speaks its encoded story of order and noise. But I would contend that *not* to articulate audibly the violent dimensions of music so strongly marked with deviation and resistance – to reduce it to orderliness – is to practice a more pernicious form of violence: *forceable silencing.*

Finally, I would propose the age-old strategy of rewriting the tradition in such a way as to appropriate Bach to our own political ends. Just as Renaissance mannerists justified their subjective excesses by appealing to principles of ancient Greek theory,[61] so each group since the early nine-

[59] Adorno's descriptions of a selection of Bach's fugues in 'Devotees' are excellent recipes for exciting, dialectical performances, though I know of no recording that seems informed by them. One has to play the fugues oneself in accordance with Adorno's interpretations in order to hear them as he describes them.

[60] There are performers of Bach's music who are extremely dynamic and in whose performances one can hear enacted the strains to which Adorno points. These include (among others) Gustav Leonhardt, Franz Brüggen, Nicolas Harmoncourt, and the Kuijkens. For remarkable presentations of the extravagantly theatrical side of Bach's production, listen to Edward Parmentier, a young American harpsichordist.

[61] For instance, Nicolo Vicentino, in his *L'antica musica ridotta alla moderna prattica* (1555), tried to legitimize his use of prohibited chromaticism and dissonances by appealing to the chromatic and enharmonic genera of Greek theory, hitherto empty categories in Renaissance musical practice. Vincenzo Galilei, in his *Dialogo della musica antica e della moderna* (1581), sought to replace what he regarded as the decadence of contrapuntal polyphony with popular-song style by making use of Aristotle's descriptions of Greek music.

teenth century has found it necessary to kidnap Bach from the immediately preceding generation and to demonstrate his affinity with the emerging sensibility.[62] My portrait of Bach presented earlier clearly exhibits characteristics of the post-modern eclectic, of the ideologically marginalized artist empowering himself to appropriate, reinterpret, and manipulate to his own ends the signs and forms of dominant culture. His ultimate success in this enterprise can be a model of sorts to us all. In actively reclaiming Bach and the canon in order to put them to our own uses, we can also reclaim ourselves.

[62] See the Schoenberg references in n. 50 and also the description of Bach by Wagner in David and Mendel, eds., *The Bach reader*, p. 374. This latter is clearly also a self-portrait of Wagner himself (in his own mind the never-sufficiently-appreciated nineteenth-century genius/artist); yet it is strikingly more consonant with my post-modern eclectic Bach than are the objectified, orderly versions of Bach favored by the editors of *The Bach reader*.

Music, domestic life and
cultural chauvinism: images of
British subjects at home in India[1]

RICHARD LEPPERT

Culture is supposed to assume concern for the individual's claim to happiness. But the social antagonisms at the root of culture let it admit this claim only in an internalized and rationalized form.

Herbert Marcuse, 'The affirmative character of culture' (1937)

In this essay I wish to examine the mediating role played by two of the arts, music and painting (or drawing), in the racial estrangement that gradually developed in India between the native peoples and their conquerors, the British, in the late eighteenth and early nineteenth centuries. Specifically, I shall address myself to a small number of paintings and drawings with musical subject matter set in domestic surroundings, produced by European artists active in India who painted immigrant British sitters (to whom I will hence refer for convenience as Anglo-Indians).

'The great endeavour of all commercial states, is to draw the productions of other countries to its own center', wrote Alexander Dalrymple in 1711 in *Observations on the present state of the East India Company; and on the measures to be pursued for ensuring its permanency, and augmenting its commerce* (p. 6). Chartered by Elizabeth I in 1600, by the reign of Charles II the East India Company held rights to 'acquire territory, coin money, command fortresses

[1] I wish to acknowledge financial support received from the American Philosophical Society, the John Simon Guggenheim Memorial Foundation, the National Endowment for the Humanities, and the University of Minnesota Graduate School. I am grateful to the private collectors and public institutions for granting permissions to reproduce the objects illustrated in this study. This paper is part of a larger project which will address the relationship between music, domestic life and ideology in eighteenth-century England.

and troops, form alliances, make war and peace, and exercise both civil and criminal jurisdiction.' In 1689 its directors resolved in writing that 'The Increase of our revenue is the subject of our care . . .' 'tis that must make us a nation in India.' Indeed, the Company profited. And the British government shared in the benefits of this great trade organization in ways directly tied to its own political affairs, most obvious in loans made by the Company to the British government (including one in 1742 for one million pounds to help finance war with France). Over time the development of trade in India was secured and increased by the acquisition of territory, sufficiently vast by 1757 that the British government began its own direct involvement in the country, gradually pushing aside the East India Company, a process finally completed in 1858.[2]

The intrusion of the British political system – and burgeoning bureaucracy – into India in the 1760s not only coincided with but also was a direct cause of the racial estrangement which climaxed in the early nineteenth century in the establishment of rigid distinctions between both peoples at all levels of interaction. This situation was distinctly different from what had existed before, particularly in the early history of the East India Company and its Anglo-Indian employees.

Throughout the seventeenth century and well into the eighteenth the bulk of East Indiamen (and, later, the British military) were of low class status, though the Company's rolls also included some of the high born – usually younger sons or ne'er-do-wells. Many were very young, often still in their teens. (If they survived the climate and tropical diseases – many died within weeks or months of their arrival – they had a good chance of returning to England within a few years substantially richer. Those who were talented and chose to stay with the Company might eventually return with a veritable fortune.)[3] The formative years of these young men were shaped by the new culture to which they were daily exposed. While there were obviously some who maintained their life in India as close to English models as possible, secluding themselves from contact with the local culture, there were also large numbers of East Indiamen who actively involved themselves in Indian life.

One strong inducement to cultural interaction was sex. In the seventeenth century very few British women made the journey to India. English factors, whose period of residency might last ten years or more at a time

2 See further Encyclopaedia Britannica, 11th ed., s.v. 'East India Company.' The quotations are from p. 834.
3 J.H. Plumb, England in the eighteenth century, The Pelican History of England, no. 7 (Harmondsworth, 1950), p. 174.

before a return to Europe, commonly took Indian women either as consorts or wives. The children from these unions were accepted into the resident European community without question. They were educated within the European tradition (mostly in India); male children frequently entered the service of the Company on equal status with their English fathers, while the female children often married Englishmen in the Company's service.[4]

But by the later part of the eighteenth century dramatic changes occurred. Many of the British now coming to India were adults, fully formed Westerners, already holding positions of social status as politicians, clergy, doctors, attorneys, and sons of landed families. Men no longer came as employees of the East India Company but as civil servants to administer the colonial government or as military men to secure British control. A growing consciousness of race developed as the formerly exclusive interests of Anglo-Indians in trade and commerce were gradually channelled toward the demands of imperialism. All in all, however, the racial estrangement which began in the 1760s did not become inevitable until the Governor-Generalship of Charles Cornwallis which began in 1787. Cornwallis excluded all Indians from higher governmental posts, in an effort to streamline the bureaucracy and stamp out corruption; in the process he struck a fatal blow – at the highest level – to racial understanding and cooperation.[5] As the colonial administration developed, and with the growing numbers of Anglo-Indians establishing themselves temporarily or permanently in the country, contacts between the two races and cultures naturally increased, but understanding declined. Increasingly, Indian culture came to be held in contempt as 'irrational, superstitious, barbaric and typical of an inferior civilization'.[6]

Large numbers of British men who were already married came to India with their wives and children.[7] Throughout the social spectrum the increased presence of English women profoundly affected race relations, notably in the steady decrease of racially mixed families. Thus in addition to the immigration of entire families, single women made the journey as well, hoping to marry into the resident British community, thereby reenforcing insular prejudices.[8]

[4] R. Pearson, *Eastern interlude: a social history of the European community in Calcutta* (Calcutta, 1933), pp. 65–6. See also T.G.P. Spear, *The nabobs: a study of the social life of the English in eighteenth century India* (London, 1932), p. 13.

[5] Spear, *Nabobs*, p. 137.

[6] Ibid., p. 129.

[7] Mildred Archer, *India and British portraiture, 1770–1825* (London and New York, 1979), p. 50.

[8] See Spear, *Nabobs*, pp. 140–1, and Pearson, *Eastern interlude*, pp. 171–6.

The final contribution to racial estrangement was made by evangelical missionaries who denounced Hinduism and Islam so vocally as to cast a shadow over Indians as a people.[9] In the end bigotry reigned, as the English settled by and large into a way of life made as comfortably English as possible, isolated from a culture they neither understood nor valued:

In dealing with Orientals, who were reckoned as lacking conscience or soul, to take the most and give the least became axiomatic. [Anglo-Indians] held to the smug and convenient prejudice that Orientals were innately treacherous and depraved. This was countered by Oriental distrust and dislike of Occidentals, provoked by the villainy of early traders and travelers. And strangeness alone bred mistrust. Hence, the average European made no effort to identify with the natives. He lived a virtually segregated existence, communicating with Easterners only in material matters, smugly satisfied that there was little or nothing to learn from 'barbarians' save variations of vice.[10]

Racial estrangement, based on an economy of colonialism and an ideology of cultural superiority, was obvious at all levels of society and personal interaction. But I shall consider this matter only with regard to the life of Anglo-Indians within their homes, wherein the public realities were domesticated and, more important, naturalized. It was within domestic walls where a subtler and no less invidious politics ensued between the two races than was obvious at the overt level of governmental and military activity.[11]

[9] Ibid., pp. 141–2; see also Plumb, *England in the eighteenth century*, pp. 177–8.

[10] Allen Edwardes, *The rape of India: a biography of Robert Clive and a sexual history of the conquest of Hindustan* (New York, 1966), p. 15. For more on this subject see Edward Thompson and G.T. Garratt, *Rise and fulfilment of British rule in India* (London, 1934), pp. 306–17, covering the first half of the nineteenth century. For a good general study of the violence of British colonialism in India, see Edward Thompson, *The making of the Indian princes* (London, 1943). See Peter J. Marshall, *Problems of empire: Britain and India, 1757–1813* (London, 1968), pp. 191–2, for an extract from an 1813 speech by Charles Marsh, former barrister at Madras, 'defending Hinduism against the denigration of missionaries and their supporters'.

[11] In England a man's house served as his ultimate possession, the absolute confirmation of his status. Accordingly, vast sums of money (often a family's whole substance) were spent to build, decorate, improve, maintain, and furnish the domestic enclosure. In India, where the class status of British immigrants was essentially assured by virtue of Western birth, at least relative to the native population, the house and its furnishings in both design and decoration asserted the racial superiority of its owners, thereby contributing to the estrangement of the two peoples.

Anglo-Indians, especially in major settlements like Calcutta, essentially transplanted European building styles to the tropics, with only the slightest possible accommodation to practical necessity (such as the addition of Venetian blinds to tall windows otherwise admitting too much afternoon sun, hence making rooms uninhabitable). Thus only toward the end of the century did the British acknowledge the advantages of coolness allowed by ground-floor rooms. Only slowly did they take to the practical one-storey 'bungalows' with surrounding shade-giving verandahs, in place of porticoed neo-classical structures with two-storey rooms.

Transplantation extended beyond architecture and design to surrounding parks. In India,

In about 1784 Johan Zoffany painted a group portrait of several members of the Morse and Cator families (Fig. 1), identified by family tradition as Robert Morse (d. 1816) playing the violoncello, his sister Anne Francis (d. 1823, married in 1780 to Nathaniel Middleton, a Company servant) playing the harpsichord, her sister Sarah turning the page on the music rack, and Sarah's husband William Cator (d. 1800) standing. The two men were active in India. Robert Morse served as Advocate of the Supreme Court and Sheriff of Calcutta in 1783–4; William Cator was a factor for the East India Company.[12]

at great trouble and more expense, Anglo-Indians often maintained English lawns and gardens, presumably for their value as appropriate 'framing' devices, as used in England for country houses in particular. And beyond that – whether within elegant, gigantic neo-classical mansions or more modestly scaled bungalows – they furnished their houses by and large so as to mirror the life they had left, all impracticalities and expenses of importations aside. From Spear, *Nabobs*, pp. 48–51. For a discussion of changing housing designs during the eighteenth century, together with some information on the decoration of interiors and the use of furniture, see Pearson, *Eastern interlude*, pp. 46–7, 80–2, 140–2. Mildred Archer, *Company drawings in the India Office Library* (London, 1972), reproduces a watercolor drawing of a 'classical European-style house with a garden in the foreground', cat. no. 93, plate 42. On the connection between architecture and ideology, albeit for a later period, see Thomas R. Metcalf, 'Architecture and the representation of empire: India, 1860–1910', *Representations*, 6 (Spring, 1984), pp. 37–65. On the bungalow see especially Anthony King, 'The bungalow', *Architectural Association Quarterly* 5 (1973), pp. 6–25, and Sten Nilsson, *European architecture in India 1750–1850* (London, 1968), especially pp. 176–90, on the bungalow and the relation between architectural form and climate.

[12] Zoffany, though a German, was active in England for many years. He resided in India between 1783 and 1789. For more information on his career in India, see Archer, *India and British portraiture*, pp. 130–77, and the exhibition catalogue by Mary Webster, *Johan Zoffany, 1733–1810* (London, 1977), pp. 74–81, cat. nos. 98–107, and pp. 14–16 of the introduction; William Foster, 'British artists in India, 1760–1820', *The Walpole Society*, 19 (1930–1), pp. 80–7; Sacheverell Sitwell, *Conversation pieces: a survey of English domestic portraits and their painters* (London, 1936), pp. 31–3; and Victoria Manners and G.C. Williamson, *John Zoffany, R.A., his life and works, 1735–1810* (London and New York, 1920), pp. 80–113. Manners and Williamson must be used with extreme caution; the book is notoriously unreliable. Unfortunately, it remains the only full-length monograph on the artist.

Zoffany's profits from his Indian sojourn, according to statements in several London newspapers early in 1785, were staggering: 'The emigration of artists has received an additional spur by Zoffany's having already remitted home £36,000, accompanied with a letter which states that he intends coming home as soon as he has finished the portraits that are bespoke, which will produce to the amount of £30,000 more.' Quoted from William T. Whitley, *Artists and their friends in England, 1700–1799*, 2 vols. (New York, 1928), II, p. 19. Many years later, in 1811, Zoffany's widow told a Miss Green, niece to artist George Dance, that in India her husband had 'made a considerable fortune by His paintings & drawings'. Quoted from Oliver Millar, *Zoffany and his Tribuna* (London, 1967), p. 39. See also Foster, 'British Artists', pp. 85–6. It seems that most of Zoffany's Indian earnings were realized from English sitters and not his Indian patrons.

The first professional English artist to visit India was Tilly Kettle who resided there from 1769 to 1776. He returned to England at age forty-one, having already made a considerable fortune. See James D. Milner, 'Tilly Kettle', *The Walpole Society*, 15 (1926–7), pp. 47–103 (with illustrations); pp. 64–74 cover his period in India; pp. 89–95 catalogue the paintings

The portrait was painted in India; it is this fact which first attracted my notice, rather than the image itself. In appearance the painting is fundamentally similar to scores of other examples produced in England during the same period. But the picture's function is changed by its place of origin, all the more because the place of origin is not represented: India itself has been absented. This fact problematizes the relationship between the 'objective' image and its 'subtextual' values, values visually transmitted by the metaphor of a musical performance in an (implied) domestic setting.

The thrust of my argument will be that this portrait (together with several other similar images) visually establishes a relationship between the arts of music and painting, as signifiers and transmitters of cultural values, on the one hand, and social, political and economic structures and the necessary supporting ideologies, on the other. Put another way, this oil portrait on a domestic musical subject mediates the political and social reality of British colonialism by reformulating this reality and its claimed benefits – to both English and Indian alike – into a visual language eminently attractive, seamless and unprovocative. In short, the image translates imperial policy and cultural chauvinism into the triumph and reward of Western civilization. It masks the image of *realpolitik* by erasing all evidence of that which has been subdued and of how the defeat was accomplished: by trade and labor exploitation, racial separation, bureaucratization, and the brutality of military enforcement. The image, which fundamentally demands to be read as Harmony, Unity, Order and (by association) Peace, justifies aggression for the aggressor. The question to be answered is 'How, by reference to music, is this visually accomplished?'

To begin, the portrait is a typical 'conversation piece', an informal grouping of sitters, at once casual, self-assured and homey. Except for the palatial backdrop – the conventional drapery and classically-inspired architectural and sculptural detail – the setting represents an 'ordinary' musical gathering in domestic surroundings. The sitters resonate against this (unlikely) backdrop with the perfect ease born of the very status the props serve to confirm.

The props are central to the controlled meaning of the portrait, so much

executed in India. There is also a brief reference to Kettle in Foster, 'British Artists', pp. 56–7. This study (pp. 1–88) contains brief biographical summaries of the careers of sixty-one artists. Foster updated the study in 'Additional notes to British artists in India, 1760–1820', *The Walpole Society*, 21 (1932–3), pp. 108–9; Archer, *India and British portraiture*, is the standard account on the general subject; its contents are also arranged by artist. The discussion on Kettle occupies pp. 66–97.

The Morse–Cator portrait is discussed in Webster, *Zoffany*, p. 76, cat. no. 101 and Archer, *India and British portraiture*, pp. 137–8 (illustrated), from which my information on the sitters is drawn.

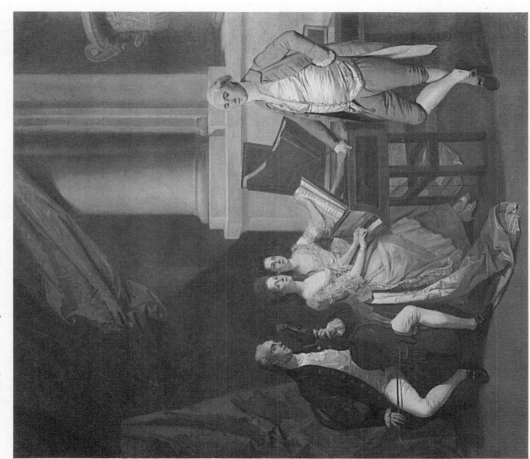

Fig. 1 Johan Zoffany (1733–1810), *The Morse and Cator Families*, c. 1784. Aberdeen Art Gallery and Museums, Scotland, inv. no. 53.2

so that two of them – the harpsichord in the foreground and the classical column at the back – occupy the center of the picture. They serve as standard-bearers of Western self-image: refinement (high culture) in the case of the former, strength and historical patrimony (civilization) for the latter. Moreover, there is a strong relationship between the two, built on contemporaneous belief in principles of 'natural' order, making them ideologically perfect reflections of Enlightenment values.[13]

Thus with regard to architecture, the eighteenth-century English stood in awe of classical or classically-inspired styles (they had very little taste for Continental Rococo). Historically, not the least attraction of this architecture was its perceived order and symmetry, embodying the rational and logical perfection of mathematics through which the proportions of the designs were realized. With regard to music, and especially music theory, the same held true, and it is this issue that I must discuss in some detail, in order to come to terms with the embedded significance of the harpsichord in the picture.[14]

[13] On the range of meanings for the word 'nature' in the eighteenth century, see the outline by Arthur O. Lovejoy, "'Nature' as aesthetic norm," *Essays in the history of ideas* (Baltimore, 1948), pp. 69–77. I wish to thank Professor Mary Bellhouse for drawing my attention to this article.

[14] Robert Morris (c. 1702–54) in his *Lectures on architecture. Consisting of rules founded upon harmonick and arithmetical proportions in building* (London, 1734) draws an explicit connection between architecture and music, as cited and explained by John Archer, *The literature of British domestic architecture 1715–1842* (Cambridge, Mass., 1985), pp. 581–2:

'Nature has taught Mankind in *Musick* certain Rules for Proportion of Sounds, so *Architecture* has its Rules dependent on those Proportions.' [Morris] conceived a hierarchy of disciplines, all based on proportion, with architecture at the top: 'The Square in *Geometry,* the Union or Circle in *Musick,* and the Cube in *Building,* have all an inseparable Proportion' (p. 74). Extending the musical analogy further, Morris established seven fundamental architectural proportions based on musical intervals, and he illustrated geometric solids based on those proportions in a plate facing page 75. The ratios of height, depth, and width in these solids are as follows: 1:1:1 (a cube), 1:1:1½ (a cube and a half), 1:1:2 (a double cube), 1:2:3, 2:3:4, 3:4:5, and 3:4:6. In the sixth and seventh lectures Morris suggested that these architectural proportions would create a kind of beauty that would lead to perception of the greater harmony of all Nature: 'Beauty, in all Objects, spring[s] from the same unerring Law in Nature, which, in *Architecture,* I would call Proportion. The joint Union and Concordance of the Parts, in an exact Symmetry, forms the whole a compleat Harmony, which admits of no Medium. . . . When I consider Proportions, I am led into a Profundity of Thought . . . If we immerse our Ideas into the infinite Tract of unbounded Space, and with the Imagination paint out the numberless Multitudes of Planets, or little Worlds, regularly revolving round their destin'd Orbs . . . we must feel Emanations of the Harmony of Nature diffus'd in us; and must immediately acknowledge the Necessity of Proportion in the Preservation of the whole Oeconomy of the Universe' (pp. 81, 101–2).

Morris's book was reprinted in 1736 and published in a second edition in 1759. I wish to thank my colleague Professor John Archer for bringing this text to my attention.

John Keeble in 1784 published *The theory of harmonics: or, an illustration of the Grecian harmonica* (Fig. 2), a treatise neither original nor unique to the period, though it attracted considerable attention at the time of its appearance. Keeble was a professional performing musician, but his book's subject was the mathematics of sound. Over the course of more than two hundred pages and with the aid of twenty-six engraved plates, he provided a detailed description of the Greek harmonic system, including by means of ratios an account of the scale across several octaves (Figs. 3–5). There is little in the

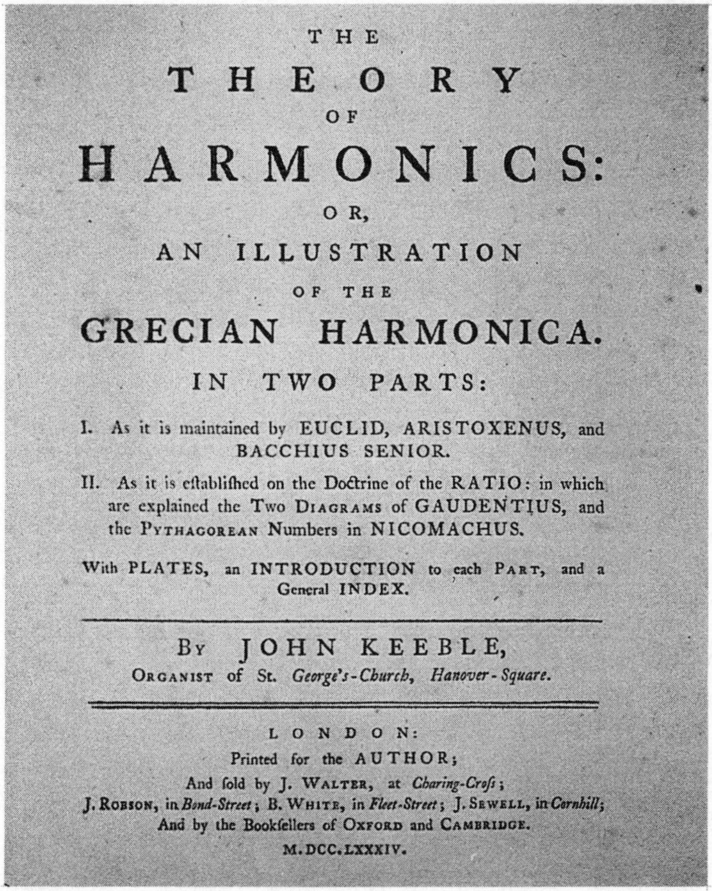
THE

THEORY

OF

HARMONICS:

OR,

AN ILLUSTRATION

OF THE

GRECIAN HARMONICA.

IN TWO PARTS:

I. As it is maintained by EUCLID, ARISTOXENUS, and BACCHIUS SENIOR.

II. As it is eſtabliſhed on the Doctrine of the RATIO: in which are explained the Two DIAGRAMS of GAUDENTIUS, and the PYTHAGOREAN Numbers in NICOMACHUS.

With PLATES, an INTRODUCTION to each PART, and a General INDEX.

BY JOHN KEEBLE,

ORGANIST of St. *George's-Church, Hanover-Square.*

LONDON:

Printed for the AUTHOR;

And ſold by J. WALTER, at *Charing-Croſs*;

J. ROBSON, in *Bond-Street*; B. WHITE, in *Fleet-Street*; J. SEWELL, in *Cornhill*;

And by the Bookſellers of OXFORD and CAMBRIDGE.

M.DCC.LXXXIV.

Fig. 2 John Keeble, *The theory of harmonics: or, an illustration of the Grecian harmonica* (1784). Title page. O. Meredith Wilson Library, University of Minnesota, Minneapolis

HARMONICS OF ROOT 1

1 B	1	2	4	8	16	32	64	128	256	512
2 B	2	4	8	16	32	64	128	256	512	1024
3 E	3	6	12	24	48	96	192	384	768	1536
4 B	4	8	16	32	64	128	256	512	1024	2048
5 G	5	10	20	40	80	160	320	640	1280	2560
6 E	6	12	24	48	96	192	384	768	1536	3072
8 B	8	16	32	64	128	256	512	1024	2048	4096

ROOT 3

1 E	3	6	12	24	48	96	192	384	768	1536
2 E	6	12	24	48	96	192	384	768	1536	3072
3 A	9	18	36	72	144	288	576	1152	2304	4608
4 E	12	24	48	96	192	384	768	1536	3072	6144
5 C	15	30	60	120	240	480	960	1920	3840	7680
6 A	18	36	72	144	288	576	1152	2304	4608	9216
8 E	24	48	96	192	384	768	1536	3072	6144	12288

ROOT 9

1 A	9	18	36	72	144	288	576	1152	2304	4608
2 A	18	36	72	144	288	576	1152	2304	4608	9216
3 D	27	54	108	216	432	864	1728	3456	6912	13824
4 A	36	72	144	288	576	1152	2304	4608	9216	18432
5 F	45	90	180	360	720	1440	2880	5760	11520	23040
6 D	54	108	216	432	864	1728	3456	6912	13824	27648
8 A	72	144	288	576	1152	2304	4608	9216	18432	36864

ROOT 27

1 D	27	54	108	216	432	864	1728	3456	6912	13824
2 D	54	108	216	432	864	1728	3456	6912	13824	27648
3 G	81	162	324	648	1296	2592	5184	10368	20736	41472
4 D	108	216	432	864	1728	3456	6912	13824	27648	55296
5 Bb	135	270	540	1080	2160	4320	8640	17280	34560	69120
6 G	162	324	648	1296	2592	5184	10368	20736	41472	82944
8 D	216	432	864	1728	3456	6912	13824	27648	55296	110592

HARMONICS OF ROOT 81

1 G	81	162	324	648	1296	2592	5184
2 G	162	324	648	1296	2592	5184	10368
3 C	243	486	972	1944	3888	7776	15552
4 G	324	648	1296	2592	5184	10368	20736
5 Eb	405	810	1620	3240	6480	12960	25920
6 C	486	972	1944	3888	7776	15552	31104
8 G	648	1296	2592	5184	10368	20736	41472

ROOT 243

1 C	243	486	972	1944	3888	7776	15552
2 C	486	972	1944	3888	7776	15552	31104
3 F	729	1458	2916	5832	11664	23328	46656
4 C	972	1944	3888	7776	15552	31104	62208
5 Ab	1215	2430	4860	9720	19440	38880	77760
6 F	1458	2916	5832	11664	23328	46656	93312
8 C	1944	3888	7776	15552	31104	62208	124416

ROOT 729

1 F	729	1458	2916	5832	11664	23328	46656
2 F	1458	2916	5832	11664	23328	46656	93312
3 Bb	2187	4374	8748	17496	34992	69984	139968
4 F	2916	5832	11664	23328	46656	93312	186624
5 Db	3645	7290	14580	29160	58320	116640	233280
6 Bb	4374	8748	17496	34992	69984	139968	279936
8 F	5832	11664	23328	46656	93312	186624	373248

ROOT 2187

1 Bb	2187	4374	8748	17496	34992	69984	139968
2 Bb	4374	8748	17496	34992	69984	139968	279936
3 Eb	6561	13122	26244	52488	104976	209952	419904
4 Bb	8748	17496	34992	69984	139968	279936	559872
5 Gb	10935	21870	43740	87480	174960	349920	699860
6 Eb	13122	26244	52488	104976	209952	419904	839808
8 Bb	17496	34992	69984	139968	279936	559872	1119744

continued

HARMONICS OF ROOT 6561

1 Eb	6561
2 Eb	13122
3 Ab	19683
4 Eb	26244
5 Cb	32805
6 Ab	39366
8 Eb	52488

ROOT 19683

1 Ab	19683
2 Ab	39366
3 Db	59049
4 Ab	78732
5 Fb	98415
6 Db	118098
8 Ab	157464

ROOT 59049

1 Db	59049
2 Db	118098
3 Gb	177147
4 Db	236196
5 Bbb	295245
6 Gb	354294
8 Db	472392

ROOT 177147

1 Gb	177147
2 Gb	354294
3 Cb	531441
4 Gb	708588
5 Ebb	885735
6 Cb	1062882
8 Gb	1417176

Fig. 3   John Keeble, *The theory of harmonics*. Plate XIV, harmonic table, first diagram (partial)

Fig. 4   John Keeble, *The theory of harmonics*. Plate XIV, harmonic table, first diagram (continued)

Fig. 5   John Keeble, *The theory of harmonics*. Plate XIV, harmonic table, first diagram (continued)

book of value either to musicians or to an understanding of music itself. Keeble himself, at the end of his lengthy exercise, seemed to acknowledge this. As he put it, 'the great advantage of discovering the magnitude of all musical intervals by the Ratio cannot but be agreeable to men of science and lovers of truth'.[15]

I am less interested in the details of Keeble's examination of Greek theory and more in what might be the reasons for his undertaking the task in the first place. One issue seems certain: his desire to link what he sees as the germ of future Western music with a culturally and historically specific paradigm of the European Enlightenment. That is, he locates music in mathematics, in phenomena which in turn can be 'objectively' measured and systematized. The system is legitimated on the claim that it is structured on 'natural' principle, and on that basis it becomes law.

To be sure, Keeble had numerous predecessors in the Middle Ages and Renaissance who likewise associated music and mathematics. But Keeble adds two components to this age old equation: Science, and a belief in the evolutionary progress of human affairs. Keeble, like others of his time, virtually fetishizes numbers as the embodying principle for both truth and progress (as opposed to, say, the medieval notion of timelessness):

Nothing contributes so much to the encouragement of Study, as the knowledge of some governing and leading principle; some visible and faithful guide, that will conduct us through the mazes of Science, and teach us to love and obey her laws. It is this that warms and animates our endeavours in the arduous pursuit, and in the end rewards our labours with success.

This governing principle shews itself in no part of human learning so much as in the various operations of numbers; whose powers, by a kind of magic, have greatly contributed to the many discoveries and improvements that have been made in all arts and sciences; nor can it be otherwise while Truth is the great object to which those powers are directed [pp. 2–3].

Science is anthropomorphized, even deified, hierarchically situated above the subjective and experiential (though, to be sure, subjectively produced and mythologized). The apotheosis Keeble implies is engendered by the recognized classificatory potential of Science/Reason, not only as a tool by which men (his gender specificity is not accidental) could come to under-

[15] From p. 200. John Keeble (c. 1711–86) was organist at St George's Church, Hanover Square, and later organist as well at Ranelagh Gardens. For the variety of critical responses to Keeble's book see Jamie Croy Kassler, *The science of music in Britain, 1714–1830: a catalogue of writings, lectures and inventions*, 2 vols. (New York, 1979), I, pp. 617–19. Kassler lists more than 50 printed texts dealing with music and mathematics, more than 200 dealing with proportions, and about 130 dealing with musical doctrines of antiquity. As one would expect, there is considerable overlapping among these three categories. Keeble's text, in other words, is representative of a much larger corpus of work generally concerned with this subject.

stand what was, but more important to *order* what could be. He sees his intellectual pursuit in developmental terms ("rewards our labours with success"), terms congruent with the 'progressive' goals of colonialism. Keeble ironically displays the deep psychological base of his argument precisely when discussing the attraction of objective powers. When he confesses 'by a kind of magic', the supposed objective foundation for his belief in rationalism slips away in an apparent ecstasy of subjectivity and superstition. He betrays in the process the ultimate magnetism of what he understands by 'governing principle', namely, governing power.

The scientific Truth he sets out to discover has no apparent use beyond the fact of its existence, since it cannot 'influence' music. But musical use is not the question. The real use value resides at the cultural level. He is out to prove the musical complement of Western cultural hegemony: 'Among the theories which have appeared at different periods, those of the Greeks seem to have all the advantages that can be wished to lead us to the true knowledge of Harmonics; for as their principles are in nature, they must be fixed and immutable' (p. 5). Put differently, Keeble's argument does not need music to be proven. Indeed, music is irrelevant and even interruptive to the discussion, for music is intensely subjective at the experiential level. Only when it remains on paper, so to speak, can it be dealt with in pure form: ideally in numbers, and thus totally contained in a logical system divorced from the world.

Keeble obliquely asserts a universal validity to his measurements when, in a comment on the human voice, he argues that it 'is tuned by this scale or gender, which is universally the same, at all times, in all countries; for as this is the scale of nature, there is sufficient reason to believe, that the principles of harmony, the number and quality of consonances and dissonances, are fixed and determined by certain laws . . .' (p. 8). He compares these laws with universals, the circulation of the blood and the law of gravity. At the close of his treatise he states his position directly: 'Could all this be by Chance? rather, is there not an absolute necessity, that All shall comply with principles found in Nature? to whose laws we must be obedient, whether they are thoroughly understood or not' (pp. 203–4).

Keeble's argument, embodied in mathematics, is that the Western system developing from the Greeks is natural and must be obeyed. It is an argument built not on 'pure' reason, but on a subjectively constituted reason at whose base lies the attraction of power and the firm conviction, held a priori to the entire discussion, that the Western system is the only one able to claim universal validity. To be sure, I am not suggesting that we get to colonialism from music theory, but rather that the musical order (theoretical systems *and* the values attached to them) defined by Keeble is constituted by, and hence reinforces, an identical ideological base of Western self-legitimization.[16]

The history of a 'scientific' theory of music owes its greatest debt to Keeble's Continental predecessor, Jean-Philippe Rameau (1683–1764). Though Keeble himself owes no explicit debt to Rameau (but rather to his teacher Pepusch), there are striking ideological similarities which underlie the work of both. Given the status – contemporaneous and later – of Rameau's musical–theoretical writings, I think it worthwhile to outline the salient features before returning to a discussion of Zoffany's painting.

In his *Traité de l'harmonie* (Paris, 1722; first published in an incomplete English translation in 1737)[17] Rameau laid out the principles of the system he further developed in later writings. For my purposes the central issue is exposed in Rameau's opening comments in his preface:

However much progress music may have made until our time, it appears that the more sensitive the ear has become to the marvelous effects of this art, the less inquisitive the mind has been about its true principles. One might say that reason has lost its rights, while experience has acquired a certain authority.

The surviving writings of the Ancients show us clearly that reason alone enabled them to discover most of the properties of music. Although experience still obliges us to accept the greater part of their rules, we neglect today all the advantages to be derived from the use of reason in favor of purely practical experience.[18]

[16] The famous, extraordinarily long and detailed histories of music written in late eighteenth-century England by Burney and Hawkins also devote a great deal of space to a consideration of ancient Greek music theory. The discussions are, to say the least, as unremittingly tedious to the modern reader as they were apparently fascinating to their authors, whose willingness to cover every aspect of the theory seems limitless, even though the theory could be associated with only a few, short musical examples. See Sir John Hawkins, *A general history of the science and practice of music*, 2 vols. (1776; reprint ed., Graz, 1969, facsimile of 1875 London ed.), I, pp. 1–68; Charles Burney, *A general history of music, from the earliest ages to the present period*, 4 vols. (London, 1776–89), I, pp. 1–108. For the short pieces reproduced by Burney, see I, pp. 86–91.

[17] See Jean-Philippe Rameau, *Treatise on harmony*, trans. with introduction and notes by Philip Gossett (New York, 1971), pp. vii–xii, for information on publication history (the text is divided into four sections, the first two of which were first translated into English only with Gossett's modern edition; sections III and IV were partially and freely translated in the eighteenth century); Kassler, *Science of music in Britain*, II, pp. 863–71, gives information on eighteenth-century editions and English published reaction to them.

  Hawkins mentions but hardly discusses Rameau's *Traité*, though his overall assessment is complimentary: 'As a theorist, the character of Rameau stands very high; and as a testimony to his merit in this particular, it is here mentioned as a fact, that Mr. Handel was ever used to speak of him in terms of great respect' (II, p. 901). Burney offers a two-paragraph reaction to the *Traité* which is little more than a challenge to its originality: 'If any one were to ask me to point out what was the discovery or invention upon which his system was founded, I should find it a difficult task' (IV, p. 612).

[18] Rameau, *Treatise on harmony*, p. xxxiii. Gossett points out in a footnote that Rameau's reference to the 'Ancients' refers to 'all musicians preceding Zarlino' (1517–90), and that 'there

Rameau's theory develops from a position that 'all music is founded on harmony, which arises from natural principles derived from the mathematical and physical bases of a vibrating body (*corps sonore*)'.[19] Rameau's method is Cartesian in its dependence on mathematical precision; it is equally Cartesian in its effects (he cites Descartes numerous times throughout the text). Notably, in the quotation from his preface, Rameau drives a wedge between experience (the body or, more specifically, the ears) and reason (the mind). He tells us that experience provides no answers to real understanding or – by implication – justification for the form modern music takes. At the same time, he canonizes rationality via the ancients (from whom come the 'true principles') and holds to a belief in historical progress.

What I think he means to assert with regard to reason and the ancients is revealed in the full title of the treatise: *Traité de l'harmonie réduite à ses principes naturels*. That is, what he claims to have discovered, like Keeble after him, is a system (a rational order) which is also *natural*, that highly charged word for the eighteenth century, equivalent of *the good*, and carrying explicit moral qualifications in its application. The importance of this assertion is evident when combined with Rameau's central principle, namely, that harmony (and not melody) serves as the underlying basis of all music. That is, Rameau conceived of harmony as the ultimate determinate in

are few direct references to Greek theory in this treatise, but in his later writings Rameau cites the Greeks more freely.'

19 Cuthbert Girdlestone, Albert Cohen and Mary Cyr, 'Jean-Philippe Rameau', *The new Grove dictionary of music and musicians*, ed. Stanley Sadie, 20 vols. (London, 1980), XV, p. 568. Cf. Rameau's definition in his *Génération harmonique* (Paris, 1737), 'La Musique est une Science Phisico-mathématique, le Son en est l'objet Phisique, & les rapports trouvés entre différens Sons en sont l'objet Mathématique; sa fin est de plaire, & d'exciter en nous diverses passions.' Quoted from Jean-Philippe Rameau, *Complete theoretical writings, miscellanea*, ed. Erwin R. Jacobi (N.P., 1968), III, p. 30 of the original, p. 29 of the facsimile reprint. This treatise was the first of his works to contain a dedication – significantly to the Académie Royale des Sciences. According to Jacobi, it represents 'a first clear indication of [Rameau's] ambitions for a closer connection with that august body and of his striving through his theoretical works to raise music to the level of a scientific discipline in the spirit of the academy' (p. xix). The publication of this treatise elicited considerable discussion in Parisian periodicals (see pp. xxi–xxix), one writer deploring 'the absence of the musician in the writer of *Génération*, finding in its place 'too much of the physicist and geometrician' (p. xxiv).

In his *Démonstration du principe de l'harmonie* (Paris, 1750) – and now having his text 'Approuvée par Messieurs de l'Académie Royale des Sciences', as proclaimed on the title page – Rameau states in the preface: 'C'est dans la Musique que la nature semble nous assigner le principe Phisique de ces premieres nations purement Mathématiques sur lesquelles roulent toutes les Sciences, je veux dire, les proportions, Harmonique, Arithmétique & Géometrique, d'ou suivent les progressions de même genre, & qui se manifestent au premier instant que résonne un corps sonore . . .' (pp. vi–vii of the original, pp. 157–8 of the facsimile reprint).

music, governed by chord relations which he defined variously as hierarchical ordering and rationalized movement (from one chord to another), and he distinguished between dissonance and consonance – in effect, between conflict and resolution. His is a musical system congruent with eighteenth- and nineteenth-century theories of political economy – from the social contract to production studies (Adam Smith) – to the extent that his theory sought to rationalize and order musical phenomena according to principles of greater and lesser (the primary versus the secondary chords), restated in political terms as a hierarchy of power relations.

It is here, I think, that the importance of the visual metaphors of architecture and, especially, music become evident in Zoffany's painting, where music and architecture stand in for political harmony. At the level of the 'rational–scientific', these images complement the philosophical–political categories of Order, Reason, the Natural, and, by implication, Right. (The domestic connection, equally important and closely related, has yet to be explained.)

Progress in the Enlightenment was a fundamental concept by which to judge history and set off the present and future from the past. Near the beginning of the preface Rameau touches on this issue:

But if through the exposition of an evident principle, from which we then draw just and certain conclusions, we can show that our music has attained the last degree of perfection and that the Ancients were far from this perfection [i.e, in their music if not their theory] . . . we shall know where we stand. . . . Persons of taste and outstanding ability in this field will no longer lack of the knowledge necessary for success. In short, the light of reason, dispelling the doubts into which experience can plunge us at any moment, will be the most certain guarantee of success that we can expect in this art [pp. xxxiii–xxxiv].

It is through Rameau's version of the Cartesian *cogito* ('evident principle, from which we then draw just and certain conclusions') that we can be certain of Progress: that is, knowledge comes from the mind, not from experience. Put another way, external reality can only be understood through a rationalization based on (mathematical) principles *antecedent* to that reality:

Music is a science which should have definite rules; these rules should be drawn from an evident principle; and this principle cannot really be known to us without the aid of mathematics. Notwithstanding all the experience I may have acquired in music from being associated with it for so long, I must confess that only with the aid of mathematics did my ideas become clear and did light replace a certain obscurity of which I was unaware before.[20]

20 Rameau, *Treatise on harmony*, p. xxxv. Gossett notes the difficulty of following Rameau's 'mathematical, pseudo-scientific explanations' which comprise book I, pointing out that 'the instinctive reaction of most readers . . . is simply to skip it' (p. xv); Kassler, *Science of*

The mathematics of Rameau and Keeble are thus heavily marked by historical situation, cultural specificity, and valuation. To the Westerner, mathematics became a primary sign of the idealized self, as well as a useful indicator of cultural difference. Thus with regard to India – and skipping to a time closer to our own – Evelyn Baring, Lord Cromer, British Agent and Consul-General in Egypt between 1882 and 1907, noted in his book *Modern Egypt* (1908): 'Sir Alfred Lyall once said to me: "Accuracy is abhorrent to the Oriental mind. Every Anglo-Indian should always remember that maxim." Want of accuracy, which easily degenerates into untruthfulness, is in fact the main characteristic of the Oriental mind.'[21]

Zoffany's painting embeds far more than the outer manifestations of taste and cultivation to be presumed by the presence of a large harpsichord, attendant musicians and audience. The instrument is a signifier for an order based on rational and 'natural' principles which define and motivate progress, hence good. The English sitters are by implication devoted to these principles and this order. Indeed, the way in which they encircle the harpsichord (the painting's compositional anchor), establishes their relationship to the cultural values for which it stands. I am arguing that the image Zoffany paints functions as the visual equivalent of what Barthes describes as political writing, the function of which 'is to maintain a clear conscience', its mission 'fraudulently to identify the original fact with its remotest subsequent transformation . . .' which Barthes sees as 'typical of all authoritarian regimes; it is what might be called police-state writing: we know, for example, that the content of the word "Order" always indicates repression.'[22]

In Zoffany, two orders, one of sound (music), the other of stone (architecture), directly or by implication bear on fundamental issues of morality and civil rights, for they supply an inherent justification for political policies later – and in another country – to be called Manifest Destiny. The realities of imperialism, *experienced* by Anglo-Indians, are neither explained

music in Britain, is by far the best source for information on this general subject. Her compendium amply demonstrates the extraordinary level of interest in the 'philosophy' and 'science' of music during the eighteenth century.

21 Quoted from Edward Said, *Orientalism* (New York, 1978), p. 38. See also p. 35. Baring served in India prior to his time in Egypt.

22 Roland Barthes, *Writing degree zero*, trans. Annette Lavers and Colin Smith (New York, 1968), pp. 25–6. See also Said, *Orientalism*, which develops the following thesis stated in the introduction (p. 3): 'My contention is that without examining Orientalism as a discourse one cannot possibly understand the enormously systematic discipline by which European culture was able to manage – and even produce – the Orient politically, sociologically, militarily, ideologically, scientifically, and imaginatively during the post-Enlightenment period.'

nor justified on the basis of this experience but, instead, by abstract principles of reason – expressed by signs of high culture – which may in fact
conflict with what experience itself suggests. As Rameau recognized, 'experience can plunge us at any moment' into doubt; only reason (i.e.,
rationalization) can save us.[23]

The sitters in the portrait are full complements to the harpsichord (and
violoncello) and architectural backdrop. They are actors: casual, informal,
and forming a tableau – striking an *attitude*, to borrow from eighteenth-
century usage. In effect they are on stage, and they are highly aware of the
audience for whom they strike their poses.[24]

In the foreground at the right, closest to the viewer, stands William
Cator, representative of business as a factor in the East India Company, the
true end of English colonialism in the eighteenth century. He is absolutely
relaxed with one hand on his hip, the other on the harpsichord, his legs
crossed. His pose is confident. His costume, like those of the others,
together with his full belly, mark status and success.

Yet the commerce in which he engages finds no reference here, except
indirectly with regard to the class status and economic situation it provides. With regard to portrait convention in eighteenth-century England,
such masking is not automatically to be expected. For example, in a portrait (Fig. 6) by Arthur Devis of Colonel James Clitherow and his wife on
the grounds of their estate, Boston House, Brentford, Middlesex, James

[23] East Indiamen at least tolerated Indian music and sometimes appreciated it in the early
decades of their occupancy. But by the late eighteenth century, 'country musick' (so called)
'was banished from public functions as it was from the army; instead European musicians
multiplied and concerts began to be given'. Whereas previously the Company itself had
regularly provided for Indian bands on great occasions, the 'general verdict was [now]
summed up by Major Blakiston when he wrote of the Indians: "in fact they have no music
in their souls"'. Spear, *Nabobs*, pp. 33–4.

About 1856 Captain George F. Atkinson produced a satire on the pettiness of British
colonials, *Curry & rice, the ingredients of social life at 'our' station in India*, on forty plates each
with an explanatory text. The book was lithographed in London and published without
date. An edition also appeared in Calcutta in 1911. No. 6, 'Our Magistrate's Wife', belittles
a woman (Mrs Chutney!) whose Englishness is sadly affirmed by her meager but loudly
proclaimed musical pretentions (much of the account describes the activities of Mrs Chutney and her lady rivals in the church choir). For a brief discussion of the performance of
European art music in India during the eighteenth century see Raymond Head, 'Corelli in
Calcutta: colonial music-making in India during the 17th and 18th centuries', *Early Music*,
13/4 (1985), pp. 548–53. See pp. 551–2, regarding the interest in the music of India on the
part of a few Anglo-Indians.

[24] The stage effects evident in this portrait are not accidentally achieved. Zoffany was on close
terms with David Garrick, whom he painted numerous times (as well as other actors) in
scenes from contemporaneous plays. Garrick in fact was Zoffany's first major English
patron. For a discussion of these pictures, see Webster, *Zoffany*, pp. 9–10, and catalogue
entries (some illustrated) 10, 15, 18, 23, 29, 33, 34, 47, 48, 50, 57–9, 65, 92, 94,
109, 110.

proudly holds a spade-like digging tool known as a 'spud', a sign of his pride in agriculture, one source of his wealth. The success of his enterprise is manifested by the well-tended park in which he stands. Clitherow's control over his land is signaled in part by the dammed river Brent directly behind him. [25] One might argue that to acknowledge agriculturally-achieved wealth was culturally acceptable in eighteenth-century England whereas that gained from business was not (the parvenue problem). But this is not necessarily the case. For example, a portrait of the Putnam family (Fig. 7) represents the patriarch at the extreme right with his hand on a globe and a ship at his back firing a salute: his wealth presumably results from foreign trade, doubly and openly acknowledged – without apology – by the ship and the globe. [26]

Cator, in the closest foreground (Fig. 1), half turns to the three other sitters, as if pointing them out to us (they are in a recessed plane and are in fact framed by him, the open lid of the harpsichord on the right, and the curtain fold at the upper left). In essence, Morse on the cello and the two women at the harpsichord stand as representatives of a culture whose values are being affirmed, in my view not only for the simple sake of these values but also (if unconsciously) as rationalized justification for the harsh realities lying beneath the surface, the semiotic 'present absence.' Any reference to the real reason these people are in India – business and the police system to keep it in place – is avoided. The musical 'harmony' of Morse's violoncello, like that produced by the harpsichord, is thus problematized: it stands in tension with that which it masks, namely, Morse's real occupation as Sheriff of Calcutta and Advocate of the Supreme Court, which is the way he really spent his time.

In precisely this way the conventional drapery at the back paradoxically takes on the metaphorical as well as literal function of a curtain. At the same time it reveals, by being pulled back to allow us to see the tableau, it also hides. It provides a limited view. By this I mean that portraits in delineating success and other attendant qualities show them only as products (arrivals) and rarely as processes. In the Morse–Cator portrait process is literally curtained off, hence hidden. We are not allowed to see the foundation of exploitation and suffering upon which this cultured scene depends. Marcuse's comment quoted at the head of this paper is relevant here.

25 The Clitherow family was a line of London merchants descended from Sir Christopher Clitherow, Lord Mayor of London in 1635. My information on this painting comes from the exhibition catalogue by Ellen G. D'Oench, *The conversation piece: Arthur Devis & his contemporaries* (New Haven, 1980), pp. 62–3, no. 37.

26 The shield mounted on the fluted pilaster at center has been in part identified: the right half corresponds with the arms of the Sussex branch of the family. See Sitwell, *Conversation pieces*, p. 99, no. 55.

Fig. 6 Arthur Devis (1712–87), *Colonel James Clitherow and his Wife, Anne, at Boston House, Brentford, Middlesex, 1789.* Private collection, London

Fig. 7 Unknown artist, *The Putnam Family.* Whereabouts unknown

I want to say something more about the harpsichord, its connection to the women, the relation of both to domesticity and, finally, the bond among all three and cultural hegemony. To begin, the harpsichord – and later the fortepiano – was first and foremost used in the home, a fact reflected in the large numbers of instruments that show up in advertisements in British newspapers for household sales throughout the century, as well as in surviving catalogues for such auctions. The references to domestic keyboard instruments are legion in stageplays on domestic situations and in countless novels. Households of modest status typically maintained a small spinet (an instrument of modest cost and limited musical means) or, toward the end of the century, a small square piano (Figs. 8 and 9). The wealthy bought single- and double-manual harpsichords (Figs. 10 and 11) and, later, large fortepianos (Fig. 12).[27] In England vast quantities of music were published for amateur musicians and made available either through outright purchase or through privately operated lending libraries (Fig. 13).

[27] Two of the most important makers of harpsichords were the Swiss immigrant Burkat Shudi (1702–73) and the Alsatian immigrant Jacob Kirckman (1710–92), both of whose firms continued after the death of their founders – Shudi's eventually passed by marriage to Broadwood after the death of Shudi's son. Shudi numbered his instruments consecutively; the highest number known to date is 1115. Kirckman's instruments were not numbered (about 110 still exist), but about 2,000 are thought to have been made between 1750 and 1800.

As for costs, Shudi charged between thirty-five and forty guineas for single-manual instruments, fifty guineas for the single-manual with an added 'Venetian swell' device he invented, and eighty guineas for double-manual harpsichords with the swell. See further Donald Howard Boalch and Peter Williams, 'Kirckman', *New Grove*, X, pp. 76–8; (same authors) 'Burkat Shudi', *New Grove*, XVII, pp. 278–9, and Frank Hubbard, *Three centuries of harpsichord making* (Cambridge, Mass., 1965), p. 159. On the Venetian swell see pp. 160–1. Keyboard instruments could be bought second-hand through shops – numerous newspaper and advertiser notices make that clear – and beyond that they could also be rented.

For information on the harpsichord reproduced in Fig. 11 see Raymond Russell, *Catalogue of musical instruments*, I: *Keyboard instruments, Victoria and Albert Museum* (London, 1968), pp. 55–6. By the 1760s five firms were active in and around London in the manufacture of fortepianos; by the 1770s there were 15, by the 1780s 27, by the 1790s at least 38. During the 1790s the Broadwood firm alone was probably producing about 400 square and over 100 grand fortepianos a year, though this number greatly exceeds the output of competitive firms. See further Derek Adlam and Cyril Ehrlich, 'Broadwood', *New Grove*, III, p. 324, and Derek Adlam and William J. Conner, 'Pianoforte,' *New Grove*, XIV, p. 695. My information on piano firms was compiled from the list of makers in London and its environs, 1760–1851, in Rosamond Harding, *The Piano-forte: its history traced to the Great Exhibition of 1851* (1933, reprint ed., New York, 1973). She provides a history of the Shudi workshop and the Broadwood firm. See especially pp. 9–132.

According to Head, 'Corelli in Calcutta,' p. 550, harpsichords 'were shipped to India as early as the 1760s (possibly earlier although no mention of one has been traced)? Regarding the availability of pianos and other instruments during the 1780s, see pp. 550–1.

Fig. 8 Bentside spinet by Thomas Hitchcock, c. 1710. Smithsonian Institution, Washington, DC, inv. no. 303,532

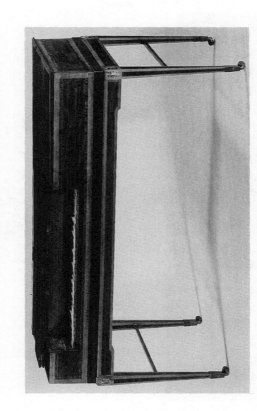

Fig. 9 Square fortepiano by John Broadwood, London, 1798. Smithsonian Institution, Washington, DC, inv. no. 315,667

Fig. 10 Single-manual harpsichord by Jacob and Abraham Kirckman, London, 1776. Smithsonian Institution, Washington, DC, inv. no. 303, 528

Fig. 11 Double-manual harpsichord by Burkat Shudi and John Broadwood, 1782. By courtesy of the Board of Trustees of the Victoria and Albert Museum, London, inv. no. W. 43-1943

Music, domestic life and cultural chauvinism

Fig. 12 Grand fortepiano by John Broadwood and Son, London, 1794. Smithsonian Institution, Washington, DC, inv. no. 303,530.

The individuals who played keyboard instruments were for the most part girls and women. The instruments were in fact both signifiers and insurers of their domestic role, as is evident in contemporaneous courtesy and conduct literature.[28] For example, John Essex, writing in 1722, produced a list of instruments which from a typical male point of view were appropriate to women, together with a list of those which were not. As is usually the case, keyboard instruments are mentioned first (instruments with phallic associations were specifically viewed as contaminating):

The *Harpsichord*, *Spinet*, *Lute* and *Base* [sic] *Violin*, are Instruments most agreeable to the Ladies: There are some others that really are unbecoming the Fair Sex; as the *Flute*, *Violin* and *Hautboy*; the last of which is too Manlike, and would look indecent in a Woman's Mouth; and the *Flute* is very improper, as taking away too much of the Juices, which are otherwise more necessarily employ'd, to promote the Appetite, and assist Digestion.[29]

28 This is a complex subject which I can only briefly touch on here. For a detailed examination of this issue see Richard Leppert, 'Men, women and music at home: the influence of cultural values on musical life in eighteenth-century England,' *Imago Musicae*, II (1985), pp. 51–133.

29 John Essex, *The young ladies conduct: or, rules for education, under several heads; with instructions upon dress, both before and after marriage. And advice to young wives* (London, 1722), pp. 84–5. As the century progressed, harpsichords were generally replaced by fortepianos, lutes by English guitars, violas de gamba ('bass viols') by violoncellos.

THE MUSICAL LOUNGE,

AND

APOLLO CIRCULATING LIBRARIES,

AT

D. CORRI's,

MUSIC SELLER TO THE ROYAL FAMILY,

No. 28, HAY MARKET,

AND AT

T. JONES's, No. 23, *Bishopsgate Street,*

Where every SUBSCRIBER will be GRATUITOUSLY entitled to the full Amount of their Subscriptions in Printed Music, either at the Time of subscribing, or at any Period within the Term subscribed for, at the Option of the Subscriber, from the Catalogue published by CORRI or JONES.

And also be accommodated, at either of the above Houses, with Apartments, and Instruments of every Description, for the Purpose of trying Music.

In Addition to which, every Annual Subscriber will have free Admission to CORRI's Quarterly PRIVATE CONCERTS, at his Great Room, Hay-Market.

THE above Libraries will contain several Numbers of the most celebrated and extensive Selections of Ancient and Modern Works, both Vocal and Instrumental, in Print and Manuscript, which will be continually increasing, by the Addition of the most esteemed Compositions that may hereafter be published in every Part of Europe, on the following Terms, viz.

	£.	s.	d.		£.	s.	d.
For a Year - - - - - -	2	2	0	A Quarter - - - -	1	1	0
Half a Year - - - - -	1	11	6	Single Book, per Day - -	0	0	6

To be paid at the Time of subscribing at either of the above Libraries.

(SEE REGULATIONS THE OTHER SIDE.)

A Musical Journal will be published every MONDAY for the Voice, Piano Forte, Harp, Flute, Violin, and Tambourine, constructed on a Plan entirely new, by D. CORRI, (Price 1s. 6d.)

N.B. The Musical Academies for Voice, Piano Forte, &c. will be continued as usual, by Mr. and Mrs. CORRI, at the above Places.

Reviord & Bailey, Printers, 54, Great Wishmin-Street, Hay-Market.

Fig. 13 Trade bill for a London music lending library, early nineteenth century. The Trustees of the British Museum, London, Department of Prints and Drawings, Banks Collection, inv. no. 88.20

The connection between music and female domesticity is repeatedly made in this literature, as in an anonymous pamphlet from c. 1778 which urges musical training even for girls showing the least propensity for it, yet not so as to form them into performers per se, but rather so they can 'amuse their *own family*, and for that domestic *comfort, they* were by Providence designed to promote'.[30] The Reverend John Bennett encouraged musical training for women, defining its benefits as increasing happiness, inspiring tranquility, and harmonizing the mind and spirits, during those '*ruffled or lonely* hours, which in almost every situation, will be your lot'.[31] Bennett's comment makes oblique reference to the limitations of women's roles in upperclass society. As Robert Burton put it in *The anatomy of melancholy* in 1621, 'Vertuous women should keepe house'; this was echoed 160 years later by Henry Home, Lord Kames: 'It is the chief duty of a woman, to make a good wife'.[32]

Zoffany's musical women at first glance appear to play merely decorative roles, in the same way that English women in eighteenth-century portraiture (and life!) generally functioned. But they are actually essential here, for they complete the sense of peace, harmony and order in this scene by making the event not merely musical but *familial*. They assure continuance of this scene and the culture it represents by means of their gender function: they are the producers of the race.[33] Their music is domestic, a signifier of the very tranquility that makes reproduction possible. In this regard it is noteworthy that both women in this painting had borne children in the months before this portrait was painted.[34]

[30] *Euterpe; or, remarks on the use and abuse of music, as a part of modern education* (London, c. 1778), p. 18. On the authorship of this essay see Kassler, *Science of music in Britain*, II, pp. 1107–9.

[31] John Bennett, *Letters to a young lady, on a variety of useful and interesting subjects calculated to improve the heart, to form the manners, and enlighten the understanding*, 2 vols. (Warrington, 1789), I, p. 234.

[32] Robert Burton, *The anatomy of melancholy* (1621; reprint ed., Amsterdam and New York, 1971), p. 704. Henry Home, *Loose hints upon education, chiefly concerning the culture of the heart* (Edinburgh and London, 1781), p. 228.

[33] Cf. Derek Jarrett, *England in the age of Hogarth* (Frogmore, St Albans, Herts., 1976), p. 126: 'One problem had not changed with the changing attitude to women and to their intellectual achievements. Whatever form masculine condescension might take . . . it still assumed that marriage and motherhood should be the goals of all feminine endeavour.' See further pp. 103–27, and Lawrence Stone, *The family, sex and marriage in England, 1500–1800*, abridged ed. (New York, 1977), *passim*.

[34] In Zoffany's painting the violoncello played by Morse strengthens the sense of a blissful union of the two families. Stringed (hence Apollonian) instruments often served in marriage portraits as signs of fidelity and the *mesure* of good relationships – all of which provides added weight to the sense of order and harmony I have been discussing. See further P.J.J. van Thiel, 'Marriage symbolism in a musical party by Jan Miense Moleneer', *Simiolus*, 2/2 (1967/8), pp. 91–9, and my own discussion of musical marriage symbolism in a portrait by Zoffany of the Cowper and Gore families (at the Yale Center for British Art) in Leppert, 'Men, Women and Music at Home', pp. 100–1, fig. 37.

Finally, it must be said that the absence of any reference to Indian culture cannot be attributed to Zoffany's rigid adherence to European portrait convention. I believe that he was instead reacting to the preferences of his sitters, for he himself was in fact genuinely interested in Indian subjects. Beyond painting portraits of rich Indian nawabs, he produced drawings of Indian life and country landscapes and he 'joined the newly founded Asiatic Society, whose researches into all branches of oriental studies were to form one of the most distinguished European contributions to oriental scholarship'.[35]

By comparison, a strikingly similar portrait from 1789 was painted by Francesco Renaldi (British-born but of Italian parentage) of Charles Cockerell and his wife, Maria Tryphena, with her sister, Charlotte Blunt (Fig. 14).[36] Cockerell was Paymaster General. His wife was the daughter of Sir Charles Blunt, another Company servant. She plays a large, expensive (especially in India) two-manual harpsichord (cf. Fig. 11), apart from house organs the costliest of musical instruments for the period. Her younger sister Charlotte turns a page of music.[37] In Renaldi's portrait as in Zoffany's nothing Indian is reproduced. It is unabashedly English: an utterly tranquil conversation piece, probably celebrating the marriage which occurred the same year, a distorting mirror of personal, economic and social triumph achieved in India, formulated once again on a musical metaphor.

At this point I need to say something about the significance of portraits as objects in the general context of this discussion. Oil paintings provided patrons with directly self-flattering signs of status and cultivation which naturally increased with the importance of the painter – Zoffany himself was highly regarded and much sought after in England and India. When produced in India, this particular visual medium proclaimed a European

35 Webster, Zoffany, p. 15. See pp. 89–91 for reproductions of some of the drawings, and also Archer, India and British portraiture, especially pp. 165–7, figs. 101–6. The Blair portrait discussed below (Fig. 20) is a further case in point.

36 For more on Renaldi's career in India, see Archer, India and British portraiture, pp. 280–97 (the Cockerell–Blunt portrait is discussed and illustrated on pp. 288–9, from which comes my information on the sitters), and Foster, 'British Artists', p. 65. A small ovular modello, reproducing the two women at the harpsichord, sold at Christie's, London, 17 March 1978, lot 63. Renaldi was active in India from 1786 to 1796.

37 This painting is also reproduced in Head, 'Corelli in Calcutta', p. 550, according to whom the harpsichord 'would appear to be . . . a Kirkman or Shudi . . . ' The image is otherwise not discussed.

After returning to England, Charlotte married Charles Imhof, the stepson of Warren Hastings (Governor-General of India from 1773 to 1785) in 1794. As for Cockerell, following his retirement he built 'a country mansion at Sezincote in the Cotswolds in which he celebrated his stay in India by incorporating in it motifs drawn from Indian architecture'. Archer, India and British portraiture, p. 288.

Fig. 14   Francesco Renaldi (1755–c. 1799), *Charles Cockerell and his Wife, Maria Tryphena, with her Sister, Charlotte Blunt*, 1789. Sold at Christie's, London, 17 March 1978, lot 62. Photo copyright Christie's

cultural hegemony by its very impracticality. India's tropical heat was detrimental to the life of canvas upon which these portraits were executed – though for many Englishmen that was not an insurmountable problem, since the usual intention was to remove oneself from India, together with acquired fortune, as soon as possible (selling the furniture to someone else who had more recently arrived or was in any event staying on).[38]

[38] The importance of oil portraits to Anglo-Indians can be measured by their willingness to pay substantial British import duties charged against pictures when they were brought home. These levies became so substantial that in the course of the nineteenth century the popularity of oil portraits 'declined until they came to be commissioned only when presentation pictures were needed for public buildings'. (In 1803 the duty for a canvas under two feet square was two guineas; for a canvas of about eight feet square six guineas. The levy was later increased.) Shipping was also expensive. See further Foster, 'British Artists', pp. 1–2, and Mildred Archer and W.G. Archer, *Indian painting for the British, 1770–1880* (London, 1955), p. 10, whence the quotation.

Two watercolors drawn at Patna in 1824 by Sir Charles D'Oyly of his bungalow's spacious drawing room in summer (Fig. 15) and winter (Fig. 16) bear on this discussion.[39] In both images the Anglo-Indian sitters are de-emphasized by their relative isolation from one another (and half of the D'Oyly family members are posed in profile or from the back). It is their possessions which direct the viewer's gaze – furniture, paintings, books, musical instruments, crystal chandeliers, sculptural (or painted) friezes, carpet, and the like.

The two musical instruments, a grand fortepiano and a pedal harp, appear in both drawings. Each enjoyed unassailable status among the European upper classes, the harp having come into its own among women in the late eighteenth century, the piano having simply supplanted the harpsichord. One issue in particular interests me as to their presence here, namely, the extra-musical status garnered by their bulk. Both instruments are large (and the piano comparatively heavy, even before the development of the iron frame); they are also oddly shaped and hence more difficult and expensive to pack and ship.[40] Like most musical instruments they are also

[39] A biographical entry on D'Oyly appears in H.L. Mallalieu, *The dictionary of British watercolour artists up to 1920* (N.P., 1976), p. 87. The only detailed assessment of his life and work is that by Mildred Archer, "The talented baronet": Sir Charles D'Oyly and his drawings of India,' *Connoisseur*, 175, no. 705 (November, 1970), pp. 173–81, from which the bulk of my information about him is drawn.

Charles D'Oyly, 7th Baronet, was born in Calcutta in 1781, educated in England, and entered in the service of the East India Company in Bengal in 1798. Between 1821 and 1832 he was stationed in Patna, on the River Ganges in Bihar, over three hundred miles northwest of Calcutta. His first assignment there was as Opium Agent, though he later served as Commercial Resident. (He retired to Italy in 1838 where he died in 1845.)

In 1819 George Chinnery painted a portrait in Calcutta of Sir Charles and Lady D'Oyly (the head of D'Oyly was soon after engraved). The painting is most notable for the costuming of the sitters. Both are in Vandyck dress, a double incongruency (time and place) – profoundly impractical (but unquestionably European) 'presentation' garb. The portrait is reproduced and discussed briefly by Richard Ormond, 'George Chinnery and the Keswick family,' *Connoisseur*, 175, no. 706 (December, 1970), pp. 250–1, fig. 7, and by Archer, *India and British portraiture*, p. 372.

[40] For information on the opium trade organized by the East India Company (opium was chiefly exported to China), see Thompson and Garratt, *Rise and fulfilment*, pp. 263–4. Instruments shipped to India became very expensive. A Broadwood grand sent to Bengal, but ultimately stranded in Canton, in 1801 was sold to 'the only Lady in this Settlement' for 130 guineas. In England at the same time Broadwood was selling grands to provincial agents (discounted) for about £73, though the price of individual instruments varied widely depending on the quality and decoration of the case. See David Wainwright, *Broadwood by appointment: a history* (London, 1982), pp. 99, 101–2, 105. By 1815 a Broadwood grand could be had for £48 with an ornamented cabinet. See Harding, *Piano-forte*, pp. 377–80.

The harp was as expensive as grand fortepianos. The London maker Johann Andreas Stumpff in 1827 charged £105 for a double-action pedal harp (although in the account from which this price is taken he indicates a willingness to offer a £30 discount). See Pamela J. Willetts, 'Johann Andreas Stumpff, 1769–1846', *Musical Times*, 118 (1977), p. 31.

Fig. 15 Sir Charles D'Oyly (1781–1845), *The Summer Room in the Artist's House at Patna*, 11 September 1824. Watercolor. Paul Mellon Collection, Upperville, Virginia

Fig. 16 Sir Charles D'Oyly, *The Winter Room in the Artist's House at Patna*, 11 September 1824. Watercolor. Paul Mellon Collection, Upperville, Virginia

delicate, hence easily damaged, and highly sensitive to climatic change. India's particularly inhospitable climate made them difficult to maintain. In short, these instruments are highly impractical to the setting.

It is precisely this degree of impracticality which increases their ideological use value. In India their significance has as much to do with a totemic function as a musical one. All of this, together with the fact that they, like most of the other furnishings, are inessential to the economic and political success of colonialism, constitutes their importance as cultural fetishes and markers of racial difference. Moreover, their delicacy parallels the male-perceived delicacy of the women who played them. That is, neither English women nor British high art and its assorted trappings could appear here until the way for them had been made safe. The presence of both represents political triumph, at the same time it masks the means by which the triumph was accomplished, as with the Morse–Cator portrait discussed earlier. Colonialism is not an arrival but a process. In this context Anglo-Indian women are essential not only for the maintenance of racial purity but also for the transmission of cultural values, especially those values which could be embodied in art. For it was in art that Europeans chose to see the clearest signs of mythologized self-justification.

This issue becomes clear if we look again to the winter room and to the vignette of Lady D'Oyly playing her harp.[41] Lady D'Oyly does not play for her own enjoyment, or even for the pleasure of her husband. She is an unwitting participant for a more important agenda, the one I have been discussing. She is the model for the making of an image-within-the-image. Charles D'Oyly sits with his back to us, and thereby draws our attention to

[41] In the summer room Lady D'Oyly is apparently accompanied on the fortepiano by a daughter. Lady D'Oyly played both harp and piano; she was judged an adapt musician by a Captain Mundy who dined at Patna with the D'Oylys in 1829 ('in the evening we heard some beautiful music'). The D'Oyly's bungalow was a gathering place for English visitors. On this point see Archer, 'Talented baronet', p. 179, whence the quotation.

The piano is shown from the front in the winter room, an angle allowing its identification as a Broadwood. Its shape and decoration appear different in the two drawings, as if to suggest that D'Oyly possessed two such instruments, whether or not this was actually the case. One instrument has a lyre-like pedal board not evident on the other. The case is plain on one instrument, whereas the other is decorated with a line of inlay (?) apparently following its circumference. On the identification of the Broadwood, see Helen Rice Hollis, *The piano: a pictorial account of its ancestry and development* (London, 1975), pp. 64–5, and Wainwright, *Broadwood by appointment*, pp. 128–9 (which repeats Hollis). Wainwright, p. 8, illustrates a Broadwood grand from 1810 that bears a marked similarity to details evident in both instruments in D'Oyly's drawings. See p. 204, regarding the Broadwood company's care and success in shipping pianos to India.

The status of Broadwoods was sufficiently great to inspire imitation. In 1803 the firm ran advertisements in English language newspapers in India asserting that in the previous nine years only three authentic Broadwoods had been sent to India (two grands and a 'small one'), all others being 'very imperfect' copies. From Wainwright, pp. 101–2.

the fact that he is sketching his wife at music. Thus it is the *image* of her at music, not the musical event itself, that matters. D'Oyly's watercolor presents an act of fetishizing in progress, the drawing reconstituting in a specific vignette the general activity the artist engaged in while producing the two watercolors. But the interior image of image-making – a woman at music – claims hierarchical supremacy in a scene filled with detail.

In the winter room, D'Oyly also illustrates a hearth scene in the background, though not apparently because the day is cold, since the doorway at the right provides a view of open French doors leading onto a garden. This vignette also can claim significance as a culturally-embedded activity relevant to the general argument I am pursuing. The association between hearth and home was central to English culture, as Derek Jarrett has pointed out: 'The social unit was not the individual but the family of the household, a fact that gave great importance to the actual houses in which these units were contained. The possession of a hearth, traditionally the centre and focus not only of the house but also of the people who lived in it, was the thing that defined a man's position and gave him a place in society.'[42]

Fig. 17   Richard Cosway (1742–1821), *Marianne Dorothy Harland (later Mrs Dalrymple)*. The Metropolitan Museum of Art, New York, gift of Mrs William M. Haupt, from the Collection of Mrs James B. Haggin, 1969, inv. no. 69.104

[42] Jarrett, *England in the age of Hogarth*, p. 132.

The pairing of hearth with wife is common in contemporaneous British portraiture, as in Richard Cosway's painting of Marianne Dorothy Harland (Fig. 17). The association between the two is so ubiquitous in fact that it even occurs in ephemeral imagery like fashion plates (Fig. 18). In these scenes there is a constancy to the inherent protectiveness provided by men who are often not present but implied. Characteristically the women are doubly cocooned in fashionable overdress and domestic overfurnishing. Marianne Harland and her anonymous fashion-plate counterpart are perfect models of femininity to the males in whose image they are made. They lead a life of comfortable boredom, metaphorically tending the fire, that is, maintaining domestic order, and – like the little dog at Ms Harland's feet – waiting, *semper fidelis*. Transplanted to India, as in the D'Oyly watercolors, the wifely motherhood and domesticity imprinted on this imagery takes on additional cultural significance as confirmation of male triumph, not simply over females who have been domesticated, but over an alien culture

Fig. 18 Robert Dighton (1752–1814), Fashion plate drawing for the month of February. By courtesy of the Board of Trustees of the Victoria and Albert Museum, London, inv. no. E34–1947

rendered harmless, hence allowing the introduction of women and their appropriate domestic trappings.

Most of what D'Oyly draws is resolutely Western; even the architectural enclosure is transplanted. Thus in the winter room, apart from the ubiquitous hookah,[43] the only reference to India is a picture-within-a-picture on the upper left depicting an Indian elephant (not surprisingly kneeling, subservient) and some Indian people, most of whom stand behind a man in British military garb. There are other signs of India's defeat, notably in the summer room where an adult and child Indian servant, physically excluded, wait to be summoned, barely visible through the doorway at the right. In the foreground of the same drawing, a tiger's skin adorns the floor: an archetypal symbol of ferocity and exoticism, now conquered, is tread upon and, worse, *made ornamental*. D'Oyly himself reiterates this defeat by nature of the drawing he holds showing a British infantryman (presumably on the march). The myriad trappings of Western culture with which the room virtually overflows, as well as the women making music, reading and drawing, all legitimate the reality of early nineteenth-century India. Ironically, theirs is an ostentation considered in good taste, in contrast to the luxury of Indian nawabs, whose wealth the Anglo-Indians mocked, as well as coveted.

Arthur William Devis' portrait of Emily and George Mason (c. 1794–5) (Fig. 19), children of Bryant Mason of the East India Civil Service,[44] is composed so as to reinforce, and even proclaim, cultural difference and racial estrangement. Only bits and pieces are visible – part of a room, a part of a chair and a harpsichord, a hint of a landscape. But we see enough. Anglo-Indian children stand in the foreground, adult Indian servants in the back. A visual tension is created between them, in spite of the physical

[43] The hookah became popular among Anglo-Indians by the middle of the eighteenth century. 'A hookah was more expensive than a pipe and required a hookahburder [a servant], and it would therefore naturally come into fashion with increasing wealth and ostentation. To the new arrivals it was a luxury, and so, in spite of all their increasingly English tastes they were devoted to its charms. By 1778 it was "universal".' The preference for the hookah among English in India declined in the early nineteenth century. Spear, *Nabobs*, p. 36. See also pp. 98–100.

[44] See further D'Oench, *Conversation piece*, p. 78, cat. no. 69; Sydney H. Pavière, *The Devis family of painters* (Leigh-on-Sea, 1950), pp. 101–41 and plates 37–48. Pavière's account represents to date the fullest study of this painter, the nineteenth child of Arthur Devis, the famous painter of conversation pieces. In addition to a short biography, Pavière provides a list of 178 works arranged alphabetically by sitter. On Devis' years in India, see pp. 101–6. The portrait of the Mason children is not included in this list of works. See also Archer, *India and British portraiture*, pp. 234–69, and Foster, 'British Artists', pp. 24–31, for an account of Devis' life and works during the years in India (1784–95).

Fig. 19 Arthur William Devis (1763–1822), *Emily and George Mason*. Yale Center for British Art, New Haven, Paul Mellon Collection, inv. no. B1981.25.5

relaxation of all the actors, because here children take precedence over adults, a visually-composed triumph virtually never found in contemporaneous English portraits,[45] a difference which would have been recognized immediately by English viewers.

[45] Zoffany sometimes approached the inclusion of Indian servants in group portraits of Anglo-Indians differently, though the semiotic effect is identical. For example, in his portrait of the Auriol and Dashwood families (1783–7) five English men and two women are attended by four adult servants, all set in a landscape park. See the color reproduction in Archer, *India and British portraiture*, plate V, discussed on pp. 158–60, and in Webster, *Zoffany*, p. 75, cat. no. 100. Similarly, his family group representing Sir Elijah and Lady Impey with their three children includes four servants and six Indian (traveling?) musicians, the latter accompanying one of the Impey children who dances. Here the scene is virtually overcrowded with native people to such an extent that the English sitters seem rather packed together, though to be sure they occupy the front picture space and the natives the back. Semiotically the native peoples mark Impey's wealth and power. The inclusion of such numbers of servants is, as far as I know, unprecedented in conversation pieces produced in England. Here, in other words, imperialism encourages the creation of a new convention in portraiture: not the absence of servants but an abundance of them. This painting is reproduced and discussed in Archer, *India and British portraiture*, p. 136.

In Calcutta at the close of the eighteenth century domestic splendor was considerable for many English immigrants – made possible in part through the cheapness of labor, made public by the numbers of laborers involved. An unmarried Anglo-Indian might command a twenty-room mansion and require the attention of several score of servants; married couples sometimes maintained a staff of a hundred or more. The jobs assigned to individuals could be ridiculously specific and confining. Thus some only waited table, and as many as a dozen served their master only when he rose or retired. Those who held the umbrella or carried the palanquin (litter) did nothing else. (Servants' liveries were distinctive and specific to each household, providing clear, publicly identifiable testimony to the greatness of their employers, and at the same time the inferiority of the wearers.)[46]

By definition servants mark the status of their employers. Indian servants also marked as well the racial and cultural superiority Anglo-Indians perceived in themselves: in England servants were never assigned tasks as profoundly inconsequential or demeaning as the ones I have just described. Within domestic settings the races interacted continuously, but only in ways which clarified the gulf between them. The home served as the perfect microcosm of imperial order, at the same time it confirmed the moral appropriateness of empire: it provided a training ground for subsequent generations of colonial bureaucrats, police and military.

The English Mason children in the foreground of the Devis portrait represent the future of colonialism. Little Emily holds a tambourine and executes a gesture of dance, metaphorically celebrating the triumphant imperialism given form by the toy infantry drum and gun held by little George (wearing standard toddler dress of the period which makes him appear androgynous). The signifiers of the new culture in India – Western, classically-inspired architecture and music – once again transform political reality into a highly palatable visual abstraction.

Zoffany's portrait of Colonel Blair (1729–1814) with his wife and two daughters (1786) (Fig. 20) is different from the other images I have been discussing. Unlike the Morse–Cator and Cockerell–Blunt portraits where the figures are placed in non-specific interiors, or the D'Oyly drawings where the specific interior has taken on the semantic aspect of a European museum, the Blair family is settled into a modest room of their house in

[46] At the bottom end of the servant class were slave boys; the East India Company traded in slaves until 1764 and only prohibited their export by proclamation in 1789. See Pearson, *Eastern interlude*, pp. 155–6, 158–9, and Dennis Kincaid, *British social life in India, 1608–1937* (London, 1938).

Fig. 20   Johan Zoffany, *Colonel Blair with his Family and an Ayah*, 1786 (?). By courtesy of the Leger Galleries Ltd., London

Cawnpore.[47] The trappings of Europe are evident in the furniture, yet not much of that is actually visible since it is covered by the figures (thus functioning more *as* furniture, less as a proclamation of British culture). The most obvious piece is the square piano,[48] yet as an instrument of the middle class it carried little of the status of the large harpsichords (or grand fortepianos) seen in the Morse–Cator or Cockerell–Blunt paintings. The mixture of furniture styles strikes me as more haphazard than purposefully eclectic – from the straight lines of the piano and the table in the right background (the latter is a purely utilitarian piece) to the curvilinear lines of the French Rococo chairs and the mirror on the back wall. Colonel Blair

[47] Colonel Blair entered the Bengal army as a major in 1768. He was made governor of Chunar Fort by about 1780 and was promoted to colonel in 1781. He resigned his commission in 1788. My information on the sitters comes from the sale catalogue, Sotheby, London, 18 March 1981, p. 64, lot no. 37 (illustrated) and Archer, *India and British portraiture*, p. 157. See also Manners and Williamson, *John Zoffany*, p. 111, catalogue entry on p. 274.

[48] This painting is also reproduced in Head, 'Corelli in Calcutta,' p. 548, according to whom the fortepiano is 'probably' by Johannes Pohlmann or Johannes Zumpe. The image is not otherwise discussed.

seems to have been ill-served by the limitations of the import market! All in all, the house and its furnishings appear to respond more to the demands of physical necessity than self-acknowledgment, at least by contrast with D'Oyly's surroundings.

The Blair portrait is particularly interesting with regard to the three paintings-within-the-painting depicting Indian life, though the precise subject matter is unclear. (It has been suggested that the three pictures represent paintings commissioned by Blair from Zoffany during a visit Blair made to Lucknow, and that this portrait commemorates the installation of the paintings in Blair's house, their having been brought down to Cawnpore by the artist himself.)[49] The images grant status to Indian culture by reason of their prominent size and compositional placement, as well as by their apparent subject matter. They are also notable for the total absence of Europeans, as far as I can make out (Fig. 21). To be sure, their existence is

Fig. 21   Johan Zoffany, *Colonel Blair with his Family and an Ayah.* Detail of painting-within-the-painting

[49] All this is uncertain since none of the paintings is known to exist, though Zoffany unquestionably executed scenes of Indian life, as I have already indicated. The smaller painting at the extreme left is almost completely indecipherable. Yet its very sketchiness adds credence to the possibility that it recalls an existing painting, since only the barest reminder of the other's form would signal the association. Archer, *India and British portraiture*, p. 157, states flatly that the three pictures reproduce paintings 'obviously by Zoffany himself'. See further the Sotheby catalogue entry referred to in n. 47.

due to Colonel Blair, whom they implicitly honor. But they are fundamentally different from D'Oyly's tiger skin (Fig. 15) or the Mason children's servants (Fig. 19), either as geographical markers or signifers of European hegemony.

The ease and genuineness of the Blairs' relationship to India is confirmed by the sitters themselves. Zoffany not only depicts them in the conventional, informal poses demanded of the genre, he also gives them an unusual warmth. The father and mother accord their daughter status by listening to her play (the music book's cover inscription seems to read 'Handel'); the devotion they feel for her is echoed in what they feel for each other (Fig. 22). Mrs Blair looks intently at her daughter, as Colonel Blair looks at his wife. They hold hands. These gestures of marital affection (especially a husband looking at his wife instead of the viewer, and the two physically touching) are highly unusual in contemporaneous English por-

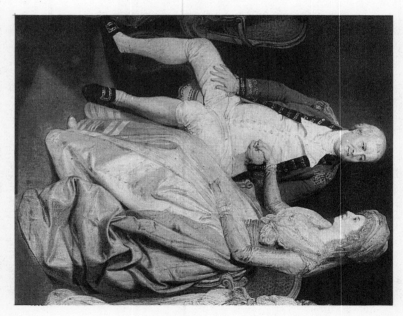

Fig. 22   Johan Zoffany, *Colonel Blair with his Family and an Ayah.* Detail of husband and wife

Fig. 23   Johan Zoffany, *Colonel Blair with his Family and an Ayah*. Detail of daughter and ayah

traits. Unlike the adult sitters in the Morse–Cator (Fig. 1) and Cockerell–Blunt (Fig. 14) portraits, the Blairs are oblivious to the viewer. The painting thus becomes more a personal memento and less a semi-public assertion of one's self and one's values.

A final, implicit (but not unproblematic) homage to India is paid by nature of the figures at the right (Fig. 23): Blair's younger daughter who pets a cat held by an ayah (a female servant). The two girls, about the same age, form an unusual image, for Zoffany treats them virtually as equals, though of course they are not. The Indian girl meets our glance head on, the same as her English companion. Both stand relaxed, totally comfortable together. In short, they appear to be friends. The family dog stands next to the ayah, as if she were a family member, and not next to the paterfamilias as is typically the case in English portraits. All in all this is a striking painting which in a small way mediates the visual norm in cultural relations between the Anglo-Indian and Indian peoples. The painting still confirms the order of colonialism and reiterates the hierarchy. But it does not acknowledge as legitimate the racial estrangement evident in the other images I have discussed. It must also be noted, however, that the ayah by the very nature of her position represents submission to the colonizer. In precisely this sense she then becomes, to the European, the 'good' native. As such she is represented sympathetically.[50]

As Fuseli expressed it, for the British, 'Portrait . . . is everything. Their taste and feelings all go to realities.' But the English portrait, as Pevsner points out, 'keeps long silences, and when it speaks, speaks in a low voice. . . . Or, to put it differently, the English portrait conceals more than it reveals, and what it reveals with studied understatement.'[51] What it tells, nevertheless, is the story of a culture and its values, and the ways in which art itself participates in the establishment and transmission thereof.

The same can be said of music. Music, that is, has always been a strong force in society, not only as it reflects and reacts to social forces but also as it helps shape a society and its culture. But with regard to the images I have considered here, music's role is limited to that of affirming a political and economic policy with epic implications for both England and India, policies of imperialist aggrandizement and suppression of human rights. This is not to suggest that music and musicians (professional or amateur), or visual artists for that matter, were responsible for the British Empire and the East India Company. But it is to suggest that the role assigned to music in the culture was primarily one of either affirming the status quo or at least not tampering with it. What is largely evident in these images, in other words, is that music and art provide evidence of the very power which their presence serves to mask.[52] In the process music and art are marginalized from participation in shaping values alternative to those of the dominant

50 Leonard Bell, 'Artists and empire: Victorian representations of subject people', *Art History*, 5/1 (1982), pp. 82–4, convincingly discusses examples from the mid nineteenth century of European versions of 'good' and 'bad' natives. As he points out, what the 'good' natives have in common (whether represented visually or in literary texts) is their docility and passivity. As such, non-European facial features are sometimes de-emphasized for 'good' natives, whereas for the 'bad' the differences are sometimes exaggerated – especially so as to make the non-Europeans appear coarse or ugly.

51 Nikolaus Pevsner, *The Englishness of English art* (Harmondsworth, 1964), p. 79. The quotation from Fuseli appears on p. 31.

52 I would describe the process of discovery undertaken in this essay to accord with Walter Benjamin's assertion, in *Ursprung des deutschen Trauerspiels* (1927), that truth is to be discovered in the *unintentional*, or as he – so characteristically and obliquely – put it, 'truth is the death of intention.' (Adorno of course adopted this premise in his later formulation of negative dialectics.) See the detailed discussion of 'unintentional truth' in Susan Buck-Morss, *The origin of negative dialectics* (New York, 1977), pp. 76–81, whence the quotation (p. 77).

ideology. Instead, they aid the hegemonic drive of imperialistic politics. Many years ago Walter Benjamin pointed out that history belongs to the victors and that the spoils of victory are what we have come to call cultural treasures. He suggested that our cultural treasures have origins to be contemplated with horror: 'They owe their existence not only to the efforts of the great minds and talents who have created them, but also to the anonymous toil of their contemporaries. There is no document of civilization which is not at the same time a document of barbarism.'[53]

The barbarism of which I speak is embodied in cultural chauvinism. Perhaps no one expressed that chauvinism more forthrightly, though apparently unknowingly, than Thomas Babington Macaulay, in his lengthy speech to the House of Commons (10 July 1833) on the subject of a draft penal code for India. 'I see', he said, 'the morality, the philosophy, the taste of Europe, beginning to produce a salutary effect on the hearts and understandings of our [Indian] subjects.' And a little later: 'Consider, too, Sir, how rapidly the public mind of India is advancing, how much attention is already paid by the higher classes of the natives to those intellectual pursuits on the cultivation of which the superiority of the European race to the rest of mankind principally depends.'

Macaulay concluded his speech by redrawing the connection between Western cultural superiority (defined as art and morality) and the suppression of India by British political power (defined as law); his remarks represent nothing less than the apotheosis of unrepentant nationalism: 'There is an empire exempt from all natural causes of decay. Those triumphs are the pacific triumphs of reason over barbarism; that empire is the imperishable empire of our arts and our morals, our literature and our laws.'[54] In the House of Commons Macaulay thus drew attention to the

[53] Walter Benjamin, 'Theses on the philosophy of history', in *Illuminations*, ed. with introduction by Hannah Arendt, trans. Harry Zohn (New York, 1969), p. 256. Bell, 'Artists and empire', pp. 73–86, undertakes a complementary examination regarding several paintings executed in the mid nineteenth century of native peoples in colonial Africa, Hong Kong, and New Zealand. He remarks (p. 73) that 'what unifies a seemingly bewildering variety of imagery is that most, if not all, of these representations had a common ideological base. They can be seen as attempts to fashion "realities" for the "natives" – "realities" primarily geared to prevailing British beliefs, values and interests – however much the "reality" asserted or implied might be at variance with socio-political, psychological and physical actualities as perceived by the "natives" themselves or by later European historians and critics.' Bell concentrates especially on the ways in which European painters reshaped or otherwise transformed the very way native peoples looked, so as to render their 'meaning' to European viewers in keeping with the fundamental tenets of colonial ideology. As he puts it, British artists were fundamentally creating "myths" or "fictions", that were important and necessary for the dominant culture in so far as they contributed to the "justification" of its actions' (pp. 73–4).

[54] Thomas Babington Macaulay, *The works of Lord Macaulay*, 12 vols. (London, 1898), XI, pp. 567, 571, 586. I wish to thank Professor Derek Longhurst for drawing my attention to Macaulay's speech.

identical relationships I have developed here, namely, that political empire is mirrored by the empire of culture: *our* arts, *our* morals, *our* literature, *our* laws. By direct implication, moreover, these cultural markers provide for him the rationalization – hence, justification – for imperialism.

On grounding Chopin

ROSE ROSENGARD SUBOTNIK

Autonomy versus contingency

The notion that society lies at the heart of music – at the heart not only of its significance but also of its very identity – is a notion, I have come to realize, that is for me not an hypothesis, not a thesis the scientific proof of which is the goal of my study. In fact I would say that this notion does not lend itself to any popularly conceived model whereby an inductive investigation of an hypothesis leads to scientific conclusion, whether one thinks of it as a general notion (the notion that music and society in general are intimately related) or as any particular version of that notion (say, the Marxist version, that music takes shape out of some set of underlying economic conditions). That is to say, not even the existence of such an intimacy, much less any particular account of it, is susceptible of scientific proof through a presentation of facts.

This is why studies based on the notion I describe are so suspect in mainstream American musicology. The latter remains dominated by positivism, defined in Webster's second edition as 'A system of philosophy . . . which excludes everything but the natural phenomena or properties of knowable things, together with their relations of coexistence and succession.' It is a discipline committed in its materials and methods to a rather old-fashioned, vulgarized notion of scientific models.

For me, and I suppose for most of the writers in this volume, the notion of an intimate relationship between music and society functions not as a distant goal but as a starting point of great immediacy, and not as an hypothesis but as an assumption. It functions as an idea about a relationship which in turn allows the examination of that relationship from many points of view and its exploration in many directions. It is an idea that generates studies the goal of which (or at least one important goal of which) is to articulate something essential about why any particular music is the way it is in particular, that is, to achieve insight into the character of its identity. This process involves decisions (which can never be definitive) as to what constitutes the significant ways in which this music differs from other forms, even related forms, of human expression.

Critics sometimes complain that authors of studies based on this assumption of social intimacy are not really interested in music but rather in philosophy or anthropology or some other 'extrinsic' discipline. This criticism is actually two-pronged in that it reveals an insistence on the autonomy not only of music but also of musicology, which positivists tend to see as an extension of the autonomous domain of music itself. As to this latter notion, I would say it is deceptive, for positivist musicologists do not derive their methods of study from the music they study any more often than serious contextualists do; on the contrary, as I hope to show, they do it less. The real objection here, I believe, is not that contextualists violate the autonomy of musicology as a strictly musical undertaking but that they look to the wrong outside disciplines for help – to philosophy and anthropology rather than to a positivistically conceived model of science.

As to the charge of non-interest in music, it seems to me patently wrong. No doubt massive collections of facts about a body of music can indicate a love, at least of some antiquarian sort, of that music. But is love not evident also in studies which, based on the assumption that society lies at the heart of the very identity of music, aim at understanding why music is the way it is? Good contextualist studies start from the music and lead back to it. In this respect contextualist studies often resemble Adorno, whose repeated assaults on the problem of social mediation remained inseparable from a concomitant, if seemingly contradictory, insistence on autonomy as the ideal condition of musical structure.

But along the way, of course, in the dialectic that occurs between the departure from the music and the return to it, serious contextualists grapple with problems that cannot be solved through the mere establishment of facts or simple models of cause and effect. Typically, contextualists alternate between following the music into its relations with its social context and reassessing their own method of studying those relationships. Serious contextualists want to go beyond questions that can be answered through 'His Life and Works' or 'The Music and its Times', studies which, like other more clearly positivistic studies, may produce information that is useful to others but need not go beyond the connections implied by 'and' in the framing of questions or methods.

Serious contextualists try to deal with the relation between music and society in a way that recognizes the complex questions raised by human forms of expression and, consequently, the need for methodological honesty, refinement, and self-critical capacity in the study of those forms. For example, recognizing, as post-Marxian or post-Freudian scholars do, that no single principle is likely to find scientific acceptance as the universal explanation of human forms of expression, serious contextualists do not thereby renounce, as do positivists, the problem of social mediation as one worthy of serious study or even, necessarily, the theories of Marx or Freud as helpful sources of insight into forms of human expression. Rather they acknowledge that they have hold of an assumption, and of theories and problems concerning that assumption, that can never be definitively proved but only asserted, manipulated, stroked, and viewed repetitively through a series of altered angles, or returned to periodically as patterns of identity strung through a medium of shifting contexts or perceptions until, it is hoped, some persuasive pattern of intelligibility emerges.

To be persuasive, of course, an account requires internal rigor; but though simple scientific models do not supply a basis of rigor for such contextualist studies, it does not follow that no such rigor is possible. Scientific structures are not the only sort that the human mind has fashioned persuasively; the rigor of religious systems, for example, has probably exercised sway over far more human minds than that of scientific models. Nor is science the only model of study available to serious contextualists. There are other forms of human expression which suggest that, while it may be difficult to convey the presence of mental rigor in connections forming patterns other than those of mechanistic causal explanation or empirical induction, it is not impossible. I think particularly of aesthetic forms of expression. The persuasive demonstration of such rigor has in fact been a central agenda of the arts themselves in the past two centuries of Western history – certainly of music since Beethoven – and the difficulty has not yet entirely vanquished the arts (though it threatens to) or eliminated them as credible instruments of human understanding. Criticism, too, tends to model itself on artistic rather than scientific patterns of connections and has had an enormous impact on a good deal of twentieth-century thought, though not on mainstream American musicology. Indeed, I would argue that the problem of trying to relate music to society *is*, fundamentally, a problem of criticism, requiring very much the same sorts of means that one would take to the interpretation of a literary text.

In choosing science over art as a paradigm for seeking truth, positivist musicology seems to believe it is safeguarding its double ideal of autonomy – in the domains of both music and musicology. But is it really safeguarding either? In actuality, the structural autonomy posited as an ideal for music by Adorno is extended by the positivist to include a number of things besides the superficially most plausible autonomous entity, the composition itself. The positivist definition of musical autonomy includes music that preceded a composition, the instruments and other material conditions of performance that figured in composition, and above all the composer's mind, the iconic status of which is shown by the massive attention given to sketch studies and especially to the making of so-called authentic editions.

Such considerations define the autonomy of music for positivist musicologists. Yet even they seem uneasily aware that this extended definition itself already involves music in a kind of heteronomy, to use that dreadful and misleading word, and that in order to work, this extended definition requires certain kinds of connections that cannot be supplied through the positivist principles of coexistence and succession.

Consider this passage from the conclusion to a recent highly regarded essay on Chopin: 'Perceptive analysis and comprehension of the sources and interpretation and evaluation of the music form, or ought to form, inseparable parts of one line of inquiry. . . . If this article has addressed a fundamental aspect of source studies in Chopin, work must now take up the associated issue: the critical reassessment of his music.' 'Work'. But whose work? And how 'associated'? Time and again we are exhorted at the end of such an article to go out and synthesize the preceding collection of facts into some account of the music itself, but we are given no clue how to approach such a synthesis, much less any reference to non-positivist work on such a problem.

Or again, consider the material and stylistic sources of music. Positivist methods can gather genuinely useful facts about instruments, orchestras, and opera houses; they can quantify certain kinds of similarities and differences between works; they can prove (though not always disprove) contact between two composers. But can they – do they – offer us any theory or account, for example, of how musical influence actually works? Judging even from my own experience as a composition student, of cribbing the opening to Mendelssohn's 'Reformation' Symphony in total ignorance of my theft, I would suspect that influence is an extremely complicated mechanism.

Or again, consider sketch studies. One frequently encounters a defensive tone in such articles as authors seek to justify the validity of the enterprise,

[1] Jeffrey Kallberg, 'Chopin in the marketplace: aspects of the international music publishing industry in the first half of the nineteenth century', Notes, 39 (1983), p. 819. This article won the Alfred Einstein Award of the American Musicological Society for 1983.

assuring us of their familiarity with the intentional fallacy and respect for it.[2] The reason for this defensiveness seems to be that here, too, as in the case of source and style studies, authors sense the inconsistencies within their received definition of musical autonomy. Likewise they probably sense the need for modes of connection which might be found in models they do not know how to construct or to justify.

Even sketch studies, it seems, which try to do no more than connect a work with earlier versions of itself – surely the narrowest extension of the concept of musical autonomy one can imagine – even these studies, to maintain their own validity, require ultimately a kind of connection-making which the positivist dares not risk. Outside the characteristically expansive last paragraph, in which they simultaneously admit and shrink back from the need to establish connections, positivists avoid asking seriously about such connections. If these scholars took up the challenge of their own concluding speculations with methodological honesty, they would soon run up against precisely the same kinds of epistemological and methodological uncertainties for which they castigate the serious contextualist. Is it any wonder that the positivist, who cannot close the conceptual gap between the sketch and the work, experiences acute discomfort in the presence of efforts to close the much larger gap between music and society? Musical autonomy as the positivist conceives it, I fear, consists less in the persuasive demonstration of musical autonomy than in the shaping of scholarly work so as to evade hard thought about autonomy.

The autonomy positivists impute to musicology, as I have already suggested in another context,[3] is no less problematical than that they impute to music. Even if we suppose, as positivists do, that musicology, though a legitimate part of the autonomous musical domain, nevertheless cannot draw its structure from music, and if we accept scientific method as an appropriate model of autonomy for work in any discipline, it does not follow that all positivist studies conform to such a model. On the contrary, many a positivist musicological study dispenses with even the simple conceptual framework of hypothesis and conclusion and presents a mere chronicle or at times even a scarcely disguised list of archival findings, in which not even verbs, much less connective theories, seem really necessary.

[2] See, for example, the conclusion to Philip Gossett's article, 'Beethoven's Sixth Symphony: sketches for the first movement', *Journal of the American Musicological Society*, 27 (1974), p. 280.

[3] 'The role of ideology in the study of Western music', *The Journal of Musicology*, 2 (Winter, 1983), pp. 1–12.

Such studies can hardly be said to present a scientifically autonomous argument.[4]

Ironically, although positivists reject everything outside of music in order to keep the study of music pure, they fail to look to music itself for the incomparable insight it could give into a problem central to their own work. I mean by this the rigorous and painstaking job of trying to fashion a persuasively whole structure exactly suited to the character of their materials themselves. Because everything included in a positivist study must be 'accounted for', everything tends to be treated as equally important. No structure is generated to serve the particular needs of materials because such needs are not seriously considered or defined.

Such conceptual limitations may in some ways actually counteract scholarly efforts to preserve for us the original spirit of earlier music. In positivist studies, for example, questions typically do not arise (because they cannot) about the inherent purposes and the results of reconstructing textual accuracy. Achieving textual accuracy is more often than not simply accepted as an *end* of musical scholarship, rather than envisioned as one part of a larger project. But even if we assume that reconstruction of a composer's exact intent is the highest duty of musical study – an assumption questioned by all the great composers who reworked the compositions of their predecessors – does it follow that textual accuracy is necessarily the best means to such a reconstruction?

In preparing this essay, I used my own old edition of Chopin's etudes, edited in 1916 by Arthur Friedheim.[5] At one point I was struck by a 'rallentando' marking and wondered if it was authentic. This question led me to Friedheim's preface, which astonished me. Friedheim openly acknowledged altering, omitting, and adding to various received markings in the music, but not thoughtlessly, or because he thought he could improve on Chopin's original markings. Rather, he had actually heard some of these

---

[4] Nor is the failure even to approximate structural autonomy limited to such extreme cases. Insisting on the self-containment of any scholarly problem, the positivist school renounces recourse to non-musical resources that might help these scholars to make distinctions concerning the importance of their musical materials and to define for them some significance. This spares them the messiness of trying to establish a dialectical relationship between the shape of an idea and the diverse materials to which it will be applied. But at the same time, lacking criteria for characterizing or assessing their materials, such studies, while needing a form, do not characteristically work out a problem in a genuinely autonomous fashion. Rather, they typically rely for their structure on models established in preceding studies of the same kind. This entire discussion is deeply indebted to the ideas of William A. Levine, a cultural theorist and colleague at the Burroughs Corporation in Chicago, where I worked at the time this essay was written.

[5] This edition was published in New York by G. Schirmer, as vol. VIII of Chopin's complete piano works.

works performed by Liszt (and by Anton Rubinstein, who was audibly influenced by Liszt); and he assumed, reasonably, that these performances preserved as well as possible Chopin's own spirit. Attempting to preserve the 'tradition at second-hand' that he had in his mind's ear, he had used the markings which were most likely to get that rendition from the modern performer.[6] This is in keeping with Adorno's idea, in 'Bach defended against his devotees', or more recently, with Richard Taruskin's idea, that to preserve the essential quality of old music, which requires maintaining its vitality in our own context, it is sometimes necessary to change the material conditions of its performance.[7] Is it not possible that the faithful rendering of Chopin's expressive markings, some of which may now have altered significance, and which to some extent reflect values different from ours, could actually bring about performances unfaithful to Chopin's intent? Positivists do give such matters some consideration at the level of the immediate editorial decision, but unlike the less scientific Friedheim, they do not ordinarily address the broader conceptual implications of such problems, let alone make room for persuasive reinterpretations.

I have no quarrel with the notion that the quality of a work of art is related in some central, though not necessarily exclusive, way to its persuasiveness in projecting its own structural wholeness. I have no thought that enlarging the domain of musicology to include the methodological concerns of contextualists would invalidate the value of formal analysis. Nor do I have any quarrel with the notion that composers, at least in modern Western history, experience the working out of a creative problem as a self-contained exercise, even when their structural solutions or materials seem actually to be drawn, at least in part, from outside the traditional musical medium.

I see no fatal contradiction between the acceptance of autonomy, in the sense of wholeness, as one sort of paradigm for interpreting structure and the rejection of autonomy as an epistemological ideology. Nor do I view various composers' experience of their own autonomy as an epistemological barrier to my view of their work as something inseparable from its environment. Rather I see such conflicting concepts as part of a dialectic that exists not only in art but also in life. In life, too, we tend to experience the working out of a problem or relationship as a self-contained activity; our preoccupation with internal relationships tends to distract us from

[6] 'Introductory', ibid., pp. 1–2.

[7] Theodor Adorno, 'Bach defended against his devotees', *Prisms*, trans. Samuel Weber and Shierry Weber (London, 1967), especially pp. 142–6; Richard Taruskin, 'The musicologist and the performer', *Musicology in the 1980s: methods, goals, opportunities*, eds. D. Kern Holoman and Claude V. Palisca (New York, 1982), pp. 101–17.

observing any connections our works and problems may have to the world beyond them.

And yet upon reflection, such experiences often make more sense to us viewed as elements of patterns which are presented, repeated, varied, or returned to in the course of our lifetime, precisely as patterns are treated in art and in aesthetically modeled studies. In fact I would argue that the structure of art and the experience of life support each other in ways that affirm the value of serious contextual studies. On the one hand, the patterns of problem-solving provided by art seem well designed as models for trying to impose coherence on – to make sense of – our experience.[8] And on the other hand, though our reflection on experience cannot pretend to a scientific sort of rigor, we are certainly in a strong position to judge the adequacy of our reflections to the undeniable hardness of our experienced reality itself.

And our reflected experience, I believe, gives us ample support for the notion that even as we define problems and relationships in apparent autonomy, we are reflecting complex interactions with society of which we are largely unconscious, and for which the most useful metaphor of explanation is not the simple one of cause and effect but the more complicated assertions and intertwinings of art. In terms of my own life, I think of the shock I experienced in coming to realize that the decisions I had made about bringing up my own children (involving patterns I had imposed on them and relationships I had developed with them), decisions which I had experienced as being drawn from an instinctive, very personal set of values, were highly characteristic of parents in my generation. Why? Was it because we were all reacting against the 'defects' of an identical inherited set of child-rearing values (how did *those* become identical?)? Because we were all working parents? Because we were all living through the same technological revolution?

Not even the most sophisticated statistical methods could sort out these elements into their 'correct' causal proportions, let alone establish conclusively their connection to my problem-solving as a parent. And yet clearly there were patterns out there in society that exactly paralleled not only the materials – the values – I brought to my activities as a parent but also the shapes of the decisions and relationships I defined. Here was a personal example of the mysteries of mediation, unscientific, and yet not necessarily less real, or less worthy in an epistemological sense of further exploration than were Piaget's observations of his own children. If I could

8 See especially in this connection the study by Phyllis Rose, *Parallel lives: five Victorian marriages* (New York, 1983), p. 6.

look into the future and hear the account given by some contextualist historian of this phenomenon, I could judge out of the hardness of my own experience whether his or her account made any sense of reality. This does not mean I would, or in fairness could, limit future explanations to my own perspective; but surely this ability to judge would validate the historian's very attempt to connect my actions to a context of which I may have been unconscious. Should not our own attempts have the same legitimacy in our studies of composers past?

Contingency in Chopin

Chopin at first blush seems to most of us an unlikely candidate to propose for any study aimed at countering the notion that music is purely autonomous. Certainly his music seems to satisfy criteria for autonomy on a number of levels. Most obviously it is mainly instrumental music, meaning it does without both voice and word, those two obtrusions of the human presence which drag music down so heavily into our own mundane world and out of the ethereal realm where early German Romantics imagined it existing as a kind of disembodied significant form. This absence is felt not as a renunciation, such as that implied by Mendelssohn's title *Songs without Words*, but as a simple and rather persuasive fact of independence. Indeed, the instrumental source is largely confined to a single instrument, the piano, which is likely to exist in the performer's home, so we can say that even in the most external sense, Chopin's music requires relatively few social resources, though of course it does require some.

Chopin's music, furthermore, is basically non-functional. True, certain works, notably the etudes and preludes, are often, though certainly not always, used as a means of improving the performer's skill. This is a time-honored function of music, and yet it does not seriously threaten the characterization of Chopin's music as autonomous at the level of which I am speaking. At most, in Chopin's case, this function seems merely a minor variant of the ideal of autonomy; the principal effect of these works is no more pedagogical than that of the other music which the instrumentalist's enhanced skill may serve. On the contrary, even the preludes and etudes can readily be taken as designed to pass through time, or perhaps to define it, in an aesthetically pleasing way. (One is never surprised to find a Chopin study piece in a recital of music designed for just this seemingly autonomous purpose of self-presentation, whereas a Clementi etude or even a Bach invention may seem a bit out of place on such an occasion.)

Certainly Chopin's music does not strike us as dedicated to state occasion or the glory of God. True, we happen to know the absence of such function from outside sources, but it is also the case that Chopin's piano pieces help define or at least conform to the shape and sound of a genre which can readily be interpreted, even without external knowledge, as essentially aesthetic, as opposed to functional, in character. Moreover, though it would not be true to say that listeners, either in Chopin's time or since, never associate Chopin's works with places, events, or other things outside of them – a point to which I shall return later – in our own time, at least, such associations are not thought necessary to make sense of those works.

Finally, Chopin's music seems autonomous to us in the sense that each piece seems to have a sensuous identity, a 'personality', so to speak, of its own. This sensuous distinctiveness does not seem to motivate the form of eighteenth-century music in quite the same way. One could argue plausibly, I believe, that with perhaps some noteworthy exceptions, typically tending towards a post-Baroque expressiveness (such as the Prelude in B♭ Minor in the *Well-tempered Clavier*, book I), Bach's preludes and fugues carve out a sensuous identity to some extent in spite of themselves. In other words, the achievement of such an identity does not seem to be what these works are principally after. Or again, even within the keyboard works of François Couperin or Rameau, works of a palpably aesthetic rather than functional character, it is not difficult to imagine mistaking one piece for another. Neither of these situations characterizes Chopin's music.

And yet the very nature of this last sort of autonomy – sensuous distinctiveness – must give us pause. Some time ago I published an analysis of Chopin's Prelude No. 2, the notorious A Minor, arguing that it represented a turn away from a belief in the possibility of truly autonomous intelligible structures, structures able to present wholly in themselves a self-evident (and hence universally intelligible) meaning.[9] I argued not only that this work failed to achieve such genuine internal structural autonomy – in my view all works ultimately fail in this respect – but more significantly, that the piece did not even project such autonomy as an aesthetic ideal. At the time one critic accused me of setting up a straw man by choosing a piece that was atypical of nineteenth-century music. This criticism surprised me, for although it is clear that there is something especially distinctive about this piece (all Chopin's pieces are distinctive but some are more distinctive than others?) I would have said it was not atypical but merely

[9] 'Romantic music as post-Kantian critique: Classicism, Romanticism, and the concept of the semiotic universe', *On criticizing music: five philosophical perspectives*, ed. Kingsley Price (Baltimore, 1981), pp. 87–95.

extreme. I thought this piece pushed to the outer limits characteristics that were very typical of Romantic music, and that for precisely this reason, as Walter Benjamin suggested more generally about extreme examples,[10] it made a good locus of style study. At any rate, I would like now to continue that line of analysis with reference to other, less controversially characteristic pieces by Chopin.

What perhaps is unusual about the Prelude No. 2 is this: its sensuous identity is so powerful that it threatens to overwhelm another sort of identity which we typically associate with Chopin's music, and which ordinarily defines a more fundamental, even ultimate ground or context for making sense of a Chopin piece. I mean, of course, Chopin's compositional identity itself. The Prelude No. 2 is unusual in that one can imagine (at least up to m. 17) not being sure the piece is by Chopin at all. On the whole this is not true of Chopin's music. We hear a work by Chopin, and our first impression, which remains throughout the piece as a kind of grounding principle, is that we are hearing a piece by Chopin.

This is no tautology. I do not deny that other composers achieved styles in the centuries before Chopin: I am told that Renaissance scholars can easily identify Josquin, and I myself have forced undergraduates to identify Dufay on listening exams. Still this is a rather specialized sort of experience. Likewise, it is possible to follow the structure of a work by Bach without having the listening experience overshadowed by the awareness of Bach's identity. And no matter how distinctive the most characteristic gestures of each may be, we can at least imagine confusing moments of Handel and Bach, or of Haydn and Mozart. Even Beethoven's personality, it could be argued, is grasped only secondarily to a sense of his energy, propulsiveness, and scale; that is, it is possible to imagine the experience of even a characteristic middle-period work preceding our recognition of Beethoven's authorship – if only there were a few such movements left that we did not already recognize! By contrast, it seems to me, the first sense we make of Chopin's music is almost always, to use the words of Robert Schumann,[12] who pointed this out repeatedly: 'This is by Frédéric Chopin.'[11]

I have sometimes been thought to look down on Romantic music,[12] and

[10] For a discussion of this issue see Charles Rosen, 'The origins of Walter Benjamin', *New York Review of Books*, 24 (10 November 1977), p. 33.

[11] Essay on the twenty-four preludes, Op. 28, Robert Schumann, *On music and musicians*, ed. Konrad Wolff (New York, 1946), p. 138. In another review (*Neue Zeitschrift für Musik*, 9 (1838, 178) Schumann writes: 'Chopin can hardly write anything now but that we feel like calling out in the seventh or eighth measure, "It is by him!"' From Leon B. Plantinga, *Schumann as critic* (New Haven, 1967), p. 230.

[12] See Lawrence Kramer, 'The mirror of tonality', *19th Century Music*, 4 (1981), p. 192.

certainly there is a school of thought that sees the establishment of this sort of personal identity in music as a sign of structural weakness. Again I am speaking of Adorno, with whom my work is often associated. For Adorno the highest achievement of music would be to define and resolve a structural problem, on a purely structural plane, uncorrupted by society. Adorno would have agreed with me that this is in practice an impossible achievement, but he associated the notion, rightly I believe, with Classicism in the sense that the ideal of such an achievement formed a constituent principle of the Classical style.

But I have never shared Adorno's negative judgment towards the music that followed Beethoven. On the contrary it seems to me that if one must make value judgments, then there is something very positive to be said about the Romantic style in general – the very thing, incidentally, that makes me see in the Romantic musical structure a more useful model for modern humanistic scholarship than those provided by Enlightenment paradigms of scientific universality. It can be argued that Classicism aimed at a high ideal of human universality, in which all rational structures would be self-evident without recourse to a supplementary knowledge of particular individuals, circumstances, or cultures. But I believe it is also true that Romanticism gave honest voice to the dawning recognition by modern Western society that such universality did not characterize human reality. Increasingly since Romanticism the human universe of discourse has been understood as an aggregate of relationships among discrete, particular individual consciousnesses, cultures, and values in which humans need always to decipher each other's meanings, whether in the case of the Rosetta Stone, a musical composition, or a television ad, using whatever external knowledge and coherent patterns of fragments they can find. In composing music that seems to require of the listener prior knowledge of Chopin's authorship, Chopin seems to me, like the very different Mahler decades later, to affirm that we draw meaning from another's expression not only from its inner structure but also from its sensuous qualities and from our knowledge of (and reaction to) the particular context in which it originated.

Furthermore I would add that within such a context of sensed fragmentation, it took great courage for Chopin to persist in efforts to create generally comprehensible structures of sound. It also took great ability to create a personal style which succeeded in functioning as a ground of meaning for large portions of society far removed from Chopin and his culture.

In the entire history of Western music, even allowing for the fact that at least in modern times it has generally been easier for composers outside the

Italo-German center to project distinctiveness of style as a central value, I think it fair to say that no composer has ever exceeded the extent to which Chopin infused the listening experience with his own identity, and that very few have matched it. And where I would agree with Adorno is in his implicit suggestion that music dependent in any fundamental way on the identity of its composer for its general intelligibility is not to be characterized as autonomous music.

For this sort of dependence is something rather different from that identity of the composer's mind and his works that positivist scholars define as autonomy in their studies of autographs and sketches. This dependence shifts attention to the composer not as an ultimate arbiter of textual accuracy but as a particular individual in a particular cultural situation existing outside of the music; and it shifts the center of meaning away from the enterprise of self-generating structure, which more than mere wholeness is what *I* understand by autonomy. Those who take my denial of Chopin's autonomy as a criticism ought perhaps to rethink their own criteria for compositional excellence. My observation casts no aspersions on Chopin as a craftsman but is, simply, a characterization of his style, of the means he used to create the style, and of the kinds of meaning and value I think can be imputed to that style. I simply do not think that Chopin's music is about, or intends to be about, the problem of creating autonomously intelligible structures. Certainly he took the trouble to give his works a generally intelligible shape, but I do not believe his pieces are to be understood as efforts to create a whole out of self-contained means.

What I do think Chopin's music is about – and I think this is true not only of the Prelude No. 2 but also of his music more generally – is something quite different. I think what this music does primarily is to recognize the reality of the contingent. I think it accords hard reality to the concrete, to the physical, to the particular, to the discrete, to the here-and-now, no matter how arbitrary, ephemeral, or fragmentary. And I think the problem of Chopin's music is how to achieve intelligibility with materials so defined – how to make persuasively intelligible structures which acknowledge the reality of the contingent at a multiplicity of levels. Saying Chopin used tonality to insure intelligibility does not do justice to his solution to this problem. Certainly he still benefited from tonality; but to avoid irreparable contradiction within his own stylistic context, Chopin had to use tonality in a way that did not allow its promise of self-evident intelligibility to overshadow his assertion of the contingent. This meant working against or in spite of the communicative virtues of tonality to a certain extent, emphasizing its cultural and sensuous particularity over its capacity for abstract structural logic. The center of Chopin's intelligibility, I believe, lies not in his tonal architecture but in his successfully projected and explicitly sensuous interweaving of the fragmentary and particular against a lingering background of tonal tension, which is now only secondary as a source of connection or 'explanation.' This sort of interweaving is extraordinarily difficult; it requires the composer to persuade his audience that the connections and relationships between contingent elements are rigorous, even necessary. The compulsiveness with which Chopin continuously polished his works, in some cases even after publication, lends credence to this vision of this style.[13] Chopin seems, like Beethoven before him, to have had a compulsive need to 'get it right', a need which is bound to be paramount in a society which no longer endorses general standards of intelligibility, and in which successful communication seems to depend on the eloquence of the individual.

Within such an enterprise, it seems to me, the achievement of an internally generated wholeness is an irrelevant criterion of musical value, for this sort of achievement has been abandoned as a possible or even desired goal of the composition. Rather, the shape of an independently existing physical entity is recognized as ultimately particular, not universal, and therefore contingent, not eternal, precisely the way in which its component details are recognized. Therefore it is perfectly consistent with the character of the undertaking for the composer to impose recognizable limits, signs of wholeness, from without. He need do no more than create generally plausible outer shapes and conclusions in order to avoid the really brute, arbitrary physical independence that emerges, say, when a symphony orchestra presents snippets of the classics to an audience of underestimated children. As long as the sensuous experience of the piece remains absorbing – and it does in no small measure because this sensuous quality can be identified as the product of a real, known person – it will be accepted as a plausible whole even if this wholeness is not projected as internally generated. What Chopin demonstrates rather explicitly is that structure need not be internally generated to be perceptibly coherent.

Stated another way, it is aesthetically acceptable if a piece by Chopin is internally fragmentary. That is a part of its particular kind of wholeness. And precisely because this is music in which style is of greater importance to intelligibility than is form, much of the same value can be obtained from the fragments or details of Chopin's pieces as from the whole. Thus the opening of the well-known Etude in E Major (Op. 10, No. 3) is not a

13 Though it attempts no theoretical interpretation of this characteristic, Kallberg's 'Chopin' (see n. 1) provides many useful examples of it.

statement of a harmonic premise that will unfold itself but a self-contained section which leads nowhere and could well stand, with just a few rhetorical changes, as an independent piece, plausible in structure and intelligible as an experience of sense or color.

Ex. 1: Op. 10, No. 3, mm. 1–21

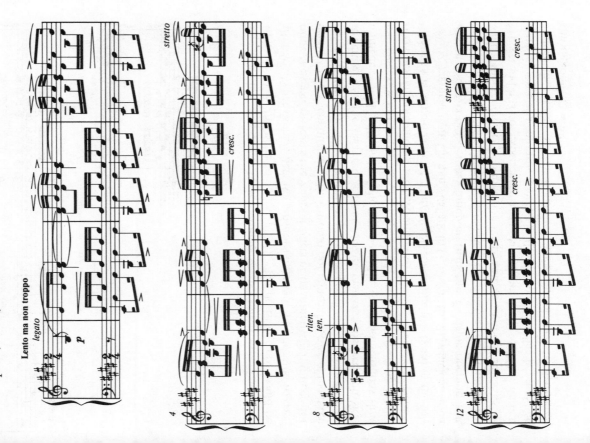

Ex. 1: (*cont.*)

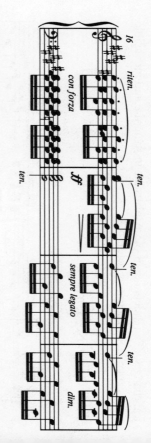

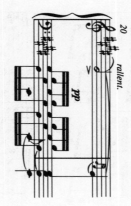

The fact that it goes on to something else is, and is experienced as, arbitrary. Were the piece to end at m. 21, that decision, too, would be arbitrary. What we have here is a sensuous fragment. The decision to continue the piece increases the values it offers us quantitatively but does not really change them qualitatively. It would not ravage the sense of the piece to end it here as it would to end at the corresponding point in a Mozart structure. For the balanced tension Mozart maintains between physical immediacy and structural implication, even in the most sensuous slow movement, is in this passage of Chopin's, not atypically, undercut by the overwhelming presence of the here-and-now.

Much the same quality of arbitrary self-containment is heard in the following fragment from Chopin's Ballade in G Minor (Ex. 2), which has even less of a conventional tonal function than the E Major opening just described. Is it a 'second theme'? Its key is E♭, not the relative major B♭, which the modulatory 'bridge' (and Classical convention) leads us to expect; and it is not experienced as a polar magnet to the opening. Rather, it makes sense as a coloristic contrast to the passage immediately preceding and as the bearer of certain motivic fragments of melody that recur throughout the work.

On grounding Chopin

Ex. 2: Ballade in G Minor, mm. 67–82

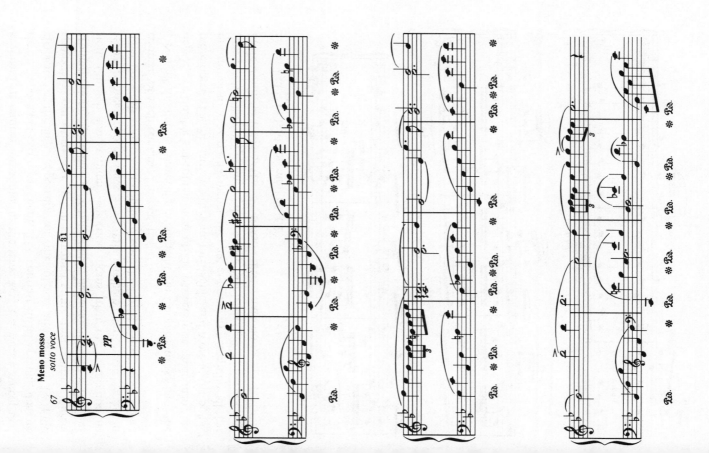

Later, after numerous fireworks and a scale descending the length of the keyboard, it returns fortissimo, in the same key, E♭, with a syncopated rhythm and rapid accompaniment. The contrast to its opening delicate character is thrilling, especially for the player, and cannot be fully appreciated out of context. Yet in structural terms, this return is purely arbitrary; nothing requires it. What Chopin has accomplished is the illusion, through almost purely coloristic means, that the connection he asserts between two passages is not only intelligible but inevitable. Yet in what does this connection consist except the varied return, in changing context, of a self-contained fragment?

Not all the details conveying intelligibility in Chopin's works have the degree of plausible self-containment of the passages just cited; many are more openly fragmentary. Yet they are intelligible, and more to the point, in contrast to Mozart's fragments, they are *as fragments* perceptibly all that they can be. Take, for example, the passage that leads back to the opening of the Etude in E Major (Ex. 3), the so-called retransition.

Ex. 3: Etude in E Major, mm. 54–62

In a classical work, such a passage is defined above all functionally (though again, Mozart, as I have argued elsewhere,[14] unquestionably begins to undermine this functional priority in his marked attention to the sensuous surface of his music at precisely such points). It has been said that such a passage in a characteristic Classical structure can instantly be located by the listener because of its clear functional definition.

This is not true of the passage at hand. When I first thought of writing this essay, it was this particular passage that came to mind, and not its function within the piece but its internal character. Here, if ever, it seemed to me, was music about the here-and-now. One could listen to it and suspend caring about where it is coming from, where it is going, whether it ever ends.

True, it has the main harmonic feature of a functioning retransition, a dominant pedal point (on B). Further, one can point to many features in this passage that by convention signify the impending return of the tonic.[15] And certainly one could not deny that the eventual return of the tonic in the reprise (m. 62) is experienced, on the level of harmonic logic, as providing closure.

And yet I would argue that the return to an all-powerful, all-clarifying, all-resolving tonic is not the primary focus of attention in this passage. However necessary harmonic coherence may be to achieving the primary focus, that focus itself is on the dense, leisurely, undulating, and iridescent quality of the so-called musical 'surface'. It is on the manipulation, the stroking, the luxuriant ornamentation, and the repetitive examining of something concrete, particular, and unchanging in a succession of slightly altered contexts. It is on the simultaneous experience of sameness and constant change, and on the imputation of reality to both the concreteness and the ephemerality of the particular.[16]

To me, this focus is so strong as to be prior to any formal musical analy-

---

[14] 'Evidence of a critical world view', *Music and civilization: essays in honor of Paul Henry Lang*, ed. Edmond Strainchamps and Maria Rika Maniates (New York, 1984), pp. 29–43.

[15] In the bass, for example, one can note the propulsive lowered-VI to V pattern (on C♮ to B). In the melodic line, always so crucial in Chopin's definition of structure, one can point out the movement downward, essentially by step, towards the tonic; the repetitive circling of the leading-tone, D♯; the prolonged postponement of a conclusive cadence on the tonic, E; and the increasing truncation of the melodic patterns (stretto). In terms of chordal texture, one can point to the recurring stress on dissonance which gives way at the last possible second (m. 61) to clear consonance.

[16] Ironically, this music points, among other things, to the positivist relations of succession and coexistence or what Comte himself called 'succession and resemblance' (as quoted in the entry on Comte in the *Encyclopedia of philosophy* (New York, 1967), II, p. 174). This is not so surprising since the two men lived in France at the same time, in a century that came to be dominated by certain aspects of empiricism.

sis.[17] In part this impression derives from a feature of Chopin's style that I have elsewhere analyzed in detail: his replacement of implicative or causal Classical structures (such as antecedent–consequent) with a reliance on discrete 'analogy' – on parallel segments and layers – that turns attention away from propulsive relationships to the immediacy of the moment.[18] On a local level, for example, one could point to the numerous adjacent, mosaic-like particles consisting of strong-beat dissonance and momentary resolution, or to the immediate presentation, in mm. 55 and 57, of ornamented repetitions, which throw substantive weight, sustained throughout the passage, on the triplet figure in the bass.

Especially characteristic of Chopin in this respect is the way in which mm. 56–7 present themselves as an analogue (rather than a consequent or resolution) to mm. 54–5. True, the two pairs of measures have the melodic alteration characteristic of tonal 'correction'; and true, the bass line in the later pair contains no counterpart to the dominant B in the bass of m. 55. Nevertheless, these measures have other features which suggest the later pair primarily as a rough transposition (or, in structuralist terms, 'transformation') of the earlier one. Not only are the two segments equal in length (which would also be the case with antecedent and consequent) and parallel in melodic shape. In addition, the tenor line in the later pair offers the same lowered-VI to V movement (but this time on G♮–F♯, with the new goal, B, now simultaneously anticipated in the bass), and the same melodic movement downward, essentially by step, towards a goal (but again, here B rather than the E of the previous two measures).

Furthermore, even the harmonic structure of these measures has analogical aspects that work against the conventional function of drive towards the tonic. One might suppose, looking at the bass line of the score, that the presence on strong beats first of B (mm. 55–6) and then of E (mm. 56–7)

[17] David Josephson of Brown University, whose help in preparing this essay was invaluable, differs sharply with my perception of this passage. For him, the functional pull of the passage outweighs its static sensuousness, which he concedes is substantial. He characterizes this passage as a study in intensified avoidances. This difference in interpretation, I would argue, which reflects no disagreement about the structural 'facts,' cannot be settled by any reference to the musical text. (Josephson would also disallow interpretations based on a post-facto knowledge of culture, whereas I believe such interpretations are not only inevitable but also, within limits of responsibility, desirable. In my view it is counterproductive to invest any text with the authority of an autonomous meaning, independent of its dialectical relation reception.)

[18] See 'Romantic music as post-Kantian critique', especially pp. 91–2. I was startled recently to learn that at the time this article appeared some colleagues took issue with its failure to 'explain' Chopin's Prelude No. 2 as a study in 'the circle of fifths.' I had hoped it was clear that this analysis was trying to deconstruct such conventional labels, that is, to bore through their often dulling effect on actual musical experience.

defines the pattern of closure (V to I) common in antecedent–consequent construction. Yet the effect of the later two measures is one not of closure but of indeterminate continuation. In actuality, both melody and bass are harmonically ambiguous in mm. 56–7, pointing simultaneously to E and B in ways that may contradict each other (such ambiguity, as well as conflict between layers, is typical of Chopin). And at a crucial point the harmony supports a hearing of the later passage as an analogue in B to the earlier one in E. For the bass note E in mm. 56–7, though technically part of a dominant–tonic cadential formula, is experienced as a passing sub-dominant on its way to B. In other words, playing upon the conventional ambiguity of the plagal relationship, Chopin presents the conventionally definitive V–I cadence in the bass as devoid of the force needed to effect persuasive resolution, and hollowed of any certainty except the identity of the pitches themselves (B and E). This means, of course, that the status of E as a tonic is suggested here as contingent. Indeed, one's reaction to the premature return of the tonic at this point, in sharp distinction to the effect of corresponding moments in Beethoven's middle-period work, is one of indifference.[19] 'So what?' one might say, or 'Plus ça change, plus c'est la même chose.'

One might even refer the entire retransition to the notion of analogy at a larger structural level: to the extent that its boundaries are emphasized, the passage as a whole suggests itself as a discrete and equal counterpart to other sections of the etude. And the argument can be made that this passage is jagged at both its ends.

The break at the opening is clear. After a pause following the extreme pitch of unresolved hysteria reached by this piece, the retransition simply takes up as if to answer a cry for help with the words, 'Now another thing.' Although the retransition may well be meant to soothe the preceding outburst, it does not really resolve it, least of all on any commensurate level of rhetorical passion. Far more, the import of the retransition seems to be, 'Are you through? Now as I was saying.' In effect the retransition seems to argue that here, in contrast to our image of the Classical development section, even a passage which attains extreme tension has no privileged claims on structure. Such a passage cannot count with certainty on altering irrevocably the ensuing action or on reaching resolution; rather than moving towards a self-determined destiny, it is just another section. The join at the end of the retransition may appear seamless. Yet here, too, especially in

[19] Unlike the self-absorption in the sensuousness of the moment or even the inescapable world-weariness suggested by Chopin's use of this device, the precipitate and explosive return of the tonic Eb on the horns just prior to the first-movement recapitulation in Beethoven's 'Eroica' seems anything but anti-climactic.

conjunction with the melodic phrasing in Friedheim's edition, one experiences between the D♯ of m. 61 and the E of m. 62 a palpable moment of discreteness. One has the sense that something of importance is being left behind, as the music leaves to take up a different, but no more privileged activity. In short, given the clarity of its boundaries as well as the intense focus on its internal content, it does not seem far-fetched to construe the retransition as a sensuous fragment.

What I am arguing is that in this passage, techniques and ambiguities that were formerly used unequivocally as means to a harmonic end are well on their way to becoming a sensuous end in themselves. The harmonic function of this retransition is so challenged by considerations of color and identity that harmonic function itself has given way, in no small degree, to harmonic identity and thus, ultimately, to sensuous color. Even the early return of the tonic is experienced here as just another coloristic element, a change rung on the basic recurring melodic pattern. We have here something very much of the physical world, inertia (defined by Webster, in part, as 'the property of matter by which it will remain . . . in . . . motion . . . unless acted upon by some external force').

Indeed, it is the rhetorical, harmonically extrinsic devices of melodic stretto and literal deceleration that ultimately serve to wind down this recalcitrant passage, forcing it finally to give way to tonal authority. Nevertheless, the sensuousness of the repetition in the last half of the passage is so mesmerizing that the anticipatory interest in the 'actual' return of the tonic very nearly disappears. One could almost imagine being happier without it, especially if one had the choice of lingering forever on the leading-tone D♯, which 'hangs' far more than it 'leads' here. Certainly it is not difficult to extrapolate from this passage the possibility of musical movement so narcissistic, or so effete, as to turn the very category of resolution into an irrelevancy.

Of course, the tension is not altogether gone. We are not yet in the wholly atemporal, post-tonal, even existential realm of Debussy (or Satie), where we are given the here-and-now with hardly the memory of a hope of anything beyond. Much of the poignance we feel so keenly in passages by Chopin such as this one comes from the remaining ability of tonality, now a ghost of its former self – unable to produce or even promise the encompassing wholeness and progress of functionality – to let us know that the thickness of the present physical moment will not last; the awareness of the impermanence is as real as the physical immediacy. Indeed, this awareness is a part of the physical immediacy, a function of it, an intrinsic element in its definition. It is in part this very use of tonal function, largely fragmented into tonal physicality, that tells us that the balance between the optimism of functional structure and the uncertainty of physical immediacy has shifted towards the latter.[20]

This same technique of repetition is used often by Chopin at various points in his composition. It appears characteristically, for example, in the coda of the Berceuse[21] (Ex. 4).

Ex. 4: Berceuse, mm. 47–63

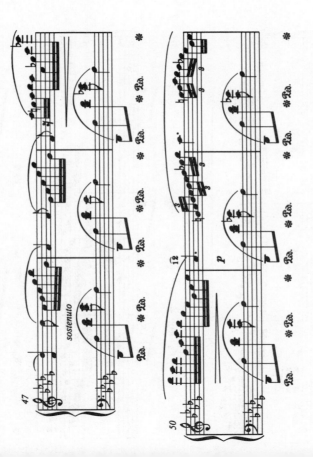

[20] At the time this paper was delivered, Susan McClary suggested a sexual interpretation of the analysis just given. Chopin's music, she noted, is often characterized as effeminate. Could this not be, in part, because its lingering sensuousness at such typical moments, in contrast to the masculine Beethovenian climax, evokes and affirms the quality and the rhythm conventionally associated with female sexuality? This imagery, once offered, lends itself almost irresistibly to many aspects of nineteenth-century musical style (not least the critique, suggested in so many Romantic compositions, of the no-nonsense ending).

[21] It has been pointed out that the putative function of the Berceuse, that of lulling a baby to sleep, could account for the technique of repetition at this point in this piece. The obvious value of this interpretation should not be allowed to obscure the need for further reflection on the significance of a device so pervasive in Chopin's music. An argument could be made, for example, for a dialectical relationship between the device described and the genre of the berceuse. The genre may welcome the device; but the sensibility that constantly fashions the device may also account for an attraction to a genre drawn from the womanly domain of experience.

Ex. 4: (cont.)

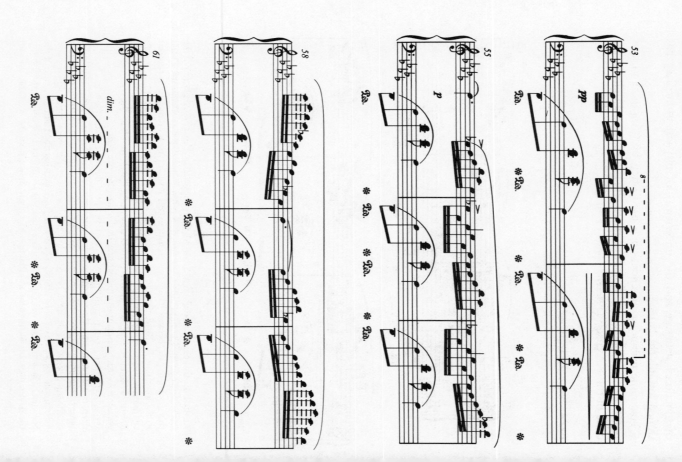

And the entire Prelude No. 4 in E Minor seems to be built in the same way, as a study of means by which to make sense of the fragmentary. Here also the experience of repetition in an endlessly shifting harmonic (or, more accurately, coloristic) context, the arbitrary decision to repeat the first section in order to get beyond its fragmentary condition, and the externally imposed, rhetorical, or dramatically expanded means with which the second part varies the first all point to a conception of the compositional problem not as the task of achieving the self-generation of form but as that of wresting sense from the intrinsically fragmentary. They point to a sensibility which recognized the ultimate reality as well as the contingency of the here-and-now, along with the tragic implications for humanity of a world vision in which the real is not the eternal but the transient.

Conclusion

These remarks, I know, open up more questions than they answer. For example what, more particularly, was the relationship of Chopin's music to the rest of his culture? And how can we go about trying to determine the significant ways in which Chopin's music resembled, as well as differed from, the other art of its culture in its principles and values?

It could be argued that what Chopin's Prelude No. 2 was to his own oeuvre, Chopin's oeuvre itself was to European art of the time, that is, the achievement of an extreme in which the cultural values at work can be most clearly deciphered. And this was not just an extreme in any old sense. It was an extreme in the sense of creating a personal style; and herein lies an important clue, I believe, to Chopin's historical significance, at least from our current vantage point. In successfully projecting his individuality, Chopin embodied in his music something paradigmatic of Romantic culture: the existential and in a sense even the essential priority it gave to the contingent, the concrete, the individual. But Chopin's particular achievement, his style, signifies even more than this for us. For style is the very medium through which modern Western culture decodes meaning in structure, as epitomized in the cliché of our times, 'The medium is the message.' It could be said that Chopin's achievement helped mark a shift in Western thought away from metaphysical beliefs, and even away from complete confidence in the innate rationality of structure, or hence ultimately, I would say, from confidence in the universal rationality of science. It helped to mark a shift away from all these things towards a fragmented, essentially aesthetic view of human reality. We take it for granted today in many areas of our lives that the achievement of a personal style signifies competence, fluency, and eloquence – that is, a mastery of what is sometimes, rather inelegantly, called communication skills; but this was not always an assumption in Western culture, which previously associated such skills far more closely with metaphysical vision or powers, with the mastery of conventional rhetoric or craftsmanship, or with logical clarity.

To obtain a more integrated view of Chopin's stylistic relationship to his culture, one would want to establish, I would argue, some dialectical sort of movement between Chopin's music, and various other selected structures in his society, seeing the extent to which patterns discerned in his work seemed relevant to those in other structures and bringing back from the latter still other patterns to test against Chopin's compositional strategies. One would want to give further attention to critical methods being developed in other disciplines. For such work to go forward beyond the level of suggestion I have offered here, American musicology would have to develop a respect, comparable to that it gives the unearthing of empirical data, for the kind of scholarship which demands from its outset an ongoing interpenetration of theory and fact. This could result, finally, in the establishment of a serious musicological discipline of criticism, which I think is what the scrutiny of forms in any medium really amounts to, and which I think holds the most promise for confronting the nature of the relationship between music and society with a kind of rigor that meets the genuine needs of this task.

I would like, though, in closing to remark on the well-known fact that many listeners, even apart from their ability to identify Chopin's style, have never really listened to his pieces as autonomous music but have made associations with them. Listeners in Chopin's time, as Edward Lippman has shown us, listened concretely rather than abstractly.[22] They attached all sorts of poetic and visual associations to instrumental music, even Chopin's. And in our own time, I believe, many listeners perceive Chopin's music as the articulation of a fairly specific mood or emotion. Earlier I suggested that the kinds of patterns I discern in Chopin's music, and which seem to characterize the modern Western experience of life. If this last is so, then perhaps the reason that Chopin's music succeeded so brilliantly in its own society and continues to have meaning for ours is that it was able to project something about the human condition in a civilization which was his and is to some extent, despite many differences, still ours. So though I

22 Edward A. Lippman, 'Theory and practice in Schumann's aesthetics', Journal of the American Musicological Society, 17 (1964), pp. 310–45.

would not advocate going back to the 'stupid titles' which so enraged Chopin,[23] or substituting newer ones of our own, I would suggest that such titles constitute not negative judgments on Chopin's lack of structural autonomy but a compliment. They may, indeed, be evidence that Chopin's music functions as an archetype of the patterns out of which Western society makes sense of its experience.

[23] Quoted in Kallberg, 'Chopin', p. 565.

Towards an aesthetic of popular music

SIMON FRITH

Introduction: the 'value' of popular music

Underlying all the other distinctions critics draw between 'serious' and 'popular' music is an assumption about the source of musical value. Serious music matters because it transcends social forces; popular music is aesthetically worthless because it is determined by them (because it is 'useful' or 'utilitarian'). This argument, common enough among academic musicologists, puts sociologists in an odd position. If we venture to suggest that the value of, say, Beethoven's music can be explained by the social conditions determining its production and subsequent consumption we are dismissed as philistines – aesthetic theories of classical music remain determinedly non-sociological. Popular music, by contrast, is taken to be good only for sociological theory. Our very success in explaining the rise of rock 'n' roll or the appearance of disco proves their lack of aesthetic interest. To relate music and society becomes, then, a different task according to the music we are treating. In analyzing serious music, we have to uncover the social forces concealed in the talk of 'transcendent' values; in analyzing pop, we have to take seriously the values scoffed at in the talk of social functions.

In this paper I will concentrate on the second issue; my particular concern is to suggest that the sociological approach to popular music does not rule out an aesthetic theory but, on the contrary, makes one possible. At first sight this proposition is unlikely. There is no doubt that sociologists have tended to explain away pop music. In my own academic work I have examined how rock is produced and consumed, and have tried to place it ideologically, but there is no way that a reading of my books (or those of other sociologists) could be used to explain why some pop songs are good and others bad, why Elvis Presley is a better singer than John Denver, or why disco is a much richer musical genre than progressive rock. And yet for ten years or more I have also been a working rock critic, making such judgments as a matter of course, assuming, like all pop fans, that our musical choices matter.

Are such judgments spurious – a way of concealing from myself and other consumers the ways in which our tastes are manipulated? Can it really be the case that my pleasure in a song by the group Abba carries the same aesthetic weight as someone else's pleasure in Mozart? Even to pose such a question is to invite ridicule – either I seek to reduce the 'transcendent' Mozart to Abba's commercially determined level, or else I elevate Abba's music beyond any significance it can carry. But even if the pleasures of serious and popular musics are different, it is not immediately obvious that the difference is that between artistic autonomy and social utility. Abba's value is no more (and no less) bound up with an experience of transcendence than Mozart's; the meaning of Mozart is no less (and no more) explicable in terms of social forces. The question facing sociologists and aestheticians in both cases is the same: how do we make musical value judgments? How do such value judgments articulate the listening experiences involved?

The sociologist of contemporary popular music is faced with a body of songs, records, stars and styles which exists because of a series of decisions, made by both producers and consumers, about what is a successful sound. Musicians write tunes and play solos; producers choose from different sound mixes; record companies and radio programmers decide what should be released and played; consumers buy one record rather than another and concentrate their attention on particular genres. The result of all these apparently individual decisions is a pattern of success, taste and style which can be explained sociologically.

If the starting question is why does this hit sound this way, then sociological answers can be arranged under two headings. First, there are answers in terms of technique and technology: people produce and consume the music they are capable of producing and consuming (an obvious point, but one which opens up issues of skill, background and education which in pop music are applied not to individual composers but to social groups). Different groups possess different sorts of cultural capital, share different cultural expectations and so make music differently – pop tastes are shown to correlate with class cultures and subcultures; musical styles are linked to specific age groups; we take for granted the connections of ethnicity and sound. This is the sociological common sense of rock criticism, which equally acknowledges the determining role of technology. The history of twentieth-century popular music is impossible to write without reference to the changing forces of production, electronics, the use of recording, amplification and synthesizers, just as consumer choices cannot be separated from the possession of transistor radios, stereo hi-fis, ghetto blasters and Walkmen.

While we can thus point to general patterns of pop use, the precise link (or homology) between sounds and social groups remains unclear. Why is rock 'n' roll youth music, whereas Dire Straits is the sound of Yuppie USA? To answer these questions there is a second sociological approach to popular music, expressed in terms of its functions. This approach is obvious in ethnomusicology, that is in anthropological studies of traditional and folk musics which are explained by reference to their use in dance, in rituals, for political mobilization, to solemnize ceremonies or to excite desires. Similar points are made about contemporary pop, but its most important function is assumed to be commercial – the starting analytical assumption is that the music is made to sell; thus research has focused on who makes marketing decisions and why, and on the construction of 'taste publics'. The bulk of the academic sociology of popular music (including my own) implicitly equates aesthetic and commercial judgments. The phenomenal 1985 successes of Madonna and Bruce Springsteen are explained, for example, in terms of sales strategies, the use of video, and the development of particular new audiences. The appeal of the music itself, the reason Madonna's and Springsteen's fans like them, somehow remains unexamined.

From the fans' perspective it is obvious that people play the music they do because it 'sounds good', and the interesting question is why they have formed that opinion. Even if pop tastes are the effects of social conditioning and commercial manipulation, people still explain them to themselves in terms of value judgment. Where, in pop and rock, do these values come from? When people explain their tastes, what terms do they use? They certainly know what they like (and dislike), what pleases them and what does not. Read the music press, listen to band rehearsals and recording sessions, overhear the chatter in record shops and discos, note the ways in which disc jockeys play records, and you will hear value judgments being made. The discriminations that matter in these settings occur *within* the general sociological framework. While this allows us at a certain level to 'explain' rock or disco, it is not adequate 'for an understanding of why one rock record or one disco track is better than another. Turn to the explanations of the fans or musicians (or even of the record companies) and a familiar argument appears. Everyone in the pop world is aware of the social forces that determine 'normal' pop music – a good record, song, or sound is precisely one that transcends those forces!

The music press is the place where pop value judgments are most clearly articulated. A reading of British music magazines reveals that 'good' popular music has always been heard to go beyond or break through commercial routine. This was as true for critics struggling to distinguish jazz from Tin Pan Alley pop in the 1920s and black jazz from white jazz in the 1930s as for critics asserting rock's superiority to teen pop in the late 1960s. In *Sound effects*[1] I argued that rock's claim to a form of aesthetic autonomy rests on a combination of folk and art arguments: as folk music rock is heard to represent the community of youth, as art music rock is heard as the sound of individual, creative sensibility. The rock aesthetic depends, crucially, on an argument about authenticity. Good music is the authentic expression of something – a person, an idea, a feeling, a shared experience, a *Zeitgeist*. Bad music is inauthentic – it expresses nothing. The most common term of abuse in rock criticism is 'bland' – bland music has nothing in it and is made only to be commercially pleasing.

'Authenticity' is, then, what guarantees that rock performances resist or subvert commercial logic, just as rock-star quality (whether we are discussing Elvis Presley or David Bowie, the Rolling Stones or the Sex Pistols), describes the power that enables certain musicians to drive something individually obdurate through the system. At this point, rock criticism meets up with 'serious' musicology. Wilfrid Mellers' scholarly books on the Beatles and Bob Dylan,[2] for example, describe in technical terms their subjects' transcendent qualities; but they read like fan mail and, in their lack of self-conscious hipness, point to the contradiction at the heart of this aesthetic approach. The suggestion is that pop music becomes more valuable the more independent it is of the social forces that organize the pop process in the first place; pop value is dependent on something outside pop, is rooted in the person, the *auteur*, the community or the subculture that lies behind it. If good music is authentic music, then critical judgment means measuring the performers' 'truth' to the experiences or feelings they are describing.

Rock criticism depends on myth – the myth of the youth community, the myth of the creative artist. The reality is that rock, like all twentieth-

[1] Simon Frith, *Sound effects: youth, leisure and the politics of rock 'n' roll* (New York, 1981).
[2] Wilfrid Mellers, *Twilight of the gods: the Beatles in retrospect* (London, 1973), and *A darker shade of pale: a backdrop to Bob Dylan* (London, 1984).

century pop musics, is a commercial form, music produced as a commodity, for a profit, distributed through mass media as mass culture. It is in practice very difficult to say exactly who or what it is that rock expresses or who, from the listener's point of view, are the authentically creative performers. The myth of authenticity is, indeed, one of rock's own ideological effects, an aspect of its sales process: rock stars can be marketed as artists, and their particular sounds marketed as a means of identity. Rock criticism is a means of legitimating tastes, justifying value judgments, but it does not really explain how those judgments came to be made in the first place. If the music is not, in fact, made according to the 'authentic' story, then the question becomes how are we able to judge some sounds as more authentic than others: what are we actually listening for in making our judgments? How do we know Bruce Springsteen is more authentic than Duran Duran, when both make records according to the rules of the same complex industry? And how do we recognize good sounds in non-rock genres, in pop forms like disco that are not described in authentic terms in the first place? The question of the value of pop music remains to be answered.

An alternative approach to music and society

In an attempt to answer these questions I want to suggest an alternative approach to musical value, to suggest different ways of defining 'popular music' and 'popular culture'. The question we should be asking is not what does popular music *reveal* about 'the people' but how does it *construct* them. If we start with the assumption that pop is expressive, then we get bogged down in the search for the 'real' artist or emotion or belief lying behind it. But popular music is popular not because it reflects something, or authentically articulates some sort of popular taste or experience, but because it creates our understanding of what popularity is. The most misleading term in cultural theory is, indeed, 'authenticity'. What we should be examining is not how true a piece of music is to something else, but how it sets up the idea of 'truth' in the first place – successful pop music is music which defines its own aesthetic standard.

A simple way to illustrate the problems of defining musical popularity is to look at its crudest measure, the weekly record sales charts in the British music press and the American *Billboard*. These are presented to us as market research: the charts measure something real – sales and radio plays – and represent them with all the trimmings of an objective, scientific apparatus. But, in fact, what the charts reveal is a specific definition of what can be counted as popular music in the first place – record sales (in the right shops), radio plays (on the right stations). The charts work not as the detached measure of some agreed notion of popularity, but as the most important determination of what the popularity of popular music means – that is, a particular pattern of market choice. The charts bring selected records together into the community of the market place; they define certain sorts of consumption as being collective in certain sorts of ways.

The sales charts are only one measure of popularity; and when we look at others, it becomes clear that their use is always for the creation (rather than reflection) of taste communities. Readers' polls in the music press, for example, work to give communal shape to disparate readers; the Pazz 'n' Jop poll in *The Village Voice* creates a sense of collective commitment among the fragmented community of American rock critics. The Grammy awards in the United States and the BPI awards in Britain, present the industry's view of what pop music is about – nationalism and money. These annual awards, which for most pop fans seem to miss the point, reflect sales figures and 'contributions to the recording industry': measures of popularity no less valid than readers' or critics' polls (which often deliberately honor 'unpopular' acts). In comparing poll results, arguments are really not about who is more popular than whom empirically (see rock critics' outrage that Phil Collins rather than Bruce Springsteen dominated the 1986 Grammys) but about what popularity means. Each different measure measures something different or, to put it more accurately, each different measure constructs its own object of measurement. This is apparent in *Billboard's* 'specialist' charts, in the way in which 'minority' musics are defined. 'Women's music', for example, is interesting not as music which somehow expresses 'women', but as music which seeks to define them, just as 'black music' works to set up a very particular notion of what 'blackness' is.

This approach to popular culture, as the creation rather than the expression of the people, need not be particular to music. There are numerous ways in our everyday life in which accounts of 'the people' are provided. Turn on the television news and notice the ways in which a particular mode of address works, how the word 'we' is used, how the word 'you'. Advertisers in all media are clearly in the business of explaining to us who we are, how we fit in with other people in society, why we necessarily consume the way we do. Each mass medium has its own techniques for addressing its audience, for creating moments of recognition and exclusion, for giving us our sense of ourselves. Pop music does, though, seem to play a particularly important role in the way in which popular culture works. On the one hand, it works with particularly intense emotional experiences – pop songs and pop stars mean more to us emotionally than other media events or performers, and this is not just because the pop business sells music to us through individual market choices. On the other hand, these musical experiences always contain social meaning, are placed within a social context – we are not free to read anything we want into a song.

The experience of pop music is an experience of placing; in responding to a song, we are drawn, haphazardly, into affective and emotional alliances with the performers and with the performers' other fans. Again this also happens in other areas of popular culture. Sport, for example, is clearly a setting in which people directly experience community, feel an immediate bond with other people, articulate a particular kind of collective pride (for a non-American, the most extraordinary aspect of the 1984 Olympics was the display/construction of the Reagan ideology of both the United States and patriotism). And fashion and style – both social constructions – remain the keys to the ways in which we, as individuals, present ourselves to the world: we use the public meanings of clothes to say 'this is how I want to be perceived'.

But music is especially important to this process of placement because of something specific to musical experience, namely, its direct emotional intensity. Because of its qualities of abstractness (which 'serious' aestheticians have always stressed) music is an individualizing form. We absorb songs into our own lives and rhythms into our own bodies; they have a looseness of reference that makes them immediately accessible. Pop songs are open to appropriation for personal use in a way that other popular cultural forms (television soap operas, for example) are not – the latter are tied into meanings we may reject. At the same time, and equally significant, music is obviously rule-bound. We hear things as music because their sounds obey a particular, familiar logic, and for most pop fans (who are, technically, non-musical) this logic is out of our control. There is a mystery to our musical tastes. Some records and performers work for us, others do not – we know this without being able to explain it. Somebody else has set up the conventions; they are clearly social and clearly apart from us.

This interplay between personal absorption into music and the sense that it is, nevertheless, something out there, something public, is what makes music so important in the cultural placing of the individual in the social. To give a mundane example, it is obviously true that in the last thirty years the idea of being a 'fan', with its oddly public account of private obsessions, has been much more significant to pop music than to other forms of popular culture. This role of music is usually related to youth and youth culture, but it seems equally important to the ways in which ethnic groups in both

Britain and the United States have forged particular cultural identities and is also reflected in the ways in which 'classical' music originally became significant for the nineteenth-century European bourgeoisie. In all these cases music can stand for, symbolize *and* offer the immediate experience of collective identity. Other cultural forms – painting, literature, design – can articulate and show off shared values and pride, but only music can make you *feel* them.

The social functions of music

It is now possible to move back to the starting point of this essay – the social functions of music and their implications for aesthetics. I will begin by outlining the four most significant ways in which pop is used and then suggest how these uses help us to understand how pop value judgments are made.

The first reason, then, we enjoy popular music is because of its use in answering questions of identity: we use pop songs to create for ourselves a particular sort of self-definition, a particular place in society. The pleasure that pop music produces is a pleasure of identification – with the music we like, with the performers of that music, with the other people who like it. And it is important to note that the production of identity is also a production of non-identity – it is a process of inclusion and exclusion. This is one of the most striking aspects of musical taste. People not only know what they like, they also have very clear ideas about what they don't like and often have very aggressive ways of stating their dislikes. As all sociological studies of pop consumers have shown, pop fans define themselves quite precisely according to their musical preferences. Whether they identify with genres or stars, it seems of greater importance to people what they like musically than whether or not they enjoyed a film or a television program.

The pleasure of pop music, unlike the pleasures to be had from other mass cultural forms, does not derive in any clear way from fantasy: it is not mediated through day-dreams or romancing, but is experienced directly. For example, at a heavy metal concert you can certainly see the audience absorbed in the music; yet for all the air-guitar playing they are not fantasizing being up on stage. To experience heavy metal is to experience the power of the concert as a whole – the musicians are one aspect of this, the amplification system another, the audience a third. The individual fans get their kicks from being a necessary part of the overall process – which is why heavy metal videos always have to contain moments of live performance

[margin handwritten note:] More important for many. Esp. god. Esp. [C] age of adolescents

(whatever the surrounding story line) in order to capture and acknowledge the kind of empowerment that is involved in the concert itself.

Once we start looking at different pop genres we can begin to document the different ways in which music works to give people an identity, to place them in different social groups. And this is not just a feature of commercial pop music. It is the way in which all popular music works. For example, in putting together an audience, contemporary black-influenced pop clearly (and often cynically) employs musical devices originally used in religious music to define men's and women's identity before God. Folk musics, similarly, continue to be used to mark the boundaries of ethnic identity, even amidst the complications of migration and cultural change. In London's Irish pubs, for example, 'traditional' Irish folk songs are still the most powerful way to make people feel Irish and consider what their 'Irishness' means. (This music, this identity, is now being further explored by post-punk London Irish bands, like the Pogues.) It is not surprising, then, that popular music has always had important nationalist functions. In Abel Gance's 'silent' film, *Napoleon*, there is a scene in which we see the *Marseillaise* being composed, and then watch the song make its way through the Assembly and among the crowds until everyone is singing it. When the film was first shown in France, the cinema audience rose from their seats and joined in singing their national anthem. Only music seems capable of creating this sort of spontaneous collective identity, this kind of personally felt patriotism.

Music's second social function is to give us a way of managing the relationship between our public and private emotional lives. It is often noted but rarely discussed that the bulk of popular songs are love songs. This is certainly true of twentieth-century popular music in the West; but most non-Western popular musics also feature romantic, usually heterosexual, love lyrics. This is more than an interesting statistic; it is a centrally important aspect of how pop music is used. Why are love songs so important? Because people need them to give shape and voice to emotions that otherwise cannot be expressed without embarrassment or incoherence. Love songs are a way of giving emotional intensity to the sorts of intimate things we say to each other (and to ourselves) in words that are, in themselves, quite flat. It is a peculiarity of everyday language that our most fraught and revealing declarations of feeling have to use phrases – 'I love/hate you', 'Help me!', 'I'm angry/scared' – which are boring and banal; and so our culture has a supply of a million pop songs, which say these things for us in numerous interesting and involving ways. These songs do not replace our conversations – pop singers do not do our courting for us – but they make

There was no consideration for public space @ the time

our feelings seem richer and more convincing than we can make them appear in our own words, even to ourselves.

The only interesting sociological account of lyrics in the long tradition of American content analysis was Donald Horton's late 1950s study[3] of how teenagers used the words of popular songs in their dating rituals. His high school sample learned from pop songs (public forms of private expression) how to make sense of and shape their own inchoate feelings. This use of pop illuminates one quality of the star/fan relationship: people do not idolize singers because they wish to be them but because these singers seem able, somehow, to make available their own feelings – it is as if we get to know ourselves via the music.

The third function of popular music is to shape popular memory, to organize our sense of time. Clearly one of the effects of all music, not just pop, is to intensify our experience of the present. One measure of good music, to put it another way, is, precisely, its 'presence', its ability to 'stop' time, to make us feel we are living within a moment, with no memory or anxiety about what has come before, what will come after. This is where the physical impact of music comes in – the use of beat, pulse and rhythm to compel our immediate bodily involvement in an organization of time that the music itself controls. Hence the pleasures of dance and disco; clubs and parties provide a setting, a society, which seems to be defined only by the time-scale of the music (the beats per minute), which escapes the real time passing outside.

One of the most obvious consequences of music's organization of our sense of time is that songs and tunes are often the key to our remembrance of things past. I do not mean simply that sounds – like sights and smells – trigger associated memories, but, rather, that music in itself provides our most vivid experience of time passing. Music focuses our attention on the feeling of time; songs are organized (it is part of their pleasure) around anticipation and echo, around endings to which we look forward, choruses that build regret into their fading. Twentieth-century popular music has, on the whole, been a nostalgic form. The Beatles, for example, made nostalgic music from the start, which is why they were so popular. Even on hearing a Beatles song for the first time there was a sense of the memories to come, a feeling that this could not last but that it was surely going to be pleasant to remember.

It is this use of time that makes popular music so important in the social organization of youth. It is a sociological truism that people's heaviest

[3] Donald Horton, 'The dialogue of courtship in popular songs', *American Journal of Sociology*, 62 (1957), pp. 569–78.

personal investment in popular music is when they are teenagers and young adults – music then ties into a particular kind of emotional turbulence, when issues of individual identity and social place, the control of public and private feelings, are at a premium. People do use music less, and less intently, as they grow up; the most significant pop songs for all generations (not just for rock generations) are those they heard as adolescents. What this suggests, though, is not just that young people need music, but that 'youth' itself is defined by music. Youth is experienced, that is, as an intense presence, through an impatience for time to pass and a regret that it is doing so, in a series of speeding, physically insistent moments that have nostalgia coded into them. This is to reiterate my general point about popular music: youth music is socially important not because it reflects youth experience (authentically or not), but because it defines for us what 'youthfulness' is. I remember concluding, in my original sociological research in the early 1970s, that those young people who, for whatever reasons, took no interest in pop music were not really 'young'.

The final function of popular music I want to mention here is something more abstract than the issues discussed so far, but a consequence of all of them: popular music is something possessed. One of the first things I learned as a rock critic – from abusive mail – was that rock fans 'owned' their favorite music in ways that were intense and important to them. To be sure, the notion of musical ownership is not peculiar to rock – Hollywood cinema has long used the clichéd line, 'they're playing our song' – and this reflects something that is recognizable to all music lovers and is an important aspect of the way in which everyone thinks and talks about 'their' music. (British radio has programs of all sorts built around people's explanations of why certain records 'belong' to them.) Obviously it is the commodity form of music which makes this sense of musical possession possible, but it is not just the record that people think they own: we feel that we also possess the song itself, the particular performance, and its performer.

In 'possessing' music, we make it part of our own identity and build it into our sense of ourselves. To write pop criticism is, as I have mentioned, to attract hate mail; mail not so much defending the performer or performance criticized as defending the letter writer: criticize a star and the fans respond as if you have criticized them. The biggest mail bag I ever received was after I had been critical of Phil Collins. Hundreds of letters arrived (not from teenyboppers or gauche adolescents, but from young professionals) typed neatly on headed notepaper, all based on the assumption that in describing Collins as ugly, Genesis as dull, I was deriding their way of life, undermining their identity. The intensity of this relationship between taste and self-definition seems peculiar to popular music – it is 'possessable' in ways that other cultural forms (except, perhaps, sports teams) are not.

To summarize the argument so far: the social functions of popular music are in the creation of identity, in the management of feelings, in the organization of time. Each of these functions depends, in turn, on our experience of music as something which can be possessed. From this sociological base it is now possible to get at aesthetic questions, to understand listeners' judgments, to say something about the value of pop music. My starting question was how is it that people (myself included) can say, quite confidently, that some popular music is better than others? The answer can now be related to how well (or badly), for specific listeners, songs and performances fulfill the suggested functions. But there is a final point to make about this. It should be apparent by now that people do hear the music they like as something special: not, as orthodox rock criticism would have it, because this music is more 'authentic' (though that may be how it is described), but because, more directly, it seems to provide an experience that transcends the mundane, that takes us 'out of ourselves'. It is special, that is, not necessarily with reference to other music, but to the rest of life. This sense of specialness, the way in which music seems to make possible a new kind of self-recognition, frees us from the everyday routines and expectations that encumber our social identities, is a key part of the way in which people experience and thus value music: if we believe we possess our music, we also often feel that we are possessed by it. Transcendence is, then, as much a part of the popular music aesthetic as it is of the serious music aesthetic; but, as I hope I have indicated, in pop, transcendence marks not music's freedom from social forces but its patterning by them. (Of course, in the end the same is true of serious music, too.)

The aesthetics of popular music

I want to conclude with another sort of question: what are the factors in popular music that enable it to fulfill these social functions, which determine whether it does so well or badly? Again, I will divide my answer into four points; my purpose is less to develop them in depth than to suggest important issues for future critical work.

My first point is brief, because it raises musicological issues which I am not competent to develop. The most important (and remarkable) feature of Western popular music in the twentieth century has been its absorption of and into Afro-American forms and conventions. In analytical terms, to follow the distinction developed by Andrew Chester at the end of the 1960s, this means that pop is complex 'intentionally' rather than, like European art music, 'extensionally'. In the extensional form of musical construction, argues Chester, 'theme and variations, counterpoint, tonality (as used in classical composition) are all devices that build diachronically and synchronically outwards from basic musical atoms. The complex is created by combination of the simple, which remains discrete and unchanged in the complex unity'. In the intentional mode, 'the basic musical units (played/sung notes) are not combined through space and time as simple elements into complex structures. The simple entity is that constituted by the parameters of melody, harmony and beat, while the complex is built up by modulation of the basic notes, and by inflexion of the basic beat.'[4] Whatever the problems of Chester's simple dichotomy between a tradition of linear musical development and a tradition of piled-up rhythmic interplay, he does pose the most important musicological question for popular music: how can we explain the *intensity* of musical experience that Afro-American forms have made possible? We still do not know nearly enough about the musical language of pop and rock: rock critics still avoid technical analysis, while sympathetic musicologists, like Wilfrid Mellers, use tools that can only cope with pop's non-intentional (and thus least significant) qualities.

My second point is that the development of popular music in this century has increasingly focused on the use of the voice. It is through the singing voice that people are most able to make a connection with their records, to feel that performances are theirs in certain ways. It is through the voice that star personalities are constructed (and since World War II, at least, the biggest pop stars have been singers). The tone of voice is more important in this context than the actual articulation of particular lyrics – which means, for example, that groups, like the Beatles, can take on a group voice. We can thus identify with a song whether we understand the words or not, whether we already know the singer or not, because it is the voice – not the lyrics – to which we immediately respond. This raises questions about popular non-vocal music, which can be answered by defining a voice as a sign of individual personality rather than as something necessarily mouthing words. The voice, for example, was and is central to the appeal of jazz, not through vocalists as such, but through the way jazz people played

---

[4] Andrew Chester, 'Second thoughts on a rock aesthetic: The Band', *New Left Review*, 62 (1970), pp. 78–9.

and heard musical instruments – Louis Armstrong's or Charlie Parker's instrumental voices were every bit as individual and personal as a pop star's singing voice.

Today's commercial pop musics are, though, song forms, constructing vocal personalities, using voices to speak directly to us. From this perspective it becomes possible to look at pop songs as narratives, to use literary critical and film critical terms to analyze them. It would be fairly straightforward, for example, to make some immediate genre distinctions, to look at the different ways in which rock, country, reggae, etc. work as narratives, the different ways they set up star personalities, situate the listener, and put in play patterns of identity and opposition. Of course, popular music is not simply analogous to film or literature. In discussing the narrative devices of contemporary pop in particular, we are not just talking about music but also about the whole process of packaging. The image of pop performers is constructed by press and television advertisements, by the routines of photo-calls and journalists' interviews, and through gesture and performance. These things all feed into the way we hear a voice; pop singers are rarely heard 'plain' (without mediation). Their vocals already contain physical connotations, associated images, echoes of other sounds. All this needs to be analyzed if we are going to treat songs as narrative structures; the general point, to return to a traditional musicological concern, is that while music may not represent anything, it nevertheless clearly communicates.

The third point is an elaboration of the suggestion I have just made: popular music is wide open for the development of a proper genre analysis, for the classification of how different popular musical forms use different narrative structures, set up different patterns of identity, and articulate different emotions. Take, for example, the much discussed issue of music and sexuality. In the original article on rock and sexuality I wrote with Angela McRobbie at the end of the 1970s,[5] we set up a distinction between 'cock' rock and teenybop narratives, each working to define masculinity and femininity but for different audiences and along different contours of feeling. Our distinctions are still valid but we were looking only at a subdivision of one pop genre. Other musical forms articulate sexuality in far more complicated ways; thus it would be impossible to analyze the sexuality of either Frank Sinatra or Billie Holiday, and their place in the history of crooning and torch singing, in the terms of the 'cock' rock/ teenybop contrast. Even Elvis Presley does not fit easily into these 1970s accounts of male and female sexuality.

5 Simon Frith and Angela McRobbie, 'Rock and sexuality', *Screen Education*, 29 (1978/9), pp. 3–19.

The question these examples raise is how popular musical genres should be defined. The obvious approach is to follow the distinctions made by the music industry which, in turn, reflect both musical history and marketing categories. We can thus divide pop into country music, soul music, rock 'n' roll, punk, MOR, show songs, etc. But an equally interesting way of approaching genres is to classify them according to their ideological effects, the way they sell themselves as art, community or emotion. There is at present, for example, clearly a form of rock we can call 'authentic'. It is represented by Bruce Springsteen and defines itself according to the rock aesthetic of authenticity which I have already discussed. The whole point of this genre is to develop musical conventions which are, in themselves, measures of 'truth'. As listeners we are drawn into a certain sort of reality: this is what it is like to live in America, this is what it is like to love or hurt. The resulting music is the pop equivalent of film theorists' 'classic realist text'. It has the same effect of persuading us that this is how things really are – realism inevitably means a non-romantic account of social life, and a highly romantic account of human nature.

What is interesting, though, is how this sort of truth is constructed, what it rests on musically; and for an instant semiotic guide I recommend the video of *We are the world*. Watch how the singers compete to register the most sincerity; watch Bruce Springsteen win as he gets his brief line, veins pop up on his head and the sweat flows down. Here authenticity is guaranteed by visible physical effort.

To approach pop genres this way is to look at the pop world in terms rather different from those of the music industry. Against the authentic genre, for instance, we can pitch a tradition of artifice: some pop stars, following up on David Bowie's and Roxy Music's early 1970s work, have sought to create a sense of themselves (and their listeners) as artists in cool control. There is clearly also an avant-garde within popular music, offering musicians and listeners the pleasures of rule breaking, and a sentimental genre, celebrating codes of emotion which everyone knows are not real but carry nostalgic weight – if only they were! What I am arguing here is that it is possible to look at pop genres according to the effects they pursue. Clearly we can then judge performers within genres (is John Cougar Mellencamp's music as truthful as Springsteen's?), as well as use different genres for different purposes (the sentimental genre is a better source of adult love songs than the avant-garde or the artificers). To really make sense of pop genres, though, I think we need to place this grid of ideologies over the industry's grid of taste publics. To understand punk, for example, we need to trace within it the interplay of authenticity and artifice; to understand country we need to follow the interplay of authenticity and sentiment.

In everyday life we actually have a rather good knowledge of such conventional confusions. To know how to listen to pop music is to know how to classify it. One thing all pop listeners do, whether as casual fans or professional critics, is to compare sounds — to say that A is like B. Indeed, most pop criticism works via the implicit recognition of genre rules, and this brings me to my final point. Our experience of music in everyday life is not just through the organized pop forms I have been discussing. We live in a much more noisy soundscape; music of all sorts is in a constant play of association with images, places, people, products, moods, and so on. These associations, in commercial and film soundtracks, for example, are so familiar that for much of the time we forget that they are 'accidental'. We unthinkingly associate particular sounds with particular feelings and landscapes and times. To give a crude example, in Britain it is impossible now for a ballet company to perform the *Nutcracker Suite* for an audience of children without them all, at the key moment, breaking into song: 'Everyone's a fruit and nut case,' has been instilled into them as a Cadbury's jingle long before the children hear of Tchaikovsky. Classical or 'serious' music, in short, is not exempt from social use. It is impossible for me, brought up in post-war popular culture, to hear Chopin without immediately feeling a vaguely romantic yearning, the fruit of many years of Chopinesque film soundtracks.

There is no way to escape these associations. Accordions played a certain way mean France, bamboo flutes China, just as steel guitars mean country, drum machines the urban dance. No sort of popular musician can make music from scratch — what we have these days instead are scratch mixers, fragmenting, unpicking, reassembling music from the signs that already exist, pilfering public forms for new sorts of private vision. We need to understand the lumber-room of musical references we carry about with us, if only to account for the moment that lies at the heart of the pop experience, when, from amidst all those sounds out there, resonating whether we like them or not, one particular combination suddenly, for no apparent reason, takes up residence in our own lives.

Conclusion

In this paper I have tried to suggest a way in which we can use a sociology of popular music as the basis of an aesthetic theory, to move, that is, from a description of music's social functions to an understanding of how we can and do value it (and I should perhaps stress that my definition of popular music includes popular uses of 'serious' music). One of my working assumptions has been that people's individual tastes – the ways they experience and describe music for themselves – are a necessary part of academic analysis. Does this mean that the value of popular music is simply a matter of personal preference?

The usual sociological answer to this question is that 'personal' preferences are themselves socially determined. Individual tastes are, in fact, examples of collective taste and reflect consumers' gender, class and ethnic backgrounds; the 'popularity' of popular music can then be taken as one measure of a balance of social power. I do not want to argue against this approach. Our cultural needs and expectations are, indeed, materially based; all the terms I have been using (identity, emotion, memory) are socially formed, whether we are examining 'private' or public lives. But I do believe that this derivation of pop meaning from collective experience is not sufficient. Even if we focus all our attention on the collective reception of pop, we still need to explain why some music is better able than others to have such collective effects, why these effects are different, anyway, for different genres, different audiences and different circumstances. Pop tastes do not just derive from our socially constructed identities; they also help to shape them.

For the last fifty years at least, pop music has been an important way in which we have learned to understand ourselves as historical, ethnic, class-bound, gendered subjects. This has had conservative effects (primarily through pop nostalgia) and liberating ones. Rock criticism has usually taken the latter as a necessary mark of good music but this has meant, in practice, a specious notion of 'liberation.' We need to approach this political question differently, by taking seriously pop's individualizing effects. What pop can do is put into play a sense of identity that may or may not fit the way we are placed by other social forces. Music certainly puts us in our place, but it can also suggest that our social circumstances are not immutable (and that other people – performers, fans – share our dissatisfaction). Pop music is not in itself revolutionary or reactionary. It is a source of strong feelings that because they are also socially coded can come up against 'common sense.' For the last thirty years, for example, at least for young people, pop has been a form in which everyday accounts of race and sex have been both confirmed and confused. It may be that, in the end, we want to value most highly that music, popular and serious, which has some sort of collective, disruptive cultural effect. My point is that music only does so through its impact on individuals. That impact is what we first need to understand.

Music and male hegemony

JOHN SHEPHERD

In her criticism of British subcultural analyses, Angela McRobbie observes that 'one of the central tenets of the womens' movement has been that the personal is political. . . . Although few radical [male] sociologists would deny the importance of the personal in precipitating social and political awareness, to admit how their own experience has influenced their choice of subject-matter . . . seems more or less taboo.'[1] My own involvement in the sociology of music is as a musicologist concerned to see *all* music treated seriously as a social and cultural form and, consequently, to see 'popular' music accorded the same status as 'serious' music as an object worthy of study in university music departments. This concern dates from the cultural and musical experiences to which I was subject in the 1960s and 1970s as a young person growing up in Britain and Canada. At that time 'popular' music in particular impressed me as both pervasively social and highly personal in the impact it made on individuals. However, my own subsequent attempts to uncover the politically personal in the *structures* (rather than the *processes* and *textures*) of 'classical' and 'popular' musics[2] echoed the emphasis put by subcultural analysts such as Paul Willis and Dick Hebdige[3] on the public world of men and boys at the

[1] Angela McRobbie, 'Settling accounts with subcultures: a feminist critique', *Screen Education*, 34 (1980), pp. 38–9.

[2] John Shepherd, 'Media, social process and music', 'The "meaning" of music', and 'The musical coding of ideologies', *Whose music? A sociology of musical languages*, John Shepherd *et al.* (1977; reprint ed. New Brunswick, NJ, 1980), pp. 7–124; and John Shepherd, 'A theoretical model for the socio-musicological analysis of popular musics', *Popular Music*, 2 (1982), pp. 145–77.

[3] Paul Willis, *Profane culture* (London, 1978), and Dick Hebdige, *Subculture: the meaning of style* (London, 1979).

expense of the more sequestered world of women and girls. This is to say that previous work focused on this question was formulated without sensitivity to gender or to the kinds of insights and issues that have been introduced by feminist scholarship.

I intend this paper as a contribution to the understanding of how the politically personal may be articulated from within the internal processes of music. More specifically, I seek to elaborate a theoretical model in terms of which the parameters of timbre, pitch and rhythm, in both 'classical' and 'popular' musics, can be linked to male hegemonic processes of gender typing and of cultural reproduction and resistance.[4] In order to establish the connection between music and male hegemony, I shall first consider the broader issues of gender relations and cultural reproduction, after which I can properly focus on music itself.

Gender relations and cultural reproduction

The premise from which I begin my argument is that the worlds of culture and nature are inextricably linked through processes of social interaction. Such linking should not, however, obscure the mapping or notational function of the material world, or the different possibilities the material world presents in this regard. One of the most obvious and immediate differences presented to people by the material world is that of their own biological differences. Since the species is reproduced at the biological level through the coming together of women and men, there exists a predisposition to map processes of cultural reproduction onto processes of biological reproduction. In many societies, therefore, modes of sexual behavior and relatedness come to stand for modes of social relatedness. That which

[4] It is not my intention to explore the possible social significances of the different kinds of 'serious' or 'art' music written during this century, often as a reaction to music in the 'classical' tradition as it was practiced between approximately 1600 and 1900. There are two reasons for this omission. First, given the complexity both of these reactions and their cross-fertilizations, the analysis would necessarily move far beyond the scope of this paper. Second, the 'serious' music of this century forms a very small part of the total 'serious' music consumption as measured through record sales, the weight given to it in the concert repertoire, and its practice in music education programs.

I do not intend to valorize implicitly whatever radical potential *might* be discerned in various genres of 'popular' music as against the radical potential of different forms of 'serious' or 'avant-garde' music of this century. (On this, see Christopher Small, *Music – society – education* (New York, 1977), pp. 97–159.) Nor do I intend to valorize 'popular' music as against 'classical' music in terms of their discernibly different social significances. As I shall argue, the social significances of one music cannot be understood independently from those of the other, precisely because both musics mutually contribute to the dominant modes of social control and alienation present in Western societies.

makes social life and reproduction possible may be the fertile coming together of differentiated and *totally abstract* epistemological categories which are variously mapped or notated on aspects of the material world – such as the biological differences of women and men.

This possibility may be explored in the context of contemporary capitalist societies. Dorothy Dinnerstein has argued that the development of child-rearing in our society as an essentially female occupation has had far-reaching consequences for the creation and maintenance of traditional gender-typing. Children of both sexes, she argues, first experience their world as being almost totally constituted by a woman: 'for the girl as well as the boy a woman is the first human center of bodily comfort and pleasure, and the first being to provide the vital delight of social intercourse'.[5] But whereas girls tend to internalize this relationship with the female source of social and emotional life as being a relationship with a member of their own sex, boys do not. Boys, if one can put it this way, *tend* to internalize a relationship which is comparatively negative and vacuous. When, therefore, the boy, as an adult, finds delight in heterosexual lovemaking, 'he finds it outside himself, as before, in a female body'. The girl, however, 'now lives in the female body that was once the vital source of nourishment, entertainment, reassurance'. As a consequence, Dinnerstein concludes, 'the mother-raised woman is likely to feel, more deeply than the mother-raised man, that she carries within herself a source of the magic early parental richness. In this sense . . . she is more self-sufficient than the mother-raised man: what is inside oneself cannot be directly taken by a rival.'[6] There is a sense, therefore, in which the male adolescent enters his particular stage of life with a certain inbuilt insecurity. The source of life is always external to him, and, 'to be sure of reliable access to it he must have exclusive access to a woman'.[7]

Dinnerstein argues the classic solution to this problem is control over women. Women are necessary as the source of life, as well as potentially dangerous in their power to withdraw it. Given the necessity of leaving the warmth of the woman's world and encountering the cold reality of the 'real world', the need for women becomes that much greater and their presence that much more tenuous. The growing male adolescent consequently discovers 'that authority over a woman or women is a mark of status, respected by men'.[8] So long as women do not engage in the 'real world';

5 Dorothy Dinnerstein, *The mermaid and the Minotaur* (New York, 1976), p. 28.
6 Ibid., pp. 41–2.
7 Ibid., p. 43.
8 Ibid., p. 49.

but are kept safe at home or in traditional 'female' occupations, male supremacy in the 'real world' will go unchallenged, and women will remain a reliable source of emotional sustenance that men can draw on for their 'real world' struggles. As a consequence, women typically experience the public world vicariously, as presented and brought to them by men. Both women and men, concludes Dinnerstein, become diminished as people: men because they are undernourished as sentient beings, women because they are undernourished as people of the world.

In contemporary capitalist societies, the processes of biological reproduction – in which men figure only momentarily – come to be controlled conceptually through the processes of cultural reproduction which are mapped onto them. Women, as emotional nurturers, as the first people to 'provide the vital delights of social intercourse' for very young children, come to stand for the very process – social relatedness – through which people and societies are created, maintained and reproduced. Men, on the other hand, in controlling women as necessary adjuncts both of their identity development and their forays into the 'real world', are led to deny symbolically the process responsible for their creation as people. The male desire to control women therefore parallels their desire to control the world.

There is, of course, a paradox here, which is that men cannot ultimately deny the relational and emotional because they have a very real need of it. As a result, the relational and emotional is downgraded to a second-class status – something vaguely undesirable and intimately associated with women – to be controlled by superior, 'rational' men. To be sure, social relatedness implies negotiability of political power. Yet as reflections of the male desire to control the world, women themselves must be controlled and manipulated. This is accomplished by means of their isolation and objectification. The conceptualization of people as objects decontextualized from social relations implies the possibility for uncontested, unilateral control. The objectification of women thus becomes a crucial step in the mystification of social relatedness. If women symbolize the source of life, the social interactions that are the source of our being as people, and if sexual relatedness provides a biological code for these same processes, then women tend to become equated with sex. In order to be 'successful' in a male-dominated society, they must package themselves (or be packaged, as in advertising images) as objects amenable to control by men.

Male-defined culture is projected back onto nature; women as objects are in turn equated with a natural or material world thus susceptible to unilateral control by men. Control of cultural reproduction compensates for a lack of centrality in biological reproduction, and nowhere is this control more effectively exercised than on the mapping and notational procedures – among which music figures prominently – which both facilitate and constrain processes of cultural reproduction. It is no accident that the vast majority of noetic and scribal elites have been male, for by this means men preserve themselves paradoxically as independent and in control of the very social relations which produce them.

Male hegemony is essentially a *visual* hegemony. Touch reminds us constantly of our relatedness to the world, and sound brings the world to us both circumambiently and circumjacently. Vision by contrast is the silent and inert sensory channel which allows us not only to distance ourselves from the phenomena of the world but also to interject ourselves into the world from a distance. It is the sensory channel which allows us, from a single point of view, to order discrete objects into their uniquely structured locations in space.

The consequences of the supremacy of vision are explored by Geraldine Finn. And while her immediate concern is with the effect on the male viewer of the pornographic image, the implications of her assessment carry well beyond the specificity of her topic:

A subjectivity which is external to its world, as the observer–subject is, deprives itself of nourishment which only the world can supply; and as a result becomes increasingly impoverished and isolated, and estranged from itself, from others and from the reality of the world it aspires to know and control merely by looking. Sights, appearances pried away from their meaning (their contexts and their history) are silent. Dead objects are mute. In the world of the voyeur, therefore, there is no dialogue, no relationship, no speech and no response, and therefore no understanding, neither of the self nor of the objects 'known'.⁹

Male hegemony is constituted through strategies whereby men render silent and inert a social world that is bubbling, evanescent and constantly rubbing up against us. Conceptually, this requires that life must not be allowed to originate above the level of the material, where it can be seen and controlled. By locating prime causation for social processes ultimately and exclusively within material productive forces, therefore, traditional Marxist analyses eradicate knowledge both of subjects and dialogue between subjects. However, the above observations suggest that notions of human sexuality, and the consequent 'freezing' and projection of women as sexual objects, constitute little more than a cultural construct representing male dominance in the world.

A result of these observations is that the omissions noted previously both in the work of Willis and Hebdige and in my own socio-musicological

⁹ Geraldine Finn, 'Patriarchy and pleasure: the pornographic eye/I', *Canadian Journal of Political and Social Theory*, 9/1–2 (1985), pp. 89–90.

analyses begin to speak volumes. Each of these studies, in their different ways, is concerned with issues of class (and ethnicity) and thus revolves around the question as to which males should exercise political power. This question now appears peripheral to understanding processes of cultural reproduction and resistance: the seeds of cultural reproduction are not sown in the public world of men, but, as Dinnerstein has so persuasively demonstrated, in the home.

My position is that social stratification, with its differentiated cultural realities and modes of alienation, is more likely to be a projection of the logic of gender relations than gender relations a projection of the logic of social stratification. The emphases placed on questions of social stratification, both by the general public and by different schools of social analysis, can themselves be viewed as a consequence of the particular forms of male hegemony that developed during and after the Renaissance.

The capacity for unilateral control implied through male conceptualizations of people as objects decontextualized from social relations is powerfully realized through the social structures of industrial capitalism. The *centralized* control and consequent patterns of alienation which characterize these structures could not, however, have come into being without a stress on an overall uniformity of social existence. As Harry Braverman argues, the habituation of workers to capitalist modes of production was achieved through the destruction of *all other forms of the organization of labor, and with them, all alternatives for the working population*.[10] Relations of consumption and self-identity soon followed suit,[11] so that capitalist social relations soon appeared not only simply as the *only* kind possible, but, as given, natural and unquestionable. McLuhan[12] has argued that such homogeneity of social relatedness – not to mention of thought and perception – could arise only if relatedness between people was ultimately filtered through one channel of communication to the relative exclusion of all others. The emphasis on the visual, resulting from the increasing importance in the lives of 'educated' post-Renaissance men of analytic/phonetic literacy and moveable-type printing, gave rise to a whole series of inter-related concepts (for example, objectivity, spatialized time, straight-line cause-and-effect analysis, deterministic rationality and control). These concepts were eminently successful as tools of organization and as means for manipulating the physical environment.[13]

[10] Harry Braverman, *Labor and monopoly capital* (New York, 1974), p. 149.
[11] Stuart Ewen, *Captains of consciousness* (New York, 1976).
[12] Marshall McLuhan, *The Gutenberg galaxy* (Toronto, 1962), and *Understanding media* (Toronto, 1964).
[13] See further Donald Lowe, *History of bourgeois perception* (Chicago, 1982).

Music and male hegemony

Consequently, 'educated' men were seduced by them. They quickly thought themselves into the entirely mythical position of being separate from the world, of being able analytically to pin down physical, human and social existence as a unidimensional, static display having relevance only for the gaze of the beholder.[14] The individual became supreme. But precisely because such an approach to the world is mythical, precisely because people can only become people and remain people through an interaction with others (which necessarily implies a creative and dialectical relationship with the physical environment), this fiction of unilateral physical and social control implied a control over self that is both unconscious and invisible. In surrendering to the seductive possibility that post-Renaissance culture was a culture without myth, post-Renaissance men surrendered their birthright and, through that, the birthright of all others in society under their sway. At worst European society became a reification without people: a perfect but mythical bureaucratic system where essentially human values could only survive among the powerless in cracks and margins. The comparative experiential and emotional richness of proletarianized and minority ethnic cultures[15] can in this sense be viewed as a projection through social stratification of values more fundamentally associated with the world of women.

Music, gender and social stratification

The argument I wish to develop is that the visual stress on controlling and structuring the public world has had certain consequences for the development both of 'classical' and 'popular' musics. These consequences can best be approached by understanding first that *the very fact of music*, based as it is on the physical phenomenon of sound, constitutes a serious threat to the visually mediated hegemony of scribal elites.

To repeat: vision, smooth and silent, stresses separation at a distance. It is the sense that allows us to inject ourselves into the world, to operate on the world over time and space, rather than simply having the world come in on us circumambiently and simultaneously. Touch is the sense basic not only to activating an awareness of ourselves, but also to making the fundamental distinction between us and the not-us. Sound, by contrast to both vision and touch, is a medium that, in bringing the world to us, stresses the integrative and relational. It tells us that there is a world of depth sur-

[14] Shepherd, 'Media, social process and music', pp. 18–42.
[15] Shepherd, 'Theoretical model', pp. 154–65.

musics can be approached. The argument I wish to pursue is that the sounds essential to meaning within the 'classical' tradition have been stripped down as far as possible to a small number of basic units or atoms susceptible to the exigencies of control through an analytic music notation,[18] and have come to constitute a fundamental harmonic–rhythmic framework that is elaborated into individual pieces of music through complex and extended developments according to principles intrinsic to the framework itself.[19] Notes stripped of much of their inherent sonic possibilities become a social code for the brand of individualism characteristic of industrial capitalist societies. However, the individualism of those with power and influence is not at all the same as the rich, emotive, individuality-in-community of proletarianized cultures. It may be an individualism necessarily capable of initiative and a singular point of view, but it is, at the same time, an individualism that is standardized by imperatives of social acceptability and demonstrated loyalty. Individualism among those with power and influence must be underpinned and controlled through a structured homogeneity. As McLuhan puts it: 'individualism, whether in the passive atomistic sense of drilled uniformed soldiery or in the active aggressive sense of private initiative and self-expression, alike assumes a prior technology of homogeneous citizens'.[20] As this homogeneity has been generated, maintained and controlled by an all-inclusive stress on visual channels of communication, so it has been in the generation, maintenance and control of sounds admissible to the tradition of 'classical' music.

Such standardization of musical components does not however mean that people are 'excluded' from musical processes in the tradition of 'classical' music. The ideal of perfect intonation and mathematically precise rhythms that derives from analytic music notation (that is, a notation that is 'fully analytic' of the pitches and rhythms essential to musical significance) is just as mythical as the ideal of a perfectly bureaucratic social system. Good performances in the 'classical' tradition *depend* on subtle deviations from the notational norms of pitch and rhythm, and many instruments are either tuned slightly out of tune (as with the three strings for each note on a piano) or played with an appreciable degree of vibrato so that a certain brilliance of sound is generated. Without such brilliance, the sounds of instruments would become dead, and they would lose much of their power to communicate. However, in the same way that personal

18 Ibid.
19 Shepherd, 'Theoretical model', pp. 154-65.
20 McLuhan, *Gutenberg galaxy*, p. 209.

initiative in the 'social' realm must be constrained through imperatives of social acceptability and demonstrated loyalty to bureaucratic ideals, so individual musical initiative as expressed in performances through deviations from notational norms of pitch and rhythm must be constrained through relatively tight adherence to those norms.

A similar observation may be made with respect to composition in the 'classical' tradition. One could argue that the music of many 'great' composers attempts to compensate for the loss of spirituality implicit in the harmonic-rhythmic framework of 'classical' music precisely through the creation of extended and architectonically complex pieces of music according to principles intrinsic to the framework. It may be the *ultimate* futility of this exercise that guarantees much music in the 'classical' tradition its very considerable power in speaking to the politically personal in people. Nevertheless, both musical interpretation and musical creativity in the 'classical' tradition render themselves safe, harmless and ultimately subservient to the dictates of a bureaucratized norm through a priori adherence to sounds which are *initially* admissible to musical practice.[21]

It is the ideal homogeneity of pitches, rhythms and timbres that enables 'classical' music to be exclusively articulated through a finite, closed and infinitely repeatable musical system echoing and giving expression to the closed, finite and infinitely repeatable nature of capitalist social relations. In the same way that the management of capitalist social relations as uniform and 'all-pervasive' requires that contexts always be made clear, that meanings and terms be explicitly spelled out and that logical connections always be made apparent,[22] so 'classical' music is articulated through a musical system where ambiguity of function is ultimately not permitted.

Capitalist social relations are not only thought of as given, natural and unquestionable because they are the only ones possible, but because their logic of bureaucratic rationality is made manifest in their very articulation. There *seems* to be no mystery to existence. Everything *seems* clear and transparent. So it is with 'classical' music. Its logic, its underlying rationale is made manifest in its very articulation. The scale that relates adjacent keys is articulated in the here-and-now of any musical utterance. As Richard Crocker has argued, this crucial step towards the development of 'classical' music was taken when the finals of previously autonomous medieval modes were themselves conceived as being related on a scale. 'This step

[21] Graham Vulliamy and John Shepherd, 'The application of a critical sociology to musical education', *British Journal of Music Education*, 1 (1984), pp. 247–66.
[22] Basil Bernstein, 'Social class, language and socialization', *Language and social context*, ed. Pier P. Giglioli (Harmondsworth, 1972), pp. 157–78.

led outside of and beyond any one final.[23] As a consequence, previously autonomous melodic shapes eventually became subservient to a unified harmonic scheme. It was not sonic events themselves which were henceforth important, but the various functions that could be visited on them. As homogenous building blocks facilitating the construction of extended and complex architectonic structures, notes directed the ear not to their internal qualities, but outwards and away to their unambiguous relationship with other notes. Typically, people hear only the external surface of notes in the 'classical' tradition, not the interior richness that remains even after analytic notation has done its work. 'Classical' music is, then, yet another justification of the ideology whereby people become objects and systems dominate individuals.

With 'classical' music, processes of classifying and marking out relations can be heard directly because they are immanent in the music itself. That is why traditional analyses of pieces of 'classical' music usually *seem* self-evident in their significance. The basis of the analysis is contained in the music itself. It is for this reason that 'classical' music has *appeared* to many to approach the condition of music itself, a self-sufficient and purely formal mode of aesthetic expression essentially divorced in its processes of signification from the social and cultural contexts of its creation and consumption.

In this sense it is no different from what Barthes has termed *écriture classique*,[24] the style of writing pre-eminent in France from the mid-seventeenth to the mid-nineteenth centuries which appeared not as a style at all, but as inevitable, right, and suitable for all times and places. However, as Barthes has pointed out, there is no such thing as 'white writing', writing which in its clarity seems to constitute an innocent reflection of reality. Just as there is no society, no reality that is not mythical (despite the myths of post-Renaissance 'rational' men), so there is no writing and indeed no music that is not opaque, structuring the world in one way rather than in any other. All writing, all music is style and, as such, 'clarity is a purely rhetorical attribute, not a quality in general which is possible at all times and in all places'.[25]

The particular structuring of the world implicit in 'classical' music can only be properly penetrated, deconstructed, when it is realized that the dominant myth of post-Renaissance 'educated' Western culture *is* that it is

[23] Richard Crocker, 'Hermann's major sixth', *Journal of the American Musicological Society*, 25/1 (1972), p. 33.
[24] Ronald Barthes, *Writing degree zero*, trans. Annette Lavers and Colin Smith (London, 1967).
[25] Ibid., p. 64.

the culture without myth. Reality seems really real, essentially divorced from human volition, ultimately discoverable and therefore communicable through the passive, inconsequential media of *écriture classique*, three-dimensional, representational oil painting, and, by implication, 'classical' music (although there have been some problems in this area, as expressed through debates in music aesthetics, because music is essentially a non-denotative medium). In music, art, literature and, indeed, science, post-Renaissance 'educated' culture has worn its logic on its sleeve. It not only appears transparent, clear, lucid and self-evident, but also, therefore, self-sufficient. It is a culture that one either takes or leaves. To use Walter Benjamin's terminology, it does not absorb the spectator, it is 'readerly'.[26] It does not allow the spectator in to complete the meaning.

'Classical' music thus reproduces the experiential alienation of those with power and influence. As with 'readerly' texts, there is little *jouissance*,[27] little the possibility for a meaningful dialectic between music and listener, little opportunity for an appreciable assertion of subjectivity through an active role in meaning construction. Much 'classical' music appears as inscrutable and impenetrable because there is a myth of vacuousness, of a complex and rich interiority that no longer exists because its logic, its rationale has been seemingly devolved onto a smooth and urbane exterior for all to hear. More often than not 'classical' music simply confronts the brilliant, reflective surface of its own logic and builds outwards and away in increasingly complex fashions. It is, however, through a very *real* elasticity in its technical characteristics, through the silences behind its inscrutable exterior, that 'classical' music allows for the simultaneous expression of a social reality and the mythical, contradictory ideology that supports it.[28]

Some 'popular' forms of music, on the other hand, do know a certain *jouissance*, do assert an appreciable degree of subjectivity, and do subvert, *if only partially*, the bureaucratized norms of 'classical' music. The structures of many Afro-American and Afro-American influenced 'popular' musics reflect the situation of proletarianized peoples contained by social institutions that they cannot influence or affect in any consequential fashion. Expressive musical statements are made within the sharply defined harmonic–rhythmic framework derived from 'classical music' through devices such as inflection of pitch, rhythm and timbre, individuated 'dirty' timbres and improvisation.[29] People who are dispossessed instrumentally

26 Ronald Barthes, *S/Z*, trans. Richard Miller (London, 1975).
27 Ronald Barthes, *The pleasure of the text*, trans. Richard Miller (London, 1976).
28 Shepherd, 'Theoretical model', pp. 154–65.
29 Ibid, pp. 165–73.

thus reproduce the social/musical framework which contains them and communicate personally within it. But in so doing, they create a tension, not only between their inflectionally and timbrelly individuated musical utterances and the harmonic–rhythmic framework which contains them, but within the framework itself. Experiencing considerable alienation, proletarianized peoples attempt to win back what cultural space they can, whether on the shop floor in terms of soldiering, sabotage and horseplay,[30] or musically, by altering harmonic sequences (for example, I^7, V^7, IV^7 instead of I, IV, V^7) and metric stress patterns (for example, 1 **2** 3 **4** instead of **1** 2 **3** 4). Such reordering and re-contextualization, as well as the expressive devices which are in tension with the reordered and re-contextualized framework, have as their origin the musics of black Africa, the Caribbean and Latin America.

It is important to understand, however, that there are limits to such re-ordering and re-contextualization. Like those with power and influence, proletarianized peoples seem to recognize the inscrutability and 'natural-ness' of capitalist social relations, to internalize them as such, and then to reproduce them, externalizing them in a form consistent with their own image of their own material and intellectual dispossession. This, perhaps, goes some way to explaining the traditional conservatism of many proletari-anized cultures. People in these cultures have no more secure a basis than do those with power and influence to get behind the apparently seamless logic of the industrial capitalist world. So it is musically. However much the harmonic–rhythmic framework is stretched, suspended, reordered and dismembered as part of a creative, interpretive act, Afro-American and Afro-American-influenced musics seldom approach a true transcendence and dissolution of that framework. It is nearly always there, a seemingly inevitable coathanger on which to place more immediate and significant personal statements.

Timbre and gender

In both 'classical' and 'popular' musics, timbre, the core of sound, is in different ways constrained by the same harmonic–rhythmic framework. In the case of 'classical' music this constraining takes the form of an insistence on standardized purity (which students are carefully taught to achieve) which compensates for timbre's insusceptibility to being fully notated and thereby being *visually* controlled a priori to its actual realization in time.

[30] James Rinehart, *The tyranny of work* (Toronto, 1975), pp. 78–81.

This insistence has in turn resulted in the unexamined assumption that timbre in 'classical' music is a neutral and largely unimportant element, having little to do with the expressive quality of the music. But perhaps the assumption of timbral innocence is unfounded. Perhaps the purity of timbre in 'classical' music is no more neutral and innocent than the supposed naturalness of *écriture classique* or 'white writing'. If there can be no 'white writing' – or at least if the color of such writing does not designate purity and innocence – then, equally, white or pure timbres are not as neutral and innocent as supposed. For like white writing, pure timbres are not simply the open route through which intended meanings pass: they are themselves intended meanings. White writing and readerly texts seem to make all connections apparent, all logic visible. In the same way, pure timbres, within the technological limitations of each instrument and voice, *seem* to reveal all there is to be known about the inherent sonic qualities of each instrument and voice, precisely by their inclusion of (again, ideally) all possible harmonics. Pure timbres – like explicit musical languages, readerly texts and the impenetrability of traditional, representational visual images[31] – are all highly alienating, in that in their apparent 'completeness' they admit of little participation: they seem to 'say it all'.

The manner in which timbres in 'popular' musics are constrained is rather more complex. 'Dirty' or 'un-pure' timbres as heard in various genres of 'popular' musics (apart from those electronically generated) only use some of the harmonics inherent in the ideally pure sound of the voice or instrument. This, it can be argued, renders such timbres immediately implicit or 'writerly' because they invite completion from the outside. In this sense, it may be suggestive that the vast majority of the world's music does *not* display pure timbres. If people can only become people through interaction with other people, then modes of musical utterance and timbral qualities must leave the door open for immediate interaction unmediated by a centralized or standardized bureaucratic norm. Only in highly industrialized cultures does there appear to exist a hegemonic bureaucratic rationality that attempts to squeeze the spiritual and personal out of itself, thus giving rise to a music in which conversation, call-and-response, and 'incomplete' timbres are inadmissible.

It is now appropriate for me to lay out this argument against the mediations brought on by gender. If the timbres of 'popular' musics seem, through their 'incompleteness', to offer the possibility for meaningful dialogue between subjects, then such a possibility, at the cultural level of gender relations, is rendered extremely difficult because of the nature of

[31] John Berger, *Ways of seeing* (London, 1972).

male hegemony. This thesis can be explored by reference to two kinds of 'popular' music, hard or 'cock' rock and 'soft' rock or 'Top 40'/AM ballads, the particular gender identities with which they are traditionally associated, and the vocal timbres that they typically spawn.

'Cock' rock, as Frith and McRobbie have noted, tends to be 'an explicit, crude and often aggressive expression of male sexuality'.[32] Archetypal examples of 'cock' rock are provided not only by performers such as Mick Jagger, Rod Stewart and Bruce Springsteen, but also by 'Heavy Metal' groups such as Iron Maiden, Mötley Crüe and Twisted Sister. 'Cock' rock performers tend to be 'aggressive, dominating, boastful and constantly seeking to remind their audience of their powers, their control'.[33] But at the same time, they may also be reminding themselves, and their *male* audience, that these are traditional male characteristics that need to be adopted and internalized. And the reminder is all the more necessary because of the precariousness of the male gender identity, particularly during adolescence: 'Numerous cock rock songs . . . express a deep fear of women, and in some cases . . . this fear seems pathological, which reflects the fact that the macho stance of cock rockers is . . . a fantasy for men. . . . Rock, in other words, carries messages of male self-doubt and self-pity to accompany its . . . confidence and aggression.[34]

The traditional bastion of male security (from fear of female fickleness) is male solidarity. It is no surprise, then, that such solidarity is reflected in the rock world, where women's role is essentially peripheral and over-determined by men: 'The male-ness of the world of rock is reflected in its lyrics, with their assertions of male supremacy, narcissism, and self-pity; but, for musicians, what is most significant is women's exclusion from the heart of their lives: exclusion from their friendships and work together as comrade craftsmen in the studio, on the road, in performance.[35]

The reverse side of 'cock' rock is 'soft' rock or 'Top 40' pop. This latter music is based traditionally on the sentimentality of the ballad form, which is infused, to a greater or lesser extent, with elements drawn from main-stream rock music. 'Soft' rock speaks, in various ways, to three different gender locations. Through songs of artists such as Anne Murray, it speaks first of all to the young girl or housewife who uses her source of life to attract and nurture the vulnerable male. Secondly, through the songs of artists such as the younger Donny Osmond and David Essex (not to men-

32 Simon Frith and Angela McRobbie, 'Rock and sexuality', *Screen Education*, 29 (1979), p. 5.
33 Ibid.
34 Ibid., p. 13.
35 Simon Frith, *Sound effects: youth, leisure and the politics of rock 'n' roll* (London, 1981), p. 85.

tion some of the early Beatles' songs, and Frank Sinatra in his earlier incarnation), it describes the situation of the young and vulnerable male: 'the image is of the boy next door: sad, thoughtful, pretty and puppy like'.[36] The gender symbiosis is here complete, for what the strident, aggressive male needs in his weaker moments of self-doubt 'is not so much someone to screw as a sensitive and sympathetic soulmate, someone to support and nourish the incompetent male adolescent as he grows up'.[37] Finally, through the songs of artists such as Shirley Bassey and Sheena Easton, 'soft' rock and 'Top 40' ballads speak to the woman as sex object, attracting men through an initial visual 'come-on'. In these three different ways, 'soft' rock and 'Top 40' pop therefore speak to the structural position of young girls as they discover the 'freedom' 'to be individual wives, mothers, lovers . . . to be glamorous, desirable sex objects for men'.[38]

Both 'cock' rock and 'soft' rock seem to have archetypal timbres associated with them. The typical 'cock' rock vocal sound is hard and rasping (for example, Mick Jagger singing 'Have You Seen Your Mother, Baby, Standing in the Shadow?'), produced overwhelmingly in the throat and mouth, with a minimum of recourse to the formants of the chest and head. Its origins seem to lie in what is regarded as the typical Delta blues sound of performers such as Willie Brown, which then found its way north to Chicago and into various forms of rhythm-and-blues and rock music. The sound relies on a highly constricted use of the vocal chords, presumably reproducing physiologically the tension and experiential repression encountered as males engage with the public world.

The typical vocal sound of woman-as-nurturer (for example, Anne Murray singing 'Snowbird'), on the other hand, is very different. It is soft and warm, based on a much more relaxed use of the vocal chords and using the formants of the chest in particular in producing a rich, resonating sound. The physiology of sound production in this case seems to speak to a person more fully aware of her inner, experiential being in offering herself as a source of emotional nourishment. The typical sound of 'the boy next door' (for example, Paul McCartney singing 'Yesterday') is also soft and warm by comparison with the hard and rasping 'cock' rock sound, but the softness and warmth here depends not so much on the use of formants in the chest as it does on the use of head tones. The sound is consequently much more open than that of the typical 'macho' voice. However, the physiology of the sound production still reflects an experiential emptiness in avoiding the formants of the chest cavity, and for this reason the sound

36 Frith and McRobbie, 'Rock and sexuality', p. 7.
37 Ibid.
38 Ibid., p. 12.

is typically light and thin compared to the dark, rich tones of the woman-as-nurturer. The music of the vulnerable male is thus essentially 'head' music, an appeal for emotional nurturance that does not, however, abdicate the supposed supremacy of traditional rationality. The typical sound of woman-as-sex-object involves a similar comparison. The softer, warmer, hollower tones of the woman singer as emotional nurturer become closed off with a certain edge, a certain vocal sheen that is quite different from the male-appropriated, hard core of timbre typical of 'cock' rock. Tones such as those produced by Shirley Bassey in 'Big Spender', for example, are essentially head tones, and it could in this sense be argued that the transition from woman the nurturer to woman the sex object represents a shift, physiologically coded, from the 'feminine heart' to the 'masculine head', with its stress on a cerebral, intellectual, controlled *view* of the world.

It would appear to be the case that the harmonics produced in articulating the hard, rasping timbres of 'cock' rock are typically not those produced in articulating the sounds more characteristic of 'Top 40' pop (and vice versa). The production processes are, in the case of 'macho' and 'female nurturer' timbres in particular, mutually exclusive to an appreciable degree. From the perspective of culturally constituted gender relations, it might seem as though there exists the potential for two essentially different and opposed timbral components to come together to form something that is greater than the sum of its parts.

However, this potential does not seem to be fulfilled in the case of 'cock' rock, especially in its more recent manifestations. Soft timbres, if heard at all, address male vulnerability rather than the warm nurturing of female receptiveness. 'Cock' rockers establish their personality against a bureaucratic norm by leaving themselves timbrelly open. But they do not let anyone in for completion. Their vision is inward looking and narcissistic.[39] They attempt to complete themselves, and in this sense the masturbatory symbolism of guitar playing is not without significance. It is hardly surprising that the ideal-typical male identity displays an element of self-doubt and self-pity. It seeks, at least timbrelly, fulfillment through self-denial: male reproduction attempts to be 'homosexual' or 'homosocial'.[40] The rasping timbres of 'cock' rock in particular can thus be interpreted as an attempt, through the exclusion of typically female timbres (whether these be the timbres of woman-as-nurturer, the 'masculinized' tones of woman-as-sex-object, or the 'feminized' tones of the 'boy next door') to control the

[39] Jenny Taylor and Dave Laing, 'Disco-pleasure-discourse: on "rock and sexuality"', *Screen Education*, 31 (1979), pp. 43–8, and Frith, *Sound effects*.
[40] Rosabeth Kanter, *Men and women of the corporation* (New York, 1977), p. 48.

female world, to keep women external to the man's life and 'in their place'.

The relationship of 'macho' timbres to the timbres of 'classical' music is, however, a little more complex. On the one hand, male timbres expunge the femininity symbolic in industrial capitalist societies for social process. Moreover, male timbres are in tension with the harmonic–rhythmic framework whose logical timbral expression is that of an explicit purity. On the other hand, although the timbres of 'cock' rock are in a sense atrophied and those of 'classical' music, *through their 'completeness'*, contain both the male and female elements of the timbre/gender equation, it seems that the timbres of 'cock' rock speak to a greater sense of individuality than those permitted in the tradition of 'classical' music.

The point is that the timbres of 'classical' music, although containing both male and female elements of the timbre/gender equation, do not speak to the full personal and social constructiveness that would result from unfettered male/female relationships. The 'completeness' of timbres in 'classical' music results not from the fertility of relatively unfettered male/female *gender* relationships, but from being a reflection, presumed white, innocent and neutral, of the rationality of the harmonic–rhythmic framework of 'classical' music. It is this framework which encodes musically the desire of post-Renaissance 'educated' man visually to pin down and control the material world *en route* to the control of processes of cultural reproduction and resistance. Social male/female fertility is thus both contained and *aurally* denied through the timbral completeness of 'classical' music. To use Barthes' terminology, the grain of the voice is flattened to filter out *jouissance*, thrill, erotic ecstasy.[41] In reflecting the essentially male, bourgeois, bureaucratic explicitness of harmonies in 'classical' music, 'classical' timbres render fertility unimportant, transparent and androgynous – just as in the aural and visual image portrayed by Julie Andrews in *The Sound of Music*. And that, in a world deemed susceptible to frozen, explicit control, is how it should be. The fertility of social relatedness becomes redundant, and gender relations are rendered safe and non-threatening. Gender relations are heard through male, bourgeois ears, thus making irrelevant Henry Higgins' gnawing question: 'Why can't a woman be more like a man?'

Such androgyny, such bourgeois male dominance and recontextualization of gender relations can only occur through a rejection of what the female gender could in actuality offer were this offering not downgraded to a second-class status or even to a status of non-knowledge. Male culture

⁴¹ Roland Barthes, 'The grain of the voice', *Image–music–text*, trans. Stephen Heath (New York, 1977), pp. 179–89.

attempts to be self-sufficient, although the attempt is ultimately doomed to failure because that which is fundamental to human existence can never ultimately be denied. However, the *attempt* at closure on the part of traditional male culture implies the necessity for an attempt at closure on the part of traditional female culture. The logic of the gender symbiosis of industrial capitalist societies is, to put it briefly, that if men are hard, women are soft. That is the way that *potentially* constructive gender relations are set up in an essentially male, bureaucratic world.

However, masculine hardness rarely calls out feminine softness precisely because the generation of hardness denies softness at the same time as implying it. The assertive, successful male has little need of female nurturing, traditionally choosing to demonstrate his power and influence, *inter alia*, through the presentation of a masculinized version of femininity. The woman-as-sex-object, as John Berger[42] has argued, subscribes to the vision that man has of her. So masculine hardness calls out feminine hardness, the woman-as-sex-object whose airbrushed fleshtones speak to an explicit exterior sheen that hides and denies the person within. Equally, if masculine hardness calls out a potentially depersonalizing hardness in women, then male softness calls out female softness, the self-doubt, self-pity and vulnerability of warmer male timbres requiring the interiority of the person rather than the exteriority of a sex object. Softness and hardness in gender relations, it can be argued, oscillate in a never-ending circle.

If the rasping timbres of 'cock' rock are symptomatic of a control of women through an exclusion of other, frequently softer timbres, then they represent equally an attempt to deny and contest an urbane, bourgeois 'asexuality' through the assertion of an *individualized*, aggressive, and essentially male constituted 'sexuality'. But although denial is possible, a successful contest is not. If rock 'n' roll and other forms of 'cock' rock are 'screw and smash' music (i.e., 'screw the girls and smash the opposition'),[43] then it has to be conceded that while one is possible, the other is not. So if the timbres of 'cock' rock attempt to smash the urbane 'asexuality' implied in 'classical' timbres, then the attempt is doomed from the beginning precisely because it is couched in technical musical characteristics that confirm the very logic of that 'asexuality'.

The same observation may be made with respect to female timbres. Soft female timbres (as well, it may be added, as soft male timbres) are usually acceptable to male-dominated culture, because they variously represent what is left behind when the male first moves into the world. 'Macho' vocal

---

[42] Berger, *Ways of seeing*, especially pp. 46–7, 51–64.
[43] Mike Brake, *The sociology of youth culture and youth subcultures* (London, 1980), p. 147.

sounds are, in a manner of speaking, 'all mouth', all projection into the public world with little behind them. The timbres of woman-as-sex-object are also acceptable, if a little more challenging, because they speak to a male image of femininity.

However, the vocal sheen of woman-as-sex-object changes perceptibly when women singers actually begin to occupy male locations in the social structure. It is interesting, for example, that the vocal timbres of many female classic blues singers are harder than those of many white women singers who portray stereotypic 'sexual' images. This may be because the 'sexual' aura so powerfully projected by singers such as Ma Rainey and Bessie Smith translated, for many black women, into unstable and frequently ephemeral relationships with men. Black women (both Ma Rainey and Bessie Smith personified this in their lives) frequently needed to develop a 'masculine' assertiveness and independence to survive while, at the same time, remaining 'women'. While, therefore, a song like 'A Good Man is Hard to Find' reveals many head tones in Bessie Smith's singing, there seems to be greater evidence of throat constriction and of emphasis on the mouth as a formant. This tendency becomes even more interesting with a figure such as Memphis Minnie. There is, for example, in a song like 'Give it to Me in My Hand' (performed with Kansas Joe McCoy), a striking similarity between the voice tones of female and male singer.

The vocal sheen and vocal hardness that characterizes the woman-as-sex-object and the woman moving towards a male location in the social structure can become exaggerated to stridency when the woman singer as rock artist attempts to carve out a niche for herself. Although the stridency of female rockers such as Janis Joplin has represented a clear challenge to the status quo, this stridency as a form of cultural resistance is also doomed to failure because it derives from the same splintered notions of 'sexuality' that also give rise to the rasping timbres of 'cock' rock. The 'cock' rocker finds it difficult to *communicate* with the feminine underside of his masculinity, seeking rather to possess it, absorb it wholesale through an externalized, objectified form. In the same way, by invoking closure of her 'intrinsic' femininity to provide that same objectified form, the woman-(singer)-as-sex-object runs the risk of losing touch with her already atrophied self, of being taken over by a masculine image of her 'own' inner nature. The initial inscrutability and unapproachability of the woman-as-sex-object that represents an initial 'come-on' for the male, and holds out the promise of eventual 'sexual' and personal encounter, can become with the female rocker a total closure that prevents any such encounter. The masculinity appropriated in the process of actively generating a 'sexually desirable' female image steps over into the masculinity adopted in actively becoming 'one of the boys'.[44]

Conclusion

In view of the above analysis, it can be suggested that the vast majority of music consumed in the Western world is concerned with articulating, in a variety of different ways, male hegemonic processes. 'Classical' music is founded on a notational control of pitch and rhythm which in turn implies an androgynized sense of self as expressed through pure and standardized timbres. The 'incomplete' or 'dirty' timbres of much 'popular' music speak to a greater sense of subjectivity, and they are, in many cases, in clear tension with the harmonic–rhythmic framework which contains them. But the logic of the individualized masculine identity, as expressed through the archetypal timbres of various forms of 'cock' rock, ensures that, at the cultural level, there is little meaningful dialogue between different gender identities as thus overdetermined. The qualities of sound which speak so strongly in various 'popular' music genres to a sense of individual identity therefore achieve little but a reinforcement of the traditional gender types that both result from and serve to reproduce an essentially masculine view of the world.

It should not be imagined, however, that the voice types described above are the only ones possible within an overdetermined male hegemony. There is, for example, the 'pure virgin' voice of Annie Lennox, the 'little girl' voice of early Kate Bush, not to mention what can only be described as the highly self-conscious and clearly ironic 'virgin/slut' voice of Madonna. Equally, it should not be supposed that individual singers use only one voice type. It is more usual for individual singers to move between voice types in performing a song in order to keep an audience interested.

In 'A Good Man is Hard to Find', for example, Bessie Smith frequently begins a vocal phrase with a growl of 'sexual' aggressiveness appropriated from the traditional 'macho' timbre, then moves to her standard, hard, 'woman-as-sex-object' timbre for the majority of the phrase, and then lets the phrase fall away with a hint of the softer 'woman-as-nurturer' timbre. Such changes in voice tone imply a dialogue with the unseen male-as-voyeur, initial aggressiveness and closure moving to the openness of personal encounter. In this sense it is quite possible for women singers to engage in a kind of 'vocal striptease', the 'revelations' of the striptease as a visual act

[44] Frith and McRobbie, 'Rock and sexuality', p. 9.

translating into the 'revelations' made possible through an oscillation between traditional female voice types. (The undeviating hardness of Memphis Minnie's voice, by comparison, seems to give notice that there is no intention to enter into any such dialogue.)

Finally, and most significant, it is important to emphasize that traditional notions of gender and 'sexuality' are not phenomena that are 'given' or 'natural', phenomena that 'popular' music either expresses or controls.[45] If, as I suggested above, traditional notions of gender and 'sexuality' have essentially been constructed by men in the interstices between culture and nature in order to control culture through nature, then they are notions that remain eminently negotiable. 'Popular' musicians do not as a consequence inevitably find themselves in a position of relating to something over which they have no influence in giving expression to senses of individual identity. Traditional notions of gender and 'sexuality' can be renegotiated by 'popular' musicians, and this, as Frith[46] has pointed out, is a process that became increasingly common during the 1970s.

Negotiation is the key concept in understanding how the politically personal is articulated from within the internal processes of music. There is nothing technically immanent about the meanings and relevancies analyzed in this paper as being articulated from within the qualities and relationships of pitch, rhythm and timbre. As material phenomena the various technical characteristics of music may both favor and constrain the articulation of certain cultural and social messages, but they cannot determine them. The technical characteristics of music in this sense represent little more than sites over and through which power may be mediated textually. The theoretical model elaborated in this paper assumes nothing more than that: a basic and partial map of *what*, stereotypically, is being negotiated by performers *and* consumers alike, over and through the different technical characteristics of music. No performers, not even the ones mentioned here as being associated with traditional gender/timbre types, simply and passively reflect a given gender type or notion of sexuality any more than individuals simply and passively consume them. The deconstruction of meaning in music requires not only a catholicity of theories and methodologies, but also a variety of entry points.[47] However, without the elaboration of some initial theoretical models, it is difficult to conceive a way into understanding the technical characteristics of music as sites for the textual mediation of politically personal power.

[45] This point is made by Simon Frith in 'Confessions of a rock critic', *New Statesman*, 110/2840 (1985), pp. 21–3.

[46] Ibid.

[47] John Shepherd, 'Music consumption and cultural self-identities: some theoretical and methodological reflections', *Media, Culture and Society*, 8 (1986), pp. 305–30.

The sound of music in the era of its electronic reproducibility

JOHN MOWITT

With every tool man is perfecting his own organs, whether motor or sensory, or he is removing the limits to their functioning. In the photographic camera he has created an instrument which retains the fleeting visual impressions, just as the gramophone disc retains the equally fleeting auditory ones; both are at bottom materializations of the power he possesses of recollection, his memory.

Sigmund Freud

Is it 'live' or is it Memorex?

To emphasize the importance of reproductive technology when analyzing the social significance of music is to privilege the moment of reception in cultural experience. What follows is organized around the acknowledgment of such a moment. Put succinctly, reception has acquired its analytic importance as a result of socio-historical developments within the cultural domain. I can best illustrate this by turning to a concrete example – an example that will indicate why music is a decisive reference point for an understanding of these developments. My aim in the analysis of this example will be to introduce the category of a structure of listening, on the basis of which I will argue for the priority of reception within the social determination of musical experience. Central to this argument is the notion that subjectivity acquires its irreducibly social character from the fact that experience takes place within a cultural context organized by institutions and practices. Today, these include institutions that technically fuse the contexts of cultural production and reception. I will elaborate this in terms of the problem of the place of memory in musical experience – a problem which has come to receive its strongest formulation within the phenomenological tradition. By drawing on a reading of the psychoanalytic account of memory, I will also reflect in detail on the social constitution of experience which is conspicuously underdeveloped in phenomenology. Once the socio-technological basis of memory is elaborated and used to establish the sociality of music, I will address the political issues raised by

173

this development. By turning to the debates within critical theory, I will not only be able to specify these issues, but I will be able to sketch out the emancipatory dialectic of contemporary musical reception.

A recent advertising campaign for a major cassette tape producer underscores the key socio-historical developments that have shaped contemporary musical reception. I am thinking of the Memorex Corporation's well-known television commercial featuring Chuck Mangione and Ella Fitzgerald that centered on the interrogative phrase, 'Is it live or is it Memorex?' A brief reconstruction of the commercial's narrative and *mise en scène* will enable me to unpack the main points of my illustration.

The scene is a recording studio. The television audience arrives upon the scene just as the final cadence of Mangione's 'hit' fades. Two acoustic spaces are joined: the space of the recording and the space of the commercial. A cinematically fostered structure of identification situates us in the control room of the studio along with Fitzgerald who is watching and listening to the session. The juncture of acoustic spaces means that both Fitzgerald and the television audience are listening to Mangione's piece through the playback monitors in the control room. A voice-over narrator gives us the details of a test that is going to be conducted to establish the quality of the Memorex product.[1] Fitzgerald is to turn her back on the control room window and, simply by listening once again to the monitors, determine whether the music she is listening to is 'live' or Memorex, that is, electronically reproduced. Because of our proximity to her in the narrative space, we are being invited in effect to submit to the test and its conclusions as well. The melodic 'hook' of Mangione's piece returns on the audio track, Fitzgerald indicates uncertainty, and Mangione and his group resolve her dilemma by screaming to her from within the studio, 'It's Memorex!' The voice-over narration reaches closure with the requisite repetition of the product's name embedded in the memorable phrase: 'Is it live or is it Memorex?'[2]

[1] The test organizing the Memorex commercial strongly evokes the 'blindfold test' that has been a feature in the monthly music magazine *Downbeat* for decades. Used as a forum for critical exchange, the 'blindfold test' pits a recognized musician against a record whose jacket has been kept hidden. The featured musician listens to the record and is then asked to identify the performers while commenting on their performances. Crucial to one's performance in the test is the ability to remember someone's 'sound'. Beyond the fact that musical reproduction is central to this test, it is important to stress that musical recognition is again situated here within the opposition between looking and listening.

[2] Prior to the advertisement featuring Ella Fitzgerald and Chuck Mangione, Memorex ran a commercial that featured Fitzgerald and Melissa Manchester. Two fundamental differences characterized the earlier example. First, the generational scheme was reversed: Manchester listened to two versions of a performance by Fitzgerald. Second, the race and gender of the 'original' were respectively transformed and reversed: a white woman listened to a

Many themes and problems have been paraded before our eyes and ears: memory, fidelity, production, reception, music, looking and listening. In regard to these, the issue at stake in the ad is not, in fact, whether 'The First Lady of Song' is really deceived by the King of Memory (Memo Rex). Our basic precritical cynicism assures us that this is not worth caring about because we know that Fitzgerald is being paid by the Memorex Corporation to appear in the commercial. Instead, what made this commercial and its slogan one of the most successful in the industry was its accurate and reassuring evocation of a contemporary structure of listening, a structure that is now in decline. Detailing this structure will allow me to justify the importance I have attached to musical reception.

The recording studio is a cultural facility whose existence testifies to the technological advances that made the present priority of cultural consumption over cultural production possible. The social fact that more people listen to music rather than play it derives, in part, from the cultural impact of the operation of this facility. At the very core of the studio reside repetition and reproducibility. Indeed, in the contemporary musical world (and this is not restricted to the West) repetition now constitutes the very threshold of music's social audibility. In actual recording practice this phenomenon has penetrated musical material to the point where performances themselves are immanently shaped by both the fact and the anticipation of repetition.[3] Moreover, recording has profoundly altered the improvisational idioms in music essentially by providing them with a form of notation. Besides making it possible to study the 'scores' of jam sessions, reproduction – particularly in these instances – restricts interpretation to the recorded notation of specific performances of the piece. While this can be seen as contributing to the musicological temptation to reduce interpretation to execution, it is also important to recognize that the replacement of scores with records (and tapes) has been an indispensable component of the explosion in 'nonprofessional' composition.

Significantly, in the Memorex commercial we encounter music in the studio, ostensibly the site of its production. But consider again the drama that unfolds there. The primary reason Chuck Mangione appears in the ad is that he and his music are recognizable. They are recognizable – and

black woman. While the reversal of the generational scheme in the second commercial introduced the appropriate but unorthodox theme of an inverted temporality (the younger man coming before the older woman), its recoding of the 'original' invoked a tradition begun in the recording industry by RCA Victor's slogan, 'His Master's Voice'.

[3] I am thinking here, first, of the relatively common recording practice of splicing different takes together to assemble the 'right' performance, where repetition establishes the very texture of the recorded surface; and second of the well-known temporal restraints that organize composition around the anticipated strictures of the radio 'plugging' format.

therefore commercially valuable – because of the 'plugging' mechanism made possible by the impact of recording on musical performance. Mangione's very presence then derives from the location in which we find him. What is more important, though, is that by joining the two acoustic spaces I have delineated, the ad fuses our *recognition* of Mangione's 'hit' with a representation of the moment of its original inscription. What could be reduced here to an instance of mere temporal deception can be more fruitfully read as an indication of the radical priority of reception. The ad does not merely record a moment of musical production: it registers the social construction of music. To clarify this we need to re-enter Fitzgerald's dilemma.

When we join her she has just witnessed a 'take'. Together we are then confronted with another performance of Mangione's piece. This is a test. We have to remember what the performance our eyes told us was 'live' sounded like and compare that with what subsequently comes over the playback monitors for fidelity. Who or what controls Fitzgerald's memory and, therefore, her access to the telling difference in musical listening? Clearly it is the recording facility itself, since she is represented as never having heard Mangione's piece except as it has been mediated by the recording apparatus. But what has happened to those of us who took up the invitation to share her dilemma? I believe we end up baffling ourselves. The ad presents us with the fact that even a Black musician, who in our culture is still deemed genetically (rather than culturally) rooted in music, cannot tell the difference between a sound and its reproduction. But we screen ourselves from a recognition of the electronic colonization of listening by cynically consuming the *spectacle* of our fetishized listener's failure. In short, following Fitzgerald's example, we resort to listening with our eyes and reducing the qualitative significance of musical expression to the technical perfection of its reproduction. Put more emphatically, the baffle that protects us from having to acknowledge our 'loss of hearing' becomes a concrete visual (Baudelaire might have said 'synaesthetic') supplement to listening. As such, the scandal of contemporary hi-fidelity is not that one cannot actually hear it, but that we persist in regarding the perfection of listening as essentially beyond all forms of social determination.

If recording organizes the experience of reception by conditioning its present scale and establishing its qualitative norms for musicians and listeners alike, then the conditions of reception actually *precede* the moment of production. It is not, therefore, sufficient merely to state that *considerations* of reception influence musical production and thus deserve attention in musical analysis. Rather, the social analysis of musical experience has to take account of the radical priority of reception, and thus it must shift its focus away from a notion of agency that, by privileging the moment of production, preserves the autonomy of the subject. My argument, therefore, develops on the basis of two complementary assertions: (1) that individuals are made up of the society their associations produce and (2) that human subjectivity, as a general structure of experience, is socially engendered. The Memorex ad can serve as a convenient point of reference to highlight the problems that subjectivity raises when its authority is no longer taken for granted.

In the ad Fitzgerald is not shown hearing; she is shown listening, that is, paying a particular sort of attention to the performance of Mangione's 'hit'. What distinguishes her attention from mere hearing is its interpretive character – she is trying to make sense of what she hears. Barthes and Havas, in their essay entitled 'Listening', argue that it is precisely in the activity of interpretation that what distinguishes the 'human' from the 'animal' arises within the auditory realm.[4] It is certainly fair to say then that Fitzgerald recognizes herself as a human subject as she listens. But I can be more specific than that. Meanings not only occur to her, but her identity as a listener arises where these meanings occur. During the televised test Fitzgerald is listening to one set of sounds (a recording) while trying to remember another (a performance). As such, a human faculty, memory, is being solicited and delimited within the commercial. Significantly, at the very point where Fitzgerald's memory is shown to lack sufficient discriminating power, its proper functioning is at once defined (the flawless retrieval of an origin) and taken into custody by a facility upon which she, as a recording star, is obliged to rely for proper self-recognition. What is at stake here is less a particular memory than memory as such, since the commercial organizes her acts of listening around the philosophically charged abstractions of recollection and knowledge. That the commercial produces an experience of a faculty around which the subject organizes him- or herself – an experience which includes a specific technical and therefore social mediation – indicates how deeply experience is organized by the social process.

There is one last feature of the commercial's presentation of the structure of listening that requires elaboration: the conspicuous subordination of listening to looking that coincides with the subjugation of perception by the King of Memory. The Memorex Corporation has to find a way to manage the following problem: if Memorex is as good as it is claimed to be,

[4] Roland Barthes and Roland Havas, 'Listening', *The responsibility of forms*, trans. Richard Howard (New York, 1985), pp. 245–60.

then what good is the original? The original becomes necessary and there-fore valuable solely as a means of notarizing the copy. However, if listening cannot be trusted to differentiate between the original and the copy, how are we to perceive the validity of the original's notarization of the copy since the aural original might always already be the copy from which it can no longer be aurally differentiated? This difficulty is resolved in the ad by invoking the priority of looking. Fitzgerald knows that the first time she listened she was listening to the original performance because she watched it. The television audience knows that Memorex can replace the original, not because they heard it — that would have been impossible given the actual listening conditions — but because they saw that their representative could not tell the difference. The commercial's producers were in no danger of compromising themselves here because the ad is merely consolidating a social experience of the hierarchy of senses that came into being with the hegemony of typographic culture and that continues to ground the modern subject. That is, since the seventeenth century sight has acquired ever more primacy over hearing in the West.[5] The commercial addresses us as though we were subjects who should recognize ourselves in this hierar-chy of senses. In recognizing ourselves as the addressees of the ad, we implicitly affirm that we must be the ones whose aural memories have come to rely on a prosthesis that can be seen but not heard.

Despite my declared aims, I have not really addressed the fact that Fitz-gerald and the television audience are listening to a piece of music. It is thus time to remedy this. What I have stressed is that music, as an organi-zation of noise or sound, arises within the structure of listening I have outlined. Music's social significance derives from the role it plays in the stabilization of this structure, that is, how it articulates and consolidates structurally necessary practices of listening. By sanctioning specific techni-cal mediations of listening as subjectively normative, musical reception supplies the social order sponsoring such mediations with an experiential confirmation. There is therefore a political issue here which I have yet to pose adequately: an issue having to do with the concrete character of the social order that stands confirmed within the contemporary structure of listening. This will be easier to do once the proper context has been estab-lished. Most immediately then, music needs to be characterized in a manner that enables us to understand how it can meet these rather general social demands while at the same time providing in its texture the details that occasion listening pleasure. Such a characterization is provided in

5 Donald Lowe, *The history of bourgeois perception* (Chicago, 1982), chapter 6. There is also an important summary of the issues at stake here in the introductory chapter.

Jacques Attali's *Noise: the political economy of music*, where he writes, 'All music, any organization of sounds, is then a tool for the creation or consolidation of a community, of a totality.'[6] While this formulation clarifies the tremendous theoretical importance given to music by Attali, it does not clarify the way in which it belongs within the context I have established for it. We still need to know why the structure of listening evoked by the Memorex Corporation was organized around a piece of music rather than a fragment of ambient noise no less 'live' than Mangione's 'hit'. Before pursuing this, more concentrated scrutiny must be devoted to the conceptual series: memory, music, community. Only then will it be possible to take up the socio-political questions raised by my title.

The stuff of which memories are made

Five years before he perished at Buchenwald, Maurice Halbwachs wrote 'The collective memory of musicians' (1939) which formed part of an extended inquiry into the collective character of human memory in general.[7] Characteristic of all of Halbwachs' work on memory was the effort, explicitly informed by Bergsonian phenomenology and Marxism, to situate a properly subjective faculty deep within the social process. The consequence of thus situating subjectivity was that 'society' was reconceptualized beyond the limits of positivist sociology. Though very few practitioners of cultural criticism have paid serious attention to this short text,[8] its framing of the analysis of music is significant to the development of my position.

Put simply, Halbwachs' essay explores the difficulty and necessity of remembering music for performers and listeners alike. The structure of his argument is typical of his work. He first sets out to show that memory is fundamental to music; he then illustrates how musical memory is necessarily collective or social; and he concludes by arguing that music, even in its transcendent sublimity, is a social experience. Since I plan to examine certain points of his argument, I will reconstruct a few of its key elements.

[6] Jacques Attali, *Noise: the political economy of music*, trans. Brian Massumi (Minneapolis, 1985), p. 6. The entire chapter entitled 'Repeating' is worth consulting if one is interested in another analysis of the issue I am examining in this paper.

[7] Maurice Halbwachs, *The collective memory*, trans. Francis J. Ditter and Vida Yazdi Ditter (New York, 1980), pp. 158–86.

[8] The exception here is Alfred Schütz who, in his 'Making music together', *The collected papers of Alfred Schütz* (The Hague, 1964) II, pp. 158–78, rather polemically differentiates himself from Halbwachs only to settle for a phenomenologically abstract account of the specifically social character of music.

What justifies the importance Halbwachs attaches to music in this context is the opposition he establishes in the opening of the essay between linguistic signs and musical (or, perhaps more generally, sonic) signs. Memory of linguistic signs is facilitated by our daily use of the language from which they derive and by the practice of writing which, for reasons I will later allude to, Halbwachs does not regard as a mere derivative of language. The ordinary use of language establishes conventions which restrain the effects of the arbitrary relation between the signifier and the signified, making communication possible. According to Halbwachs, musical signs, though they can and must be notated, do not enter into or derive from a language whose daily use has stabilized their significations. They are, therefore, harder to remember and retain, but precisely because of this, memory is all the more fundamental to musical communication. What is meant here is that, since musical signs refer primarily to the context of their own utilization, memory is indispensable for the structuring of this context and the reception of the significations it authorizes. One thinks here of Adorno's quip that, 'structurally, one hears the first bar of a Beethoven symphonic movement only at the very moment when one hears the last bar'.[9] Memory is not only necessary for this type of listening; its very capacity is informed by these demands. These are, in fact, the sorts of demands that oblige Halbwachs to insist upon the importance of musical notation, since he finds it doubtful that either performer or listener could retain the relevant contextual markers without a complex mnemonic device. Reluctant to treat either music or memory as a pretext for the other, Halbwachs grounds them both in the spiral of reproduction and recognition.

In order to sustain his focus on the musician, Halbwachs has to locate the listener (even an 'untrained' one) within the musician's experience of memory. He does this through recourse to the Bergsonian notion of a 'schematic model'. At issue here is the following: when a listener retains from a piece of music something that might serve as the basis for articulating the piece's meaning, Halbwachs argues that this is due to the listener's ability to reproduce (typically through humming) the traces left in his or her brain by the musical signs. The configuration of these traces is what serves as the schematic model for the remembrance of the piece. The more times this configuration is accurately replicated, the clearer the memory of the piece and the more competent the listener will be to articulate its significance. However, what determines the listener's memory of the piece

9 Theodor Adorno, 'The radio symphony: an experiment in theory', *Radio research 1941* (New York, 1941), p. 116.

is not the brain, but rather the history of the replications of the piece – a history mediated by the listener's relations to others. I will have to consider the impact on this history of a reproductive technology that promises to displace the 'original' musical signs in favor of copies which eternally return as the same. More is at stake here than the mere inscription of improvisational spontaneity.

The ordinary listener's experience differs from the musician's only in degree, and Halbwachs introduces a marvelous metaphorical figure to establish this. In describing performing musicians, he situates them before their scores. Many of them know their parts 'by heart' and refer to the scores only intermittently: many repetitions have necessarily interceded, and the scores can be said to serve as 'material substitutes for the brain'. As with the listener, a particular history and technology of reproduction supplements the musician's memory. After introducing this provocative image of an eccentric (from the standpoint of the classical subject) memory, Halbwachs goes on to compare musical signs to the footprints Robinson Crusoe found while hiking on 'his' island. What authorizes the comparison is Halbwachs' conviction that musical signs, and not merely notated signs, are indices of the action exerted on a performer's brain by the 'colony' of other brains. The significance of these signs arises within the horizon established by this structuring of memory – a memory that is at once fundamental to music and profoundly social. Halbwachs insists that without executed notational commands there would be no action inscribed as a schematic model in the listener's brain. In the absence of this inscription there could be no memory, no recognition and no meaning.

What connects specific actions on the part of musicians to specific notational commands is a code that formalizes and therefore records an intricate social history of conventions. This social history leaves its traces, its footprints, in the brains of musician and listener alike. Memory is, therefore, not only indispensable to music; it is, as it were, 'colonized' by the reception of music. As Attali put it, music is a form of community or, perhaps more strongly stated, the musical organization of memory is a formation of community. This latter point is not emphasized by Halbwachs. In fact, his essay strikes one as peculiarly insensitive to some of its obvious political and perhaps less obvious philosophical implications. (It is curious, for example, that in his discussion of Defoe's novel Halbwachs implicitly associates Friday's footprints with the presence of a 'colony' precisely at the point where he draws on Robinson's experience of an 'other' as a metaphor for collective memory. The specificity of this collectivity is misrepresented in that Robinson is more properly associated with the imposed collectivity of the colony.) As a consequence, Halbwachs neglects the political questions arising from the social control over the means of cultural reproduction. One should be entitled to ask: Which community is forming in the musical organization of the collective memory, and what is its relation to those technologies that facilitate the exact reproduction of musicians' actions for listeners?[10]

In order to broach the political problem whose themes I have been underlining, I want to turn once again briefly, within the context of Halbwachs' essay, to the relation between subjectivity and memory. As I indicated in my introductory remarks about this text, Halbwachs is attempting to situate a properly subjective faculty deep within the social process. But his argument sets aside the specificity of the social collectivity at the core of memory – the subjective corollary to which is his reluctance to question seriously the reduction of the subject to consciousness. In other words, Halbwachs' demonstration stops at the point where individual memory is shown to be dependent on social memory. He fails to consider whether this dependence is not also the precondition for the experience of independence that paradoxically defines the social bond within the bourgeois era. What his essay shows is that the structure of the autonomous subject includes something which is anterior to it – not merely in the sense of coming before it, but in the sense of preconditioning the subject to the point of displacing or preempting it. Halbwachs is content to call this the collective, or society. The fact that the subject's own memory comes *before* his or her consciousness does not shake Halbwachs' confidence in the temporal simplicity of the subject. It could be that Halbwachs' reluctance to confront the political specificity of the collective is due to his sense that the subject he feels himself to be is in no way threatened by its proximity. But in any case, the essay exhibits a version of an omnipotent fantasy, presenting us with a subject that is not merely social, but that is society itself. Against this it should be stressed that music not only brings the subject into relation with the collective memory, but it collectivizes the subject at the level of memory.

Freud, a contemporary of Halbwachs, was less reluctant to draw the consequences of the peculiar anteriority of memory. In fact, in Jacques Derrida's reading of the evolution of the scriptural metaphor in Freud's texts, the memory trace is drawn upon to show how potentially unsettling Freud's model of the psychical apparatus was.[11] It was far more unsettling

---

[10] The political stakes of a particular memory – our memory of the 1960s – is very carefully articulated by Simon Frith, 'Rock and the politics of memory', *The 60s without apologies*, eds. Sonya Sayres, *et al*. (Minneapolis, 1984), pp. 59–69.

[11] Jacques Derrida, 'Freud and the scene of writing', *Writing and difference*, trans. Alan Bass (Chicago, 1978), pp. 196–231.

than my epigraph, a citation from *Civilization and its discontents* (p. 38), would lead one to believe. There, the phonograph is treated as an instrumental extension of memory. For Derrida, Freud's mature theory of memory, as embodied in the figure of the 'Mystic Writing Pad', advances the possibility that the subject is itself the prosthesis of a mechanism that precedes it. What authorizes this possibility is Freud's conviction that within the psychical apparatus 'consciousness arises instead of a memory trace'; that is, the subject centers itself in consciousness on the site where memory traces have established the infrastructure for such centering. Derrida designates this uncanny mechanism as 'writing' and argues that 'writing supplements perception before perception even appears to itself'.[12] This is the temporal contradiction of the subject, its displacement by a reproductive apparatus that precedes it. In the final pages of the printed text, Derrida turns his reading of Freud in the direction of those questions Freud refused to raise. Specifically, he takes up the issue of the status of the 'material supplement' to memory that is essential to Freud's discussion of the psychical apparatus. Appropriately, he stresses that this notion not only problematizes the subject, but it obliges us to rethink the 'sociality of writing'. Though his formulations are only suggestively abstract, Derrida does manage to articulate what remained repressed in both Freud and Halbwachs: that is, the socio-technological character of the reproduction that comes before the subject or the social.

With the reintroduction of the concept of a reproduction that supercedes 'life', I have returned to my point of departure. It is time now to open an examination of the thesis I have been assembling: namely, that the contemporary structure of listening, with its dependency on memory, is given its social significance by the reproductive technologies that organize it. This can be done by situating this thesis within a political debate on cultural reception in the era of the culture industry. The debate I am referring to is the one realized in the intertextual field established by Walter Benjamin's 'The work of art in the age of mechanical reproduction' and Theodor Adorno's 'The fetish-character of music and the regression of listening'.[13]

[12] Ibid., p. 224.

[13] Walter Benjamin's essay is contained in *Illuminations*, trans. Harry Zohn (New York, 1969), pp. 217–51, Theodor Adorno's in *The essential Frankfurt School reader*, eds. Andrew Arato and Eike Gebhardt (New York, 1978), pp. 270–99. Though from a slightly later period the section titled 'Modes of listening' from Adorno's *Philosophy of modern music*, trans. Wesley Blomster and Anne Mitchell (New York, 1980), pp. 197–201, functions as an interesting supplement to the essay on fetishism by introducing two models of what I have called here 'structures of listening'. The reader who consults the later essay will realize that I am working with a somewhat more general notion – one that is less centered in composition as such.

Film/music and the dialectic of aura

When Benjamin and Adorno debated the socio-political significance of mass cultural forms, the technologies of cultural reproduction on which these forms rested were in their infancy. Nonetheless, the intellectual and political integrity of their positions has contributed to the formation of our own alertness to developments they neither knew nor could anticipate. Electronic reproducibility is the name I have given to what they did not yet know.

Benjamin and Adorno confronted and challenged each other most directly on the significance of the opposition between 'contemplation' and 'distraction' proposed by Benjamin for analyzing the cultural experience of reception. In his essay, Benjamin characterized contemplation as the affective state in which the subject receives auratic art. This was because auratic art was embedded in an unproblematic tradition and consummately embodied in a 'masterpiece' whose spatio-temporal singularity obliged one to approach it by way of secular pilgrimage. The experience serving as the basis of the subject's act of interpretation was one of awe-inspiring distance. Because subjects always encountered auratic art in the fabric of tradition (on the wall of a cathedral for example), Benjamin argued that the activity of cultural interpretation was reduced to an absorption of the meaning that arose for subjects in their identification with the power the tradition had over them. The continued celebration of this aesthetic experience, once others became possible, troubled him. (As those who are familiar with the text know, Benjamin had the 'poor taste' to call this experience by its name – fascism.)

Against contemplation Benjamin posed the concept of distraction which was designed to account for the cultural experience of mechanically reproduced art. This was necessitated by the disintegration of the reception conditions that had sustained auratic art – a disintegration precipitated by the emergence of mass culture. Mechanical reproduction, which for Benjamin was paradigmatically embodied in photography and *silent* cinema, made it possible to remove the work of art from its traditional context. Pilgrimage was superceded by 'crowding' as reproduced art enabled several large, socially heterogeneous groups to experience the 'same' work simultaneously. Once the art work lost its traditional footing, the activity of interpretation inevitably began to accentuate the interests that prevailed in the regional contexts of its appropriation. Art's function in the codification of collective memory was reorganized by the increasingly politicized intervention of regional hermeneutic interests within the cultural sphere. Mechanically reproduced art did not, however, only fray the fabric of tradition; it was itself fragmented. Again, film and its organizational principle of the frame was the model here. Because post-auratic art operated in accordance with the principle of the fragment, the subject's reception of it was characterized by distraction. Benjamin did not mean by this that one was unable to pay attention to the work, but rather that one could make sense of it without surrendering to its traditionally sanctioned patterns of identification. Unwilling to abandon significance for the 'play of the signifier', Benjamin emphasized the socially critical character of distraction and the habits of critical literacy that could form under its influence. In a rare discussion of music he in fact designated his own writing as a practice that required the presence of what we would now call 'ambient' music.[14]

What impressed Benjamin about cinema was its apparatus and the testimony it bore to the saturation of modern reality by equipment. Though it was nearly impossible to avoid the shock of montage, the cinematic fragment or frame took effect below the threshold of subjective experience. To this extent, the fragment marked one of the sensory boundaries of the post-auratic subject. Through editing, a segmented world could be given the *real* appearance of seamlessness. By the same token, as a cultural apparatus, cinema embodied the adjustment of reality to the social presence of the masses. It was, in other words, the technical realization of a political demand. Distraction, therefore, was the affective state in which a proletarianized subjectivity experienced what could no longer bear the name 'art'.

Adorno accepted the terms of Benjamin's argument, but he reversed its conclusions. Surprisingly, Adorno did not even contest Benjamin's advocacy of silent cinema. This is odd because when Adorno collaborated with Hanns Eisler in writing *Composing for the films* during the 1940s, film's role in the standardization of listening was soundly criticized (and it was, after all, listening with which Adorno was preoccupied).[15] Granted, there is a marked difference between silent and sound film, and I will have occasion to take up the problem of the division between looking and listening more directly later. This and other oddities notwithstanding, Benjamin and Adorno contradicted one another directly. The convergence of terms only intensifies the suspicion that their positions are aptly opposing views of an experience that solicits both responses but that resists thematization from either side. I would suggest that this experience has to do with the post-Renaissance structure of the hierarchy of senses (seeing

[14] Walter Benjamin, *Reflections*, trans. Edmund Jephcott (New York, 1978), p. 80.
[15] Hanns Eisler (and Theodor Adorno), *Composing for the films* (New York, 1947), pp. 109–11.

over hearing) grounding modern cultural reception. Adorno's text deserves more detailed consideration before we can decide this one way or another.

Adorno had been tolling the death knell of 'serious' music since the early 1930s. When he responded to Benjamin in 1938, mourning had given way to the melancholia that was to remain his thematic signature. 'The fetish-character of music and the regression of listening' opens with a sketch of what Adorno took to be the necessary theoretical description of the social totality. This totality, which could only be articulated theoretically, authorized the assessment of the cultural significance of any particular practice. Ironically, the fact that the social totality existed nowhere but within critical theory itself (as a necessary analytic category) was a clear intellectual sign of the disintegration of aura – a disintegration Adorno was consciously forced to intensify by persisting in the rigorous elaboration of theoretical discourse.

I will skip directly to Adorno's discussion of the opposition between contemplation and distraction. Without addressing Benjamin's political characterization of contemplation as intellectual fascism, Adorno underscored its dialectical character and reappropriated its positive side, namely, its relation to theoretical reason. He justified this by elaborating the two themes of fetishism and regression. In a virtuosic series of maneuvers, Adorno transcribed Lukács' analysis of reification – wherein the production of commodities is tied to the desocialization of class consciousness – for an analysis of modern (both 'serious' and 'popular') music.[16] Crucial to this project is the demonstration that exchange value, as the front line of capitalist expansion, has reduced music to the status of a commodity. This is not difficult to do with 'popular' music, but Adorno, in homage to Lukács, insisted upon confronting a sociological tradition transfixed by the notion of objectivity with the problem of a general social transformation of subjectivity. He was less interested in the conditions of 'popular' music production and more interested in what he liked to refer to as the 'infantilization' of all listening subjects. The demonstration of the commodity character of music focused on the 'babytalk' used by 'popular' music as its language, which affected the reception of even 'serious' music. Significantly, at least with regard to the dispute with Benjamin, this demonstration hinged on an interpretation of the cultural significance of the fragment or detail.

Following Benjamin's presentation of the problematic of technical reproduction, Adorno argued that 'plugging' and what he later called 'standardization' – both examples of the incursion of exchange value within music –

---

[16] Georg Lukács, *History and class consciousness*, trans. Rodney Livingstone (Cambridge, 1968), pp. 83–110, and *passim*.

had come to replace the function of musical form in the determination of interpretive value for the details of musical composition. [17] For example, instead of melody taking on its significance as a function of a rigorously conceived musical structure, Adorno argued that it takes on its function from a merely reproductive consideration: namely, the recognizability that allows the regressive listener to identify (with) the familiar but necessarily forgettable 'popular' song. Melody here became a fragment or detail detached from the musical whole. As such, it became the object of distracted listening. [18]

Adorno carried this reversal of Benjamin's opposition into the very heart of the human subject through the notion of distracted or 'regressive listening'. With this notion he succeeds in situating even 'serious' music listening within the framework of the 'popular'. What was crucial for Adorno was the recognition that listening, as a sensory and cognitive structure of experience, occurs within the reception institutions organized by the capitalist mode of production. Characteristic of these institutions is their reflection of the fragmentation and exchangeability that defines this mode of production. Listeners are themselves atomized under these conditions even prior to their exposure to music. The fact then that the music predominating under capitalism is itself organized by the principle of the detail means that both the subject and its culture are entering into a regressive spiral. As music is colonized by the commodity form – its use becomes the exchangeability of its uses – listeners regress to the point where they will not listen to that which is not recognizable without first protecting themselves with an inoculation for the exotic. Connoisseurs of 'serious' music cannot help but listen in the distracted manner promoted by the consumer discourse of classical programming and by those musicological traditions that seek paradoxically to rescue music from the clutches of exchange by treating it as the gold standard. That the Wagnerian 'motiv', as a compositional principle reflecting the triumph of the detail, still influences musical composition, is the sign that not just listeners have been

[17] Theodor Adorno and George Simpson, 'On popular music', *Studies in Philosophy and Social Science*, 9 (1941), pp. 17–24.

[18] However much Adorno's impulse towards totalization and the cultural judgments it authorizes strikes one as offensive, the relative merits of such an impulse manifest themselves when one contrasts his analysis of listening with Aaron Copland's. A year after 'The fetish character of music and the regression of listening', Copland published *What to listen for in music* (1939). This text devolves into a 'self-help' guide for the musically perplexed because it sanctifies the problem it seeks to overcome by refusing to analyze it. Though Copland's considerable efforts to democratize listening are not to be trivialized, one should remember that only under questionable ideological circumstances is it primarily the thought that counts. Listening cannot be improved if it is misunderstood. Unfortunately, 'do-it-yourself' repair manuals avoid the issue of planned obsolescence as a matter of principle.

affected.[19] The decay of musical aura and the triumph of distraction within mass cultural experience meant for Adorno that listeners could no longer make sense of music's portrayal in its own materials of the social contradictions that isolated it. Instead, music's isolation was seized upon as the guarantee of its transcendental stature. The familiarity of 'popular' music does not save it from the incomprehensibility that bonds it with its revered twin.

It is on the basis of this analysis of the contemporary listener that Adorno advocated the cause of Schoenberg whose inaccessible style was the guarantee of his integrity. This was the only option for 'serious' music that sought to avoid the ravages of the commodity form. Those who have struggled to listen to this music know that even rapt contemplation is inadequate. It is, in many respects, a notated music: that is, a music meant to be seen and not heard. As such it is curiously synchronous with the structure of listening evoked in the Memorex commercial. Setting this aside for the moment, it is clear that Adorno preferred the peculiarly classical isolation of the avant-garde to Benjamin's proletarianized public.

Resisting the impulse to choose sides allows one to recognize the profoundly political character of the differences between Adorno and Benjamin. These irreducible differences notwithstanding, what unites the two positions beyond their idiolect is the strategy of politicizing the social organization of the subject's boundaries. Significantly, the subject's boundaries are situated, in both texts, on the terrain of cultural reception which is organized around the experience of the fragment or detail. In Benjamin, it was the fragment as film frame that both shocked and radicalized subjects while eluding them. In Adorno, it was Schoenberg's austere retotalization of the fragment in the tone-row that radicalized listeners by becoming unlistenable. For both writers the question of which cultural processes precede – and therefore set the limits of the subject – is the crucial one. Though, on the face of things, they would appear to be interested in two different sensory and cognitive boundaries (looking as opposed to listening), I have already suggested that even Adorno's position quietly concedes the priority of looking within the contemporary hierarchy of the senses. Both distraction and contemplation, however otherwise opposed, are meant to be politically evaluated in relation to the struggle within cultural reception over the constitution of a subject for whom looking comes first. This is the subject of theory (a term which derives from the Greek term for

[19] Theodor Adorno, *In search of Wagner*, trans. Rodney Livingstone (London, 1981), pp. 43–61. In this chapter Adorno even goes so far as to associate the 'motiv' with the compositional principle that prevails in film music. See p. 46 in particular.

theatrical spectatorship), a subject for whom writing – as an irreducibly visual phenomenon – was the indispensable 'material supplement' to memory. It is becoming increasingly apparent that this subject is not the only one worth fighting for. This recognition definitively marks the debate between Adorno and Benjamin as dated, but not because it has become obsolete. Rather, this debate seems untimely because the advances it sought to realize have become even more urgent, since the social order confirmed in our experience of the contemporary modes of cultural expression is increasingly one delimited by corporate interests. With these exemplary instances of the politicization of reproductive technologies in hand, I can how examine the fragment's relation to the contemporary mode of electronic reproduction.

Bits and pieces

At the first New Music America Festival sponsored by The Kitchen in 1979, British composer Brian Eno gave a lecture on the topic, 'The studio as compositional tool'.[20] Aside from his fascinating remarks about the effects of recording on music listening and composing, the general question examined by Eno indicated the extent to which certain of Adorno's concerns were justified. The recording studio had become an instrument with its own peculiar musical idiom – an instrument that was also its own means of reproduction. As a consequence, repetition and the precondition for 'plugging' had advanced to the point of entering the musical material itself. For example, tape 'loops' in Eno's own work have come to be used for establishing everything from rhythm to chromatic texture, and while he did not refer to the practice of 'playing' or 'scratching' records characteristic of rap music, he could have. In most of his late discussions of 'new music', Adorno criticized this type of development from an uncharacteristically romantic position: one that exempted the opposition between conception and realization from the otherwise obligatory compositional demands for total musical integration.[21] As long as aura held out the promise of the

[20] Brian Eno, *Downbeat* (July, 1983), pp. 56–7 and (August, 1983), pp. 50–2.
[21] Adorno discusses this problem even in the 1930s. See 'On the social situation of music', trans. Wesley Blomster, *Telos*, 35 (Spring, 1978), pp. 124–38. Two examples of his later writing specifically devoted to the problems of technology and technique in the new music are, 'Music and technique', trans. Wesley Blomster, *Telos*, 32 (Winter, 1977), pp. 78–94, and 'Music and new music: in memory of Peter Suhrkamp', trans. Wesley Blomster, *Telos*, 43 (Spring, 1980), pp. 124–38.

mind's autonomy, Adorno was prepared to support it, even when doing so committed him to essentialist musical fantasies. What remains undecidable and therefore decisive is whether the developments cited by Eno are the consumption of the regressive tendencies identified by Adorno, or precisely the developments whose theoretical articulation enable us to understand that the technical penetration of music is a necessary development in the present effort to formulate a critical theory of society.

During the 1970s, the Sony Corporation introduced the Walkman cassette tape player. This device offers maximally portable hi-fidelity to listeners who are, through its use, radically reindividuated while they collectively recontextualize 'masterpieces' as (among other things) the soundtracks for health routines. In effect, everything that Benjamin had defined as the revolutionary features of mechanically reproduced art is, if not contradicted, at least neutralized by the Walkman. The same might be said about television which is a device closer to the cinematic apparatus. It is nonetheless difficult to conclude that these historical developments entitle one to regard the technologies of mass culture as constitutive of fascistic subjectivity. On the contrary, our ability to theorize this possibility despite the hegemony of mass culture, underscores an aspect of the cultural tradition, *qua* tradition, that Benjamin's historical situation authorized him to set aside.

Taken together, the Walkman and the recording of the recording studio mark developments which in effect confirm the apparently antinomous diagnoses of Adorno and Benjamin by embodying the victory of what each of them opposed in the other. That is, these developments represent simultaneously the appropriation of 'serious' music by the technology of mass culture feared by Adorno and the political co-optation of the social possibilities embedded in our relation to that technology feared by Benjamin. This might suggest, in accordance with a certain dialectical perversity, that the theoretical recognition of the decay of aura – assumed by both writers – arises only once this decay is being reversed. The role of critical theory in this reversal deserves to be elaborated in accord with the reversal's dialectical character – a task far too ambitious to be attempted here. Nonetheless, critical theory should not avoid the task of attempting to articulate the conditions of the restoration of aura, even if it can be demonstrated that doing so involves a conflict of interest. If, as I have implied, aura returns through the systematization of the fragment, it is because its restoration presupposes the shift from mechanical to electronic reproduction.

The social character of the shift to electronic reproduction has been most rigorously addressed by Oskar Negt and Alexander Kluge in their *Öffent-*

lichkeit und Erfahrung.[22] In a provocative discussion of the change in the character of the traditional media wrought by the advent of electromagnetic technologies, they show how our daily-life contexts have become the objects of the media conglomerate, an institutional feature of contemporary capitalism. Their argument draws directly upon the Marxian notion that the way in which human beings associate for the purpose of transforming nature into that which satisfies their needs also serves as the organizing matrix for the human production of expressive forms. The media represent specific historical instances of the production and reproduction of expressive forms. As such, they can be correlated with various structural features of the prevalent mode of production that serves as the context for the cultural reproduction of human subjectivity. Towards the end of Marx's introduction to the *Grundrisse*,[23] for example, he argued that the expressive form of oral epic poetry is grounded in the level of control over nature attained by the Greeks. He stressed that the mythological deities central to the epic would lose their phantasmatic power in a world where subjects could fully harness natural forces. In the traditional media, which emerge in conjunction with the industrial harnessing of nature (examples being radio, photography, and cinema), subjects are predisposed towards a particular mode of cultural reception through their exposure to the segmentation and hierarchization of specific sensory tasks that characterized the mode of production within high capitalism. In the new media, which belong to the 'post-industrial' era, the practice of sensory reintegration (exemplified in the supervisory labor of the systems analyst) predisposes subjectivity towards the hegemonic mode of cultural reception. Computer-assisted video art is a good example of a medium that arises within the mode of production characteristic of this era. A dynamic correlation can thus be established between the structural organization of the institutions of media production and the sensory division of labor presupposed and reproduced by the products of these institutions.

For Negt and Kluge this represents a qualitatively new organization of the relationship between cultural production and reception, not merely at the level of structural complexity but at the level of lived experience itself. They argue that the as-yet-unmet and even unimagined needs of subjects are capable of being organized by the solicitations of the 'consciousness industry' to such an extent that what was typically defended by the protest

[22] An English translation of this important work is forthcoming from the University of Minnesota Press. To date only one chapter has appeared in English. See Oskar Negt and Alexander Kluge, 'The context of life as object of production of media conglomerates', *Media, Culture and Society*, 5 (1981), pp. 65–74.
[23] Karl Marx, *Grundrisse*, trans. Martin Nicolaus (New York, 1973), p. 110.

of 'technological determinism' is reduced to the status of a collector's item. In short, they identify as a distinctive element of post-industrial capitalism the fact that it has become impossible to separate the subject from the technologies of cultural reception. Any political critique of capitalist culture that has recourse to a non-integrated subject as the agent of social change fails to engage its object. This is not, however, a recipe for political resignation. Negt and Kluge simply insist upon locating the contradictions of experience capable of holding a political charge in the only nature we have left – culture.

Negt's and Kluge's observations concerning the correlation between the division of sensory labor within production and cultural reception invite us to reconsider the contested opposition between contemplation and distraction. Put simply, their conclusions imply that this opposition is a feature of a hierarchy of senses that has been superceded. To argue, as Adorno and Benjamin did, that distraction in looking (at silent film) was progressive while distraction in listening (to 'modern' music) was regressive, belies a commitment to a division among the senses, where what is actually at stake is the sensory and cognitive order of the revolutionary subject itself. If what characterizes the subject today is the reintegration of its senses in the cultural domain, it is perhaps just as fruitless to retain the notion of 'hierarchy' as it is to map organs and faculties onto the opposition between contemplation and distraction. Since the name for aura arose within a reception context dominated by what Negt and Kluge call the 'traditional mass media' and was therefore fastened to the moment of aura's decay, its restoration implies that the question of aura must always be posed anew, even if the question means something different each time. But in what sense can it be said that aura has been restored? My response will take the form of an elaboration of the cultural and political implications of Negt and Kluge's remarks as they bear on the status of the contemporary fragment.

Consider the most advanced form of the fragment, the bit or binary digit. It is the fundamental organizing structure of electronic information, and it is as indispensable to the surveillance mechanisms of the South African state as it is to the state-of-the-art digital recording techniques and 'simulcast' technologies that flourish in the 'advanced' countries. The bit is structured like a language. It is a doubly articulated sign that acquires its significance or value from within a matrix of differentiated values forming a synchronic system. In the categories of information theory, the bit may be said to represent the maximal rationalization of the noise/information polarity. The severely rationalized structure of the contemporary fragment facilitates the multiplication and inter-referencing of information systems. There is then a sense in which the bit is the monad come true. The most recent application of bit-centered technology in the domain of music listening, the compact disc player, promises not only to supercede the claims of reproductive fidelity made by Memorex, but to integrate, at the level of a technological continuum, the modes of production, reproduction and reception. When CD libraries match LP libraries, more of the world's music – both quantitatively and qualitatively – will be available for listening than at any other time in history. At that point the contrast between what is 'live' and what is Memorex will be irrelevant. The frayed fabric of tradition will be rewoven with optical fibers and the conditions for auratic reception will be restored.

The problematic aspects of this development are not difficult to enumerate since they are already making themselves felt. The ritual character of auratic art manifests itself in the triumphant cult of technology.[24] Simultaneously, the intellectual atmosphere created by this cult has redefined the role of tradition in the administration of cultural interpretation. On the one hand, tradition is now called upon to assure individual interpreters that the meaning they are incapable of assigning to their experience is in fact an accurate reflection of the general meaninglessness of culture. And on the other hand, tradition is invoked to reinforce the pluralistic constraint of repressive tolerance: any meaning an individual assigns to experience is valid provided it immediately renounces all claims of generality. Critical theory responded to these developments by converting the renunciation of generality into a stylistic principle – hence the fascination of Adorno, Benjamin and Horkheimer with the essay and the aphorism. This transformation of critical theory into a vanguard literary practice did not, however, protect it from the developments it sought to elude. The demise of critical theory as a vanguard discourse nonetheless allows one to perceive the possibility of a new collective cultural practice. If Marx could regard the proletariat as a concrete manifestation of theory, then perhaps contemporary music can be seen as a gateway to the new collectivity, since it situates subjects within an emergent structure of listening which offers experiential confirmation of a social configuration.

In closing I will turn once again to Attali's remarkable book. Early in the chapter entitled 'Listening', while sketching the parameters of his project, he argues that it is 'necessary to imagine radically new theoretical forms, in order to speak new realities. Music, the organization of noise, is one such

---

[24] Jürgen Habermas, 'Technology and science as "ideology"', *Toward a rational society*, trans. Jeremy Shapiro (Boston, 1970), pp. 81–122.

"Music is organized noise."

form.[25] If we connect this citation to the earlier one in which Attali linked music and community, then it is possible to articulate why music emerges as a decisive cultural practice in the social order of the bit.

Electronically reproduced art has radicalized noise by seeking to eliminate it. Standard cassette players and stereo receivers contain the various Dolby formats for noise reduction which operate according to a systematic logic that produces information out of suppressed noise. There are two levels of production here. Musical information is produced out of noise that can be rendered informative through various strategies of signal enhancement – redundancy, for example. And noise, as a *category* of sound, is produced (though at a different level) by what is made to differ from it, namely, information. As a consequence, noise arises everywhere information is produced. With the increasing cultural hegemony of bit-oriented systems, noise even functions to name that which stands opposed to the informa-tion system as a whole. The political character of this development is reflected in the history of contemporary music where the fetish of noise reduction has gone hand in hand with the aggressive marketing of distor-tion boosters and other less obvious instrumental sources of noise. In a reception context increasingly dominated by the media conglomerates, noise is thus proliferated only to be recaptured and channelled in a manner that allows the industry to profit from it. However, this does not result in total control for the industry, because it is operating within a mode of production that continually produces new needs while failing to satisfy those it is ostensibly attempting to meet. This general dynamic has its structural basis in the binary fragment. The 'post-industrial' mode of pro-duction, in its effort to convert our life-contexts into usable information, seeks to extend the domain organized by bit-centered technologies. How-ever, just as the production of needs always exceeds the capacity of the mode of production, the production of information always proliferates noise which exceeds the organizing capacity of the bit-centered system. As a collective organization of noise, contemporary music (classical and popu-lar alike) is profoundly marked by this situation. The generality of the impact on music is due to the fact that the production and reception of all music is mediated by the same reproductive technologies. However much two listeners may differ in their tastes, they are likely to share standards of hi-fidelity. Even so, it is certainly the case that only specific producers and consumers of music act so as to realize the critical potential of the emerging structure of listening. It is striking though that those who *do*, typically see

25 Attali, *Noise*, p. 4.

themselves as 'cross-overs' (that is, as members of several of the various communities of performers and listeners).

What characterizes the work of those musicians radicalized by their relation to bit-oriented reproductive technologies is the effort to raise the technical preconditions of their musical material to the level of cultural expression. That is to say, they struggle to make audible the noise/information polarity that both grounds contemporary listening and undermines its present boundaries. When Laurie Anderson played the Orpheum Theater in Minneapolis, she opened her show with an opaque projection of a digital representation of the very lyrics she would soon 'sing' through the Vocoder (a computerized voice synthesizer). Anderson's work, which is only one example among many, can be understood as an attempt to communicate or socialize the general material character of the contemporary mode of reproduction. To the extent that the material character of reproduction currently rests on the boundless noise/information opposition, the effort to socialize it gives socio-political significance to all those musics that have hitherto been listened to as noise. These musics stand forth now as the costs of the canons.

If, as I have argued earlier, subjectivity is engendered within the social process, then there are clear implications for subjects in what has been said here concerning the forms of community that circulate in contemporary music. In analyzing the Memorex Corporation's solicitation of the faculty of memory, I noted that the delimitation of this faculty went hand in hand with a structuring of subjectivity that subordinated the sense of hearing to the sense of seeing. This subordination of hearing permitted the social mediations of listening to become part of the very structure of the competent listener. The structure of listening that arises with contemporary music cannot center itself on a subject ordered by the sensing hierarchy that emerged with the art of memory embodied in printing. This is because the classical subject, whose limits had precise internal and external coordinates, came into being through cultural experiences (like reading to oneself) that have been overrun by the institutional practices and technologies of the current modes of cultural reproduction.

The bit as contemporary fragment relocates the limits of the subject in two decisive ways. Because it is fundamental to a cultural technology that can be used to communicate the material preconditions of reproduction, the bit orientates subjectivity towards what, in this case, makes the experience of listening possible. The form of community that arises within this experience situates the subjects it comprises at their very limits, that is, at the very points where the institutions and practices that precede them give them shape. Second, because the logic of the bit indicates that the system of information can condition but not determine its outside, the subject that arises under its influence stands within a potentially multi-cultural field where it is exposed to 'others' who are not the convenient foils of the classical subject. Even if we acknowledge, as we must, that the social order circulated within music performed under the regime of the bit bears a corporate imprint, we need not conclude that this condemns music to a conservative political role, for to do so would be to ignore the specificity of the current mode of reproduction. Since our reception of music cannot escape the institutions and technologies that mediate it, the collectivity which Attali insists takes form within music must then articulate the peculiar logic of the bit – a logic which forces this collectivity into a relation with its technical preconditions and the experiences that necessarily elude it. The subjects that are engendered under these conditions are themselves informed by this double relation: they listen most closely to the noises they do not recognize. Because music takes us in these unheard-of directions it can be understood to function as a cultural practice whose oppositional character derives from its ability to engender subjects who are predisposed towards others. Music's critique of society takes the post-theoretical form of a symbolically constructed collectivity. Here the estrangement and totalization we associate with theoretical discourse return as the social experience of cultural production. At a time when the aestheticization of theory is becoming increasingly prevalent, music has responded by sensualizing cultural politics. I am not sure it is possible to have greater social significance than that.

The structure of listening that confirmed the primacy of looking is in decline, as the Memorex Corporation inadvertently illustrated. What our new organization of memory and its accompanying sensory apparatus will feel like is difficult to define, but is prefigured in Reik's notion of the 'third ear', inspired by Freud, who thought a great deal about memory while listening to others. Rather than an organ, it was a location where listening took place, registering what the speaker had forgotten. In psychoanalysis, what is forgotten gives the speaker his or her identity; as Freud said, 'Where it was, I shall become.'[26] Because the syntax of this formulation evokes so strongly the logic of the bit-centered mode of production, it strikes me as a particularly suggestive way to imagine the emerging experience of listening. Music permits us to experience this form of listening through 'ears' that feel more like the tangled resonating bodies than the folds of flesh situated

26 Sigmund Freud, 'Dissection of the personality', *New introductory lectures*, trans. James Strachey (New York, 1965), p. 80.

on both sides of the head. If I have likened listening to festive dancing, it is because what is crucially new about contemporary listening is its irreducibly communal character. What joins festive dancing to the psychoanalytic notion of the third ear is the fact that the experience of collective interdependence is precisely what was forgotten by the classical subject.

The memory that will form through the new experience of listening may well enable us to grasp its ongoing relation to the moments of danger described by Benjamin in his 'Theses on the philosophy of history'.[27] What threatened memory, according to Benjamin, was the fact that the tradition resulting from its gathering necessarily put memory at the disposal of the ruling classes. In Benjamin's hands, historical materialism was thus forced to confront the fact that the future would be under the control of those who could edit the past. Missing from this discussion of historical materialism, however, was an adequate reflection on the role of the medium of cultural memory in the constitution of historical subjects. What I have argued here is that contemporary music, as an embodiment of memory structured by the bit-centered matrix, obliges memory to register its relation with precisely what threatens it: the material conditions of its communication. However much tradition may endanger memory, if the socially organized inscription of memory preserves the problematic character of its present institutionalization, then subjects may form who expect a different future. The memory produced in this context deserves to be called 'popular', as does the music that organizes it. The problem today, in the era of music's electronic reproduction, is not, as Foucault suggests, that we have failed to decapitate the King of Memory, but that in desiring to do so we continue to locate memory in our heads.[28] The continued politicization of music will involve recognizing that the memory it organizes is no longer contained in the minds of autonomous subjects and that, in fact (to paraphrase Freud), we may be becoming who we will be where it is going.

[27] Walter Benjamin, 'Theses on the philosophy of history', *Illuminations*, p. 255.
[28] Michel Foucault, 'Truth and power', *Power/knowledge: selected interviews and other writings 1972–1977*, ed. Colin Gordon, trans. Colin Gordon, *et al.* (New York, 1980), p. 121.

Index

(References to musical examples and illustrations are printed in italic type. Only significant references to individuals, works and subjects are indexed.)

Index

rounding us, approaching us simultaneously from all directions, totally fluid in its evanescence, a world which is active and continually prodding us for a reaction. Similarly, the voice, which is the paradigm of sound for people, is fundamental to the particular form of communication, language, which both facilitates and gives rise to that which is essentially human in people. The orality of *face-to-face* communication cannot help, in other words, but emphasize the social relatedness of individual and cultural existence.

With regard to music, timbre, more than any other parameter, appears to constitute the nature of sound itself. While it is possible to conceive of sound with infinite duration, sound without fixed pitch, and even sound without gradations of amplitude, it is not possible to conceive of sound without timbre. It is the very vibratory essence that puts the world of sound in motion and reminds us, as individuals, that we are alive, sentient and experiencing. As the essence of individual sonic events, timbre speaks to the nexus of experience that ultimately constitutes us all as individuals. The texture, the grain, the tactile quality of sound brings the world into us and reminds us of the social relatedness of humanity. In touching us and stroking us it makes us aware of our very existence. Symbolically, it *is* our existence.

The existence of music, like the existence of women, is potentially threatening to men to the extent that it (sonically) insists on the social relatedness of human worlds and as a consequence implicitly demands that individuals respond. When this happens music reminds men of the fragile and atrophied nature of their control over the world. Expressed in terms already outlined with regard to gender relations, the male fear of women is mirrored in 'the threat posed by uncontrollable musical experience to the "moral fibre" of the rationalistic scribe-state'.[16] But since music cannot ultimately be 'denied' any more than social relatedness, the answer to music's 'threat' for post-Renaissance men has been to isolate those components, pitch and rhythm, which can be objectified and frozen through a 'fully analytic' notation.[17] Pitch and rhythm, as spatial and temporal extensions of timbre, are thus distanced from the core of musical articulation, precisely in order to de-contextualize articulation. This parallels the way in which a material and notational control is exercised over processes fundamental to the creation of people and the reproduction of culture in general, as discussed above.

It is in these terms that the social significance of 'classical' and 'popular'

16 Trevor Wishart, 'Musical writing, musical speaking', *Whose music?*, Shepherd *et al.*, p. 128.
17 Ibid., pp. 128–51.